Management Expert Systems

The Insight Series in Artificial Intelligence

Series Editor: Tony Morgan, Systems Designers plc

Associate Editor: Bob Muller, Digital Equipment Corporation

The series derives its name from the Insight study group sponsored by Systems Designers plc, whose workshops, conferences and study visits promoted international collaboration between companies and other institutions toward the common goal of applying advanced AI technology.

Other titles in the series:

Blackboard Systems, *edited by R.S. Engelmore and A.J. Morgan*

Management Expert Systems

Edited by
Christian J. Ernst
Université des Sciences Sociales
Toulouse, France

▲▼ ADDISON-WESLEY PUBLISHING COMPANY
Wokingham, England · Reading, Massachusetts · Menlo Park, California
New York · Don Mills, Ontario · Amsterdam · Bonn · Sydney
Singapore · Tokyo · Madrid · San Juan

The programs presented in this book have been included for their instructional value. They have been tested with care but are not guaranteed for any particular purpose. The publisher does not offer any warranties or representations, nor does it accept any liabilities with respect to the programs.

Many of the designations used by manufacturers and sellers to distinguish their products are claimed as trademarks. Addison-Wesley has made every attempt to supply trademark information about manufacturers and their products mentioned in this book. A list of the trademark designations and their owners appears on p. xx.

Jacket designed by John Gibbs and printed by the Riverside Printing Co. (Reading) Ltd.
Text design by Lesley Stewart.
Typeset by Columns, Reading.
Printed in Great Britain by T.J. Press (Padstow), Cornwall.

First printed 1988

British Library Cataloguing in Publication Data
Management expert systems.—(Insight
  series in artificial intelligence).
  1. Expert systems – For management
  I. Ernst, Christian J.   II. Series
  006.3'3'024658

  ISBN 0–201–19691–3

Library of Congress Cataloging in Publication Data
Management expert systems / edited by Christian J. Ernst.
        p.   cm.—(The Insight series in artificial intelligence)
     Bibliography: p.
     Includes index.
     ISBN 0–201–19691–3
     1. Management—Data processing.   2. Decision-making—Data
processing.   3. Expert systems (Computer science)   I. Ernst,
Christian J.   II. Series.
HD30.2.M36   1988
658.4'03'0285633—dc19

                                                          88–10584 CIP

Foreword

We are confronted by a fascinating paradox in this book. Expert systems replicate human expertise in a narrow domain. Management, especially senior and top management, is about anything *but* expertise in a narrow domain. Yet this book focuses on management expert systems.

This apparent paradox holds the key to a most promising use of expert systems technology; that is as management assistants which bring together individual areas of expertise to bear on management decisions. It is widely accepted that decision-making will become harder as situations grow more complicated, needing a new (or at least enhanced) set of capabilities in management. The use of expert systems by managers needs to be aimed at enhancing capabilities for decision-making and this book starts us on this challenging path.

Although there are individual expert systems in research, development and use which can be called 'management expert systems' we are in the early days of an emergent technology as far as management use is concerned. Vital areas of research and development which will move us towards widespread management acceptance and use of expert systems are: integrating expert systems with other systems; increasing the ease of use of computer systems; and managing change effectively. Overriding these developments is the acceptance that to be successful, expert systems must be business led, not technology led.

Probably the move toward integration is the most important. This will raise the perceived value of expert systems to management from being a curiosity technology – which has hitherto been of limited value to professionals, technicians and specialized activities – to being a key enabling set of techniques which can leverage management decision-making by embedding the 'judgment' of others in decision support. One way of giving managers an appreciation of expert systems is to give them expert systems which they can use themselves in an area of need. In this way they will become aware quickly of the advantages, limitations and potential use of the technology. Only then, will managers fully be able to judge the value of expert systems throughout their organizations.

A good start along this management awareness and understanding path could be for both managers and workers in expert systems to grasp the concepts and case studies in this book. The next step would be the development and use of appropriate management expert systems. This approach, however, will soon show that the management expert systems giving the greatest leverage in the future will depend heavily on integration and cooperating expert systems. Integrated and cooperating expert systems for management would be an excellent focus for a subsequent book.

An example of how an organization has achieved true integration of expert systems can be found in Digital, where the organization has evolved a knowledge-based overview of how the company does business. The flow of information within the company was conceptualized as a 'knowledge network'; the nodes of the network are individuals knowledgeable about the products and processes that are necessary for the company to function. In this way the areas of expertise throughout the company which could be incorporated into expert systems beneficially were identified, together with the management use of combined expertise. Using this approach, Digital has been able to benefit from the development and use of expert systems, many of which are integrated. Senior management have been involved throughout the evolutionary development process, and these senior managers have been prepared for their own strategic use of expert systems.

There is one further theme to highlight: management of change. Expert systems have already been shown to be an agent of change in the highly dynamic arena of the changing patterns of national and international competition. The final chapter of this book is particularly interesting in this context. Maybe management expert systems, in their planning and design, will help to achieve the aims set out by Sir Ieuan Maddock in his papers on why industry must learn to forget. A salient message from Sir Ieuan, penned (or even computed) in 1982 warned:

'Most industrial failures in recent years are due to long forgetting curves rather than the inability of people to learn new techniques and new attitudes. . . . Schools for learning are abundant, but schools for forgetting have yet to be invented.'

There are many challenges ahead in achieving expert systems embedded within an organization, particularly if these systems are to be used successfully to help management decision-making; but substantial progress has been made on individual expert systems for managers. In this book, Christian Ernst has brought together selected results of work from artificial intelligence research, computer science and management science as well as from computer practitioners. He has brought us a synthesis of two nations which have been highly innovative in expert systems: the USA and France. This foreword is a brief contribution from a member of another nation among the leaders in expert systems: Britain. The reader must judge the success of the mixture.

Bob Muller
Digital Equipment Corporation

Preface

The aim of this book is to introduce the basic concepts, methods, and tools necessary to design and implement expert systems as decision-support systems for managers. Major efforts have been made to select outstanding contributions whose didactic qualities make them accessible to students as well as to professionals who have no specific training in artificial intelligence (AI).

Building management expert systems (MESs) is a task that concerns both students and researchers working in academic departments of computer science or business administration, and professionals in software industry involved in the development of decision-support systems. In this volume, both academics and professionals will find the main criteria they need in order to identify and carry out potential applications of expert systems in business.

Although this book is not intended expressly for AI scientists or for business practitioners, there is much they will find useful. The various chapters will not provide AI scientists with a survey of the state of the art of expert systems, but will help them assess how to meet the requirements of decision-making in business. Business practitioners will find design techniques for MES building, rather than management techniques for supporting decision-making processes.

Students and researchers of AI and management science, and designers and potential users of MESs must recognize that only by bringing together the know-how acquired by the study of real-world cases, and the expertise gained by developing basic tools, will the technology of expert systems yield significant improvements in the effectiveness of decision-making processes.

The book is divided into two parts. The first deals with problems and techniques in the design and implementation of MESs, while the second is concerned with applications and future prospects.

While management practitioners, as actual or potential users of MESs, will be more concerned with Part II, all the issues addressed in this book (basic tools and applications) are of interest to management science students and researchers. Some more theoretical aspects, as covered in Chapters 5 and 6 (and, to a lesser extent, in Chapter 4) can be skipped by MES designers if they have no basic background in mathematics and computer science. Of the aspects considered in Part I can be singled out basic concepts of expert systems (Chapter 1) and of MESs (Chapter 2), MES architecture (Chapter 3), knowledge representation languages (Chapter 4), and reasoning models (Chapters 5 and 6). The case studies presented in Part II should be considered by MES designers and users as representative of the expert-systems approach to building and exploiting business decision-support systems.

Part I begins with a general introduction to knowledge-based expert systems by Frederick Hayes-Roth (Chapter 1), then Christian Ernst gives an analysis of issues related to MES design while emphasizing their specific features (Chapter 2). MES architecture, knowledge representation languages, and reasoning models are then dealt with. Robert Demolombe underlines the importance of coupling inference engines with database management systems (Chapter 3), while Henri Farreny demonstrates the necessity of distinguishing between languages associated with expert systems according to the specific requirements of experts to express their knowledge (Chapter 4). Didier Dubois and Henri Prade closely analyze a major management problem: imprecision and uncertainty in the reasoning models of experts (Chapter 5). Building upon features of approximate reasoning, Ronald Yager finally provides a diagnostic method for decision making (Chapter 6).

Part II presents applications of MESs, starting with a taxonomy of expert systems proposed by Larry Kerschberg and John Dickinson, who go on to describe the FINEX system, an expert support system for financial analysis (Chapter 7). Jesse F. Dillard and Jane F. Mutchler examine R&D of expert systems for auditing, stressing the capability of such systems for improving the understanding of auditor decision processes and decreasing audit risk (Chapter 8). This chapter is followed by two applications of expert systems for banking. Maia Rozenholc presents a business diagnosis expert system for assessing risks related to loan granting (Chapter 9), and Véronique El Mernissi describes a financial management expert system for advising customers on investment (Chapter 10). Finally, Jaffer R. Syed and Edison Tse propose an expert system to model competitive processes in industries with a high degree of product differentiation and multiproduction units (Chapter 11).

Of course, not all aspects of MESs and their potential fields of applications have been surveyed. However, the examples presented in

Part II can be considered representative of the use of expert systems as decision-support systems. This new approach in business management emphasizes methodology, particularly at a conceptual level, and will challenge scientists and professionals for many years to come.

Acknowledgments

This book is a natural follow-up to the First National Conference on Management Expert Systems held in Toulouse, whose proceedings provided most of the contents of the first part.

I wish to give special thanks to Jean-Claude Rault, chairman, EC2 company, Paris, and Jacques Luguet, Université Paul Sabatier, Toulouse, who made this conference possible. I also wish to thank Tony Morgan, Simon Plumtree, Bob Muller and Marie-Claude Ernst for their fruitful remarks and contribution to this book.

Christian Ernst
Toulouse, December 1987

List of Contributors

The publisher would like to thank the following for giving their permission to reproduce their material:

Robert Demolombe, ONERA/CERT
  2 Avenue Edouard Belin
  31055 Toulouse Cedex, France

John Dickinson, College of Business Administration
  University of South Carolina
  Columbia, SC 29208, USA

Jesse F. Dillard, Academic Faculty of Accounting
  and Management Information Systems
  Ohio State University
  408 Hagerty Hall
  1775 College Road
  Columbus, OH 43210-1399, USA

Didier Dubois, Laboratoire LSI
  Université Paul Sabatier
  118 Route de Narbonne
  31062 Toulouse Cedex, France

Véronique El Mernissi, TECSI
  6 Cours Michelet
  Paris La Defense Cedex 52, France

Christian Ernst, Institut d'Administration des Entreprises
  Université des Sciences Sociales
  Place Anatole France
  31042 Toulouse Cedex, France

Henri Farreny, Laboratoire LSI, ENSEEIHT
2 Rue Camichel
31071 Toulouse Cedex, France

Frederick Hayes-Roth, Teknowledge Inc
1850 Embarcadero Road
PO Box 10119
Palo Alto, CA 94303, USA

Larry Kerschberg, Department of Information Systems
and Systems Engineering
George Mason University
4400 University Drive
Fairfax, VA 22030, USA

Jane F. Mutchler, Academic Faculty of Accounting
and Management Information Systems
Ohio State University
408 Hagerty Hall
1775 College Road
Columbus, OH 43210-1399, USA

Henri Prade, Laboratoire LSI
Université Paul Sabatier
118 Route de Narbonne
31062 Toulouse Cedex, France

Maia Rozenholc, EVALOG
81 Rue Michel-Ange
75016 Paris, France

Jaffer R. Syed, Petrochemicals, Polymers & Energy Center
SRI International
333 Ravenswood Avenue
Menlo Park, CA 94025, USA

Edison Tse, Department of Engineering-Economics Systems
Stanford University
Stanford, CA 94305, USA

Ronald R. Yager, Machine Intelligence Institute
Iona College
New Rochelle, NY 10801, USA

Contents

Part I : Foundations of Management Expert Systems

Part II : Case Studies

Trademark Notice
ART™ is a trademark of Inference Corporation.
DOS™ was written for the IBM PC by Microsoft Incorporated.
IBM™ is a trademark of International Business Machines Corporation.
INTERLISP™, LOOPS™ and SMALLTALK™ are trademarks of Xerox Corporation.
KEE™ is a trademark of Intellicorp.
LISP Machine™ is a trademark of LISP Machine Incorporated
M1™ and S1™ are trademarks of Teknowledge.
MS-DOS™ is a trademark of MicroSoft Corporation.
PROSPECTOR™ is a trademark of SRI International.
ROSIE™ is a trademark of Rand Corporation.
UNIX™ is a trademark of AT&T.
VAX™ is a trademark of Digital Equipment Corporation.

Part I

Foundations of Management Expert Systems

1

Knowledge-based Expert Systems: the State of the Art[†]

Frederick Hayes-Roth

1.1 Introduction

Knowledge-based expert systems, or 'knowledge systems' for short, have evolved over 15 years from laboratory curiosities of applied artificial intelligence (AI) into the targets of significant technological and commercial development (Hayes-Roth *et al.*, 1983). These systems employ computers in ways that differ markedly from conventional data processing applications, and they open up many new opportunities. Recently, many commercial and governmental organizations have committed themselves to exploiting this technology, attempting to advance it in dramatic ways and beginning to adapt their missions and activities to it. Some recent major events in the USA include the following:

(1)   The Department of Defense claimed that knowledge systems would become the front line of the nation's defense in the 1990s, and initiated its $500 million five-year Strategic Computing Program.

(2)   IBM licensed and sold its first AI software program (INTELLECT) and publicly endorsed the field as relevant and applicable.

(3)   IBM's principal competitors teamed up to form MCC and identified knowledge systems as an area of primary concern.

(4)   General Motors took an equity position in a knowledge engineering firm to hasten the introduction of knowledge systems into their business (Holusha, 1984).

[†] This chapter is published by special permission of the *Knowledge Engineering Review*.

1.1.1 Locating expert systems within the computing field

It is not possible to give a precise definition of 'expert system,' any more than it is possible to give a precise definition of 'expert.' Rather than seeking elusive precision, this paper will adopt three common practical approaches: it will state what an expert system is, what it is not, and how one is recognized.

1.1.2 What is an expert system?

An expert system is a knowledge-intensive program that solves problems which normally require human expertise. It performs many secondary functions, as an expert does, such as asking relevant questions and explaining its reasoning. Some characteristics common to expert systems include the following:

- they can solve very difficult problems as well as or better than human experts,
- they reason heuristically, using what experts consider to be effective rules of thumb, and they interact with humans in appropriate ways, including natural language,
- they manipulate and reason about symbolic descriptions,
- they can function with data which contain errors, using uncertain judgmental rules,
- they can contemplate multiple, competing hypotheses simultaneously,
- they can explain why they are asking a question,
- they can justify their conclusions.

1.1.3 What is not an expert system?

Compared to a human expert, today's expert system appears narrow, shallow and brittle. It does not possess the same breadth of knowledge or understanding of fundamental principles. It does not apparently think as a human does: perceiving significance, reaching conclusions intuitively, and examining a single issue from diverse perspectives. Rather, the expert system of today simulates an expert's thinking rather grossly. It reaches the same major decisions by elucidating many of the relevant criteria and making many of the same educated guesses that an expert would if forced to verbalize the thought process. Unlike a human, however, the expert system does not resort to reasoning from first principles, drawing analogies, or relying on common sense; neither does it learn from experience.

Suggestions to read

→ Yazdani, Masoud, ed. Artificial Intelligence:
Principles and Applications. London and New York:
Chapman and Hall, 1986.

First National Conference on Management
Expert Systems held in toulouse. Dec 87?

In contrast to advanced data-processing (DP) systems, today's expert systems seem specialized and unusual. Where conventional DP systems amass and process large volumes of data algorithmically in order to automate time-consuming clerical functions, expert systems ordinarily address small tasks typically performed by professionals in a few minutes or hours: interpreting, diagnosing, planning, scheduling, and so forth. In order to accomplish these tasks, an expert system makes judicious use of data in its reasoning process. In contrast to the algorithmic DP approach, the expert system generally either searches a large space of possibilities, or constructs a solution dynamically.

1.1.4 How to recognize an expert system

Expert systems today generally serve to relieve a human professional of some difficult task. Find a computer that performs a function that previously required an expert. Locate the expert or team of experts who now maintain the program's knowledge base. Determine whether the knowledge in the system is accessible: can you read it, ask for explanations and justifications that exploit it, and can you modify it? Confirm that the system stores a substantial body of knowledge and that it reasons with that knowledge in flexible ways. Although any good programmer can implement a procedure integrating a few heuristics, incorporating hundreds or thousands of heuristics into a computer system requires knowledge engineering. Systems employing this level of judgmental knowledge are expert systems.

Now that we have the subject more or less defined, let us consider where it fits into the field of computing. Figure 1.1 places the area of expert systems in its historical context. The figure locates the beginnings of expert systems around 1980, with the first efforts to commercialize the technology. The first company formed exclusively to promote expert systems (in the field of genetic engineering) was IntelliGenetics. Shortly afterwards Teknowledge was formed as the first knowledge engineering company. These companies were a spin-off from the Heuristic Programming Project at Stanford University, which had led the development of knowledge engineering during the 1970s.

The field of applied AI draws together techniques from three areas: symbolic programming, cognitive psychology, and work on incremental programming environments (Barr and Feigenbaum, 1981/82). From a decade of work, three primary subfields emerged: expert systems, natural language, and robotics (including vision, speech, and locomotion). Presently, a few small commercial companies in the USA occupy positions in each of these subfields.

Researchers in knowledge engineering have so far focused primarily on creating artificial experts for tackling tough practical problems. The

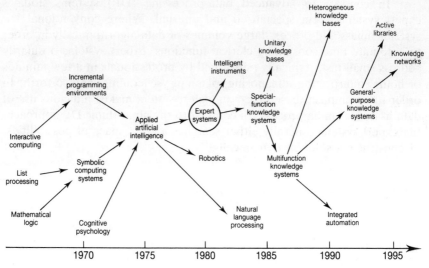

Figure 1.1   Expert systems in the evolution of computing.

Stanford group were pioneers with this approach, developing the first truly expert system, DENDRAL, the first successful learning system, META-DENDRAL, and a variety of applications in medicine. This group had a recipe for success, with two key ingredients:

- attack problems amenable to the techniques of applied AI,
- consider only important, difficult, and high-value problems.

In more detail, here is a recipe followed by many US knowledge engineers:

(1) Seek problems that experts can solve via telephone communication.

(2) Choose a problem that experts can solve in 3 minutes to 3 hours.

(3) Choose a problem whose solution requires symbolic reasoning.

(4) Prefer high-value problems.

(5) Rule out problems where different experts disagree about solution correctness.

(6) Rule out areas where initial problems cannot be solved with a limited subset of the experts' total knowledge.

(7) Select an initial class of problems to solve that require only a subset of knowledge.

(8) Identify some training problems and collect the experts' problem-solving protocol.

(9) Build a knowledge base that contains explicit and declarative representations of the experts' concepts and heuristic reasoning rules.

(10) Develop an initial expert system to solve the training problems as the experts do.

(11) Ask the experts to review the system's solutions and its lines of reasoning.

(12) Augment the system to accommodate the experts' critique.

(13) Apply the system to more training problems and augment its knowledge base incrementally.

(14) Evaluate the system's performance on novel test-cases.

1.1.5 Preview of the ideas

In surveying the state of the art and the state of commercialization, a few key points emerge:

(1) Knowledge systems transform book knowledge and private knowledge into an active inspectable form capable of performing high-value work.

(2) Knowledge today takes many different forms, necessitating a variety of tools or instruments for knowledge engineering.

(3) Knowledge systems must be integrated with DP systems, but knowledge engineering work differs greatly from conventional software work.

(4) A number of companies today make money from knowledge engineering products and services.

(5) One cannot predict the direction of commercialization.

(6) Steady, rapid growth of both the technology and the commercial applications should continue through the turn of the century.

Sections 1.2 and 1.3 explain these points and provide additional details.

1.2 Technology

Problem-solving engines organize the activity of knowledge systems to solve problems. To understand these engines, we need to relate their implementation to their design and intended purpose. Today's knowledge systems aim to solve specific problems. A knowledge engineer analyzes the problem to be solved and then adopts an overall approach generally consisting of three stages:

(1) a problem–solution paradigm, such as top-down refinement or multidirectional opportunistic search,

(2) a general-knowledge system architecture that makes specific decisions on the key system design questions, including what kinds

of knowledge to represent, in what formalism, for what kinds of inference, and affording what kinds of flexibilities,

(3)   a specific problem-solving strategy that determines what knowledge to apply in what order.

Today's problem-solving engines provide specific devices for implementing the knowledge engineer's choices. These engines provide a specific knowledge representation formalism and related interpreter, a high-level control architecture and executive, and an inference procedure and related inference engine. The knowledge representation formalism may include useful ways to describe conceptual taxonomies and conditional heuristic rules. A conceptual taxonomy includes relationships between types of object, class, and individual, and determines how properties of one apply to another. For example, many problem-solving engines can accommodate and exploit these kinds of facts:

The Warsaw Pact includes the USSR, Poland, Hungary, ...
The USSR is a country.
Cuba is a client state of the USSR.
All Warsaw Pact countries are client states of the USSR.
Every client state of any country will do whatever that country does regarding participation in the Olympic Games.

Heuristic rules represent judgmental knowledge. In fact, the conclusion reached in the example above actually represents such a heuristic. Most current problem-solving engines provide a stylized 'if then' formalism for representing such heuristic knowledge. Some examples of other kinds of heuristics that various problem-solving engines can exploit are as follows (the uncertain nature of all of these should be evident):

- If you see an oily sheen on the surface of the water, hypothesize that oil has been spilled.
- If you hypothesize that oil has been spilled but cannot smell petroleum or feel slime, rule out that hypothesis.
- If you have competing hypotheses, you can identify the correct one by trying to rule them all out.
- If all hypotheses but one have been ruled out, accept that one.
- If you need to schedule n events, schedule the most constrained one first.
- If you need to determine how constrained an event is, rate as highly constrained any event whose time and date are already fixed, and rate as weakly constrained any event such as a weekly date with a friend.

Once the knowledge engineer has adopted a particular problem-solving engine, the knowledge base for the application then needs filling out. Knowledge bases generally consist of conceptual taxonomic relations and rules. From our experience, some generally valid heuristic rules about knowledge bases are:

- An interesting demonstration of the technology requires only 50 rules.

- A convincing demonstration of the power of a knowledge system requires about 250 rules.

- A commercially practical system may require as few as 50 rules.

- An expert level of competence in a narrow area requires about 500 to 1000 rules.

- Expertise in a profession requires about 10 000 rules.

- The limit of human expertise is about 100 000 rules.

To help amass and maintain rule bases, most research and commercial knowledge engineering tools include various automated aids. These generally provide a range of support, from automatic name recognition on input and spelling correction to line-of-reasoning traces, knowledge base browsing, and automated facilities for system testing and validation.

1.2.1 Forces affecting knowledge system technology

Figure 1.2 shows the ways in which we can now see the technology expanding. In the upward direction, a variety of user needs are encouraging advances in knowledge systems technology. These needs determine the economic and functional niches the technology occupies. Specifically, knowledge systems address problems that arise from difficulties in retaining, transmitting, and applying know-how. For example, knowledge systems can preserve fragrance-blending knowledge beyond the retirement of a perfume manufacturing expert, or can disseminate to equipment service facilities worldwide the diagnostic methods of one master mechanic. In addition, they provide a means of employing know-how where it is needed, when it is needed, and at great speed. This has many attractions for factory automation, process control, safety systems, military intelligence, and weapons systems.

In the downward direction, the field will expand in response to technology drives. These include improved forms of conventional hardware and software for symbolic computing, less expensive memory and processors, standardized and increasingly reliable knowledge engineering techniques, and possibly novel non-von Neumann architectures (such as those that the DARPA and Fifth Generation programs now pursue). Throughout the world today, many groups are active in

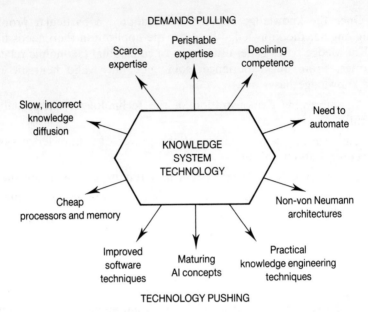

Figure 1.2   Forces of 'pull and push' that are expanding the technology.

these areas. However, the author does not foresee any short-term breakthrough changing this predicted pattern of the technology's development. Rather, steady improvements in the directions indicated should reduce the cost, expand the capability, and increase the reliability of the technology. This will make an already practical technology much more so.

1.2.2 Assessing technological capacities

To assess the state of the technology, we need better measures than those currently in existence. Table 1.1 gives estimates of the levels and rates of change of some key technology measures. To assess the rate of progress, we need a method of measuring the productivity of a knowledge engineering team. Although there are many differences between the systems that have been built so far, a reasonable first-order approximation is to treat them all as collections of heuristic rules. Typically, a knowledge engineer and an expert collaborate to create the rules that enter a system. Using the range of 500–1000 rules as the typical size of an interesting application, the author has estimated the rate of system development for numerous applications.

Figure 1.3 shows development times in terms of engineering person-hours per rule. The graph shows an approximate doubling of productivity

Table 1.1 Estimated measures of current US technology capacities.

	1984 level	1984–1985 change
Knowledge system prototypes under development	70	+50%
Knowledge systems being deployed	15	+100%
Knowledge systems being maintained	10	+200%
Knowledge engineering departments established	15	+150%
Senior knowledge engineers	40	+50%
Knowledge engineers	150	+50%
Knowledge engineer trainees	300	+100%
Applied AI graduate students	250	+20%
Undergraduate students in AI	2000	+50%
LISP or PROLOG programmers	2000	+50%
LISP or PROLOG installations	400	+100%

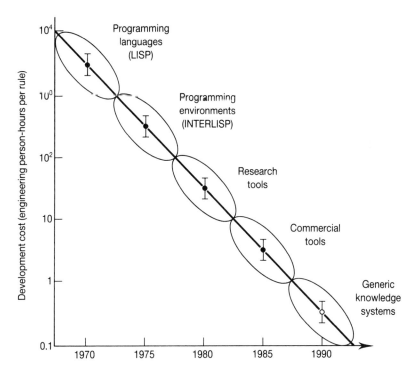

Figure 1.3 Approximate development costs for stages in the evolution of knowledge systems, showing that efficiency is doubling every two years.

every two years over the past 15 years. These improvements can be attributed to two factors:

- technological advances in the best available methods for carrying out knowledge engineering,

- typical improvements resulting from learning within a given method.

Figure 1.3 identifies five successive periods in the development of technology for knowledge system construction: programming languages, such as LISP, programming environments, such as INTERLISP, research tools, such as EMYCIN, commercial tools, such as S1, and future generic knowledge systems which will incorporate a user's own knowledge into a prefabricated heuristic problem-solving package (e.g., a personal financial planner). With the recent emergence of commercial knowledge engineering tools, many useful systems will become deployable in a year or less.

1.2.3 Weaknesses in current technology

While many applications today seem straightforward, many others present difficulties that stretch the current technology. The requirements most frequently encountered include:

- flexible and general natural language understanding, which may arise when users need to exercise initiative in directing the activities of a knowledge system,

- the incorporation of knowledge that is hard to represent, which often arises when it is required to reason with spatial or temporal problems,

- the combination and unification of the knowledge of many experts when no prior standardization has occurred,

- the application of broad bodies of knowledge quickly, as may arise in real-time command-and-control problems.

Applications today generally work around these technological shortcomings, or have to await some appropriate advance in the state of the art.

1.3 Commercialization

Knowledge systems and the tools for creating them have begun to enter the commercial world. The first systems to find regular use grew out of long-term academic research. DENDRAL, which determined molecular

structure from mass spectroscopy and NMR data, was developed over a
period of 15 years at Stanford (Lindsay *et al.*, 1980). Numerous
pharmaceutical companies access it on the national SUMEX-AIM
medical computing network. Stanford recently granted an exclusive
commercial license on DENDRAL. Similarly, MACSYMA, evolved over
many years of research at MIT (Martin and Fateman, 1971), eventually
became a superhuman expert in its area of specialty, the evaluation of
mathematical expressions. It too has been commercialized (Table 1.2).

Table 1.2 Some commercially available knowledge systems.

Area	Name	Vendor	Functions
End-user applications	Questware	Dynaquest	Personal computer HW/SW selection
	Logician	Daisy	Electronic design
	TK Solver	Software Arts	Equation solving
	SMP/Macsyma	Interference/ Symbolics	Mathematical simplification and problem-solving
Commercial applications tools	S1	Teknowledge	Industrial diagnostic and structured selection problems
	M1	Teknowledge	Microcomputer tool for small expert system applications
	OPS	DEC	VAX AI programming language used in-house
Research and experimentation	KEE	IntelliCorp	Extended programming environment; frames
	LOOPS	Xerox	Extended programming environment; objects
	ART	Inference	Varied representations and inference techniques
	ROSIE	Rand	Legible, intelligible symbolic programming language
	KL-TWO	BBN/ISI	Knowledge representation schemes

contd.

Table 1.2 *contd.*

Area	Name	Vendor	Functions
Supporting systems	COMMON LISP	DEC/LMI/ Symbolics	New attempt to standardize LISP
	INTERLISP	Xerox/ISI	Mature programming environments
	FRANZLISP	Berkeley/ Tektronix	UNIX-based LISP
	LISP Machines	LMI/Xerox/ Symbolics/ Tektronix	Integrated graphics, personal workstation
	PROLOG	Silogic/Quintus/ LMI	Formal semantics logic-based programming language
	LISP/VM	IBM	First IBM 370 LISP product

In recent years many companies have applied knowledge engineering to their own internal problems. DEC reports a $10 million annual savings from one expert system for configuring VAX orders (McDermott, 1980); Schlumberger claims that its knowledge-based Dipmeter advisor will significantly increase its revenues from interpretation services; Elf-Aquitaine expects to field a drilling advisory system which, it says, should reduce total drilling costs by more than one per cent; and numerous other companies have undertaken confidential and proprietary applications.

Recently three new types of commercial application have emerged: tools for the construction of knowledge systems, specialized hardware and systems software for general AI programming, and the commercial expert system – a problem-specific artificial advisor. These have arisen in a variety of areas including CAD, data interpretation, computer selection, and mathematical problem-solving.

Figure 1.4 illustrates the expansion of commercialization. The central hexagon represents the major ingredients of knowledge system technology, and three larger hexagons represent increasing commercialization. The innermost contains the types of commercial product presently available: supporting hardware, software, knowledge engineering tools and equipment, and knowledge applications. The next hexagon contains products expected to emerge in the near future at the time of writing, while the outermost indicates areas that should see commercial systems available by 1990.

Table 1.2 lists a representative set of products now available. The

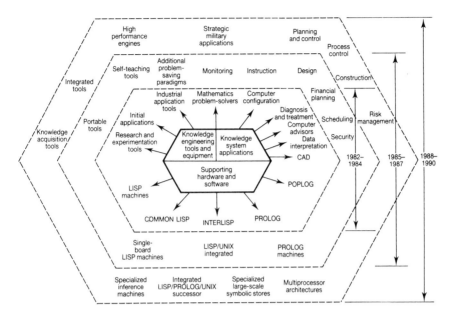

Figure 1.4   The commercialization of knowledge systems technology.

table categorizes these in four ways: end-user applications, commercial application tools, research and experimentation tools, and supporting systems. The supporting systems consist primarily of LISP and PROLOG and their variations. So far the vast majority of applications have employed LISP. Over the twenty years that AI and knowledge engineering professionals have worked in LISP, they have developed elaborate programming environments. These programming environments offer many productivity aids to programmers. However, they require considerable computing resources and this has motivated the development of specialized, personal LISP workstations. In Europe and Japan, PROLOG receives as much interest as LISP does in the USA. Although it does not yet afford a mature programming environment, PROLOG offers a simple and powerful knowledge programming system based on logic. Vendors of supporting systems emphasize its performance, price, and compatibility with existing and planned computing systems and standards.

    The current commercial situation reflects a wide diversity of products and a relatively immature market. A number of companies now have profitable lines of business based on knowledge system technology. Many independent forecasts of market growth suggest that demand should increase rapidly for at least a decade. Although this chapter has outlined the current state of commercial activity and suggested what seem to be the most likely short-term growth paths, no one can predict accurately how a new industry will develop. Because the technology addresses a fundamental problem – retaining, distributing, and applying know-how electronically – it should continue to prosper. However, we should expect this technology to combine with other emerging technologies in surprising ways. The final section discusses some of these possibilities.

1.4 Future trends

For nearly 500 years books have provided the primary means of retaining and transmitting knowledge. To achieve excellence in a profession, a person has needed to study, interpret, and memorize these books, then apprentice and train with someone who can clarify and illustrate the books' principles, then practice for years and learn practical rules from experience. The development of printing made an enormous impact on human culture by providing a means of distributing representations of human expertise to large numbers of potential practitioners. However, because it could not explain or apply its knowledge directly, the passive book left much work for the reader.

As technology progressed and economies advanced, the rate of knowledge transfer – which still relied on the printed word – became a bottleneck in cultural development. In highly advanced fields such as medicine and electronics, knowledge is acquired more quickly than it can be diffused and utilized. In information processing fields such as military intelligence and earth resources, data acquisition rates outstrip analysis and interpretation capacities. In capital-intensive industries such as automobile and electronics manufacturing, global competition based on price and quality has highlighted the need to integrate and coordinate knowledge about all phases of product development. This challenge is made greater by a very significant acceleration of new technologies and a rapid shortening of product lifetimes. In all of these areas, the same point emerges: the computer has created both the need and the opportunity to enhance the distribution of knowledge. Knowledge systems address that need.

What will the future bring? Three basic trends are certain, from US perspectives at least. First, this technology will spawn many new and speculative products. Some of these will be incredibly successful. The big success may be an expert system for advising about wardrobe colours, one about job-searching, or one about improving your personal finances. Or perhaps the big success will be an inexpert, broad knowledge system: all about the Bible, a computerized pen pal, or 'everything you always wanted to know about . . . .' We cannot predict which consumer-oriented knowledge systems will be commercial successes, but we can predict that most will be failures.

The second trend will see knowledge engineering continuing to penetrate industrial and commercial organizations on a broad front. Unlike many information processing applications, knowledge system applications often produce substantial short-term benefits. Most large organizations will find many high-value applications of this technology. For example, the typical expert system may raise the average level of performance on a task by a factor of two to ten. If an organization processes thousands of transactions of this sort annually and the benefit of such performance improvement exceeds $100 per transaction, the company can make an annual saving of up to a million dollars for each application. Since these numbers are quite typical, more and more people will perceive the attractiveness of this technology in the years to come.

The third trend is toward closer integration of knowledge systems with DP. Today, most computer-readable data elements are found in conventional databases. Many knowledge engineering applications need to access and analyze these data; in addition, many knowledge systems formulate plans for controlling other electronic systems. Both types of application will draw the two technologies closer together.

What applications, in which industrial and commercial areas, will the technology emphasize? Several areas are mentioned frequently in studies of likely ways to exploit the technology. These include expert systems for automotive and equipment repair, heuristic control systems for military functions and industrial automation, knowledge-aided design systems, knowledge-based planning aids, and automated interpretation systems for sensors and instruments. However, the technology will flow into all sectors of the economy, in an unpredictable fashion, because it provides an alternative means of supplying to industry an essential input – knowledge. Eventually the technology will become standard in most industries.

To summarize: experience gained in the USA indicates that knowledge systems technology will find several paths to commercial markets. Before the highest-value applications of the technology become apparent, many more products and uses will need to be developed and tested. The rate of success of knowledge engineering would seem to depend on the efficiency with which the field can discover new opportunities. That the technology will find several high-value targets is not, however, in doubt.

References

Barr, A. and Feigenbaum, E.A. (1981/82). *The Handbook of Artificial Intelligence*, Vols I and II. Menlo Park, CA: William Kaufman

Hayes-Roth, F., Waterman, D.A. and Lenat, D.B.; Eds (1983). *Building Expert Systems*. Reading, MA: Addison-Wesley

Holusha, J. (1984). 'GM's Silicon Valley stake', *New York Times*, May 3

Lindsay, R.D., Buchanan, B.G., Feigenbaum, E.A. and Lederberg, J. (1980). *Applications of Artificial Intelligence for Organic Chemistry: The DENDRAL Project*. New York: McGraw-Hill

McDermott, J. (1980). 'R1: An expert in the computer systems domain' In Proc. 1st Annual Conf. on 'Artificial intelligence', 269–271

Martin, W.A. and Fateman, R.J. (1971). 'The MACSYMA system' In Proc. 2nd Symp. on 'Symbolic and algebraic manipulation', 59–75

2

Management Expert Systems

Christian Ernst

2.1 Origin of management expert systems

Management expert systems are decision-making aids for managers who have to solve complex problems in their own fields. The use of this new management technology gives rise to many questions about the role of expert systems in organizations. Managers have to ask themselves what kind of decision-making problems can be tackled with this technology, and what the internal specifications of expert systems must be if they are to be effective as management assistants.

Management expert systems were born of the meeting of two fields of research: decision-support systems and knowledge-based systems. The former currently provide conceptual frameworks for a structural analysis of decision processes in the firm; the latter bring in the expert system technology, enabling designers to solve problems which were previously identified, in conceptual decision-making frameworks, as unsolvable or only poorly solvable with traditional software.

2.1.1 Decision-support systems

In the 1950s the first decision-support systems were built on the theoretical foundations of management decision-making established at the Carnegie Institute of Technology. In particular, the work by Simon (1960) provided an original conceptual framework for 'a new science of management decision' which has since been greatly improved by a large number of scientists.

This conceptual framework has established a taxonomy of decision

Table 2.1 A conceptual framework for management expert systems.

Differentiation factors	Decision-maker behavior factors	Expert system design factors
Perception	Large databases	Knowledge representation languages, rule-based systems
Rationality	Subjective rationalities	Approximate reasoning models
Action	Meta-knowledge (know-how)	Decision specification languages

processes based on generic factors which, in part, now seem particularly relevant to the paradigm of expert system design: perception, rationality, and action factors (Table 2.1).

Perception factors

Basically, a decision process is a transformation process of information into action (Figure 2.1). Indeed, the behavior of a decision-maker is determined primarily by the knowledge and messages received from the environment. The first task is to understand the problems by reference to the image of the cognitive environment perceived through a database. Consequently, a first differentiation level of decision processes is given by their degree of openness to the cognitive environment of managers: the higher the decision level in the firm, the more open to the environment are the decision processes. Following Anthony (1965), organizational theoreticians have been led to distinguish three decision levels:

- *planning control*, concerning the firm's general policy,

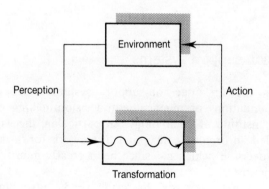

Figure 2.1 Decision processes.

- *management control*, concerning resource optimization and the objectives of the firm,
- *operational control*, concerning the firm's activities.

This categorization of decision processes provides the designers of management expert systems with the beginnings of a conceptual framework which deals with problems of representing and manipulating knowledge related to the environment of decision-makers; designers of expert systems call such knowledge **static knowledge**. This is a central issue in artificial intelligence (AI), where the aim is to build tools which give users the capability of reasoning with large databases.

Rationality factors

One of the most important contributions by Simon is his clear formalization of the 'bounded rationality principle': the efficiency of the decision-maker is restricted by the objective rationality of the firm, but judgmental knowledge sometimes gives better results because it is founded on values specific to decision-makers, and goes beyond the rational behavior which would have resulted had the outcome been determined by the objectives and structure of the firm.

The rationality of decision processes provides a second dimension for an expert system conceptual framework. It leads to the building of reasoning models; these models can be very different, depending on whether decision-makers use strongly structured management procedures or subjective and strongly context-dependent decision factors. In the latter case, designers are subject to the paradigm of **approximate reasoning**. In AI, this means that decision-making models can accommodate imprecise decision factors and the uncertainty affecting the applicability of decision processes in various contexts.

Action factors

Much of the research into systems analysis of organizations (Tabatoni and Jarniou, 1975) is devoted to the pragmatics of decision-making. It includes the study of factors determining the actions undertaken by decision-makers when facing a problem which has a space of possible solutions. The logical process of decision-making is seen to be closely associated with the management function of the decision-maker in the firm. The functional factors referred to here do not deal with the object of the management function (i.e., personnel, marketing, production, finance, etc.) but rather with principles of action. Actions taken by any manager at any decision level may be classified as follows:

- *organization actions*: allocating human, financial, or material

resources to activity units oriented toward given goals,
- *coordination actions*: maintaining the integrity and consistency of decisions made by several managers engaged in solving a common problem,
- *control actions*: reducing the distance between goals and results of activity units.

These types of action modify the manager's environment and consequently necessitate updating of the database describing this environment. They require that a manager should both be able to master the use of decision-support systems and possess a know-how based on his own experience.

The pragmatics of decision-making are based on a **context-dependent logic**: reasoning procedures used by decision-makers may be different, depending on the problem-solving context and the types of action to be taken. Moreover, pragmatics involve interactions between two levels of knowledge:

- *static knowledge*: the knowledge of managers about their environment, as stored in a database,
- *active knowledge*, or meta-knowledge: the know-how used by managers in dealing with their environment.

2.1.2 Expert systems

Expert systems are consulting systems designed to support experts' own reasoning on complex problems arising in a specific field of knowledge. They are the result of research conducted in AI over the past twenty years (Hayes-Roth *et al.*, 1983), and are currently generating a large number of commercial products. They are designed to reach as far as – or even beyond – the understanding capabilities of experts, by speeding up reasoning processes, and also to transfer expert knowledge to individuals who may require it.

Expert systems evolved from the combination of two basic ideas (Pitrat, 1984):

- that an AI program needs to be provided with a large amount of knowledge about the problem to be solved,
- that the description of this knowledge must be independent of the control procedures necessary for its manipulation.

Therefore AI researchers are concerned mainly with the representation and manipulation of knowledge. In this context, the development of management expert systems has been reinforced by two additional paradigms:

- the general paradigm of knowledge-based systems,
- the specific paradigm of deductive databases.

Knowledge-based systems

Problem-solving in AI makes use of two types of mechanism:

- *deductive mechanisms*, generally the manipulation of inference rules,
- *interpretative mechanisms*, requiring access to a database.

In decision-making in business, managers have to solve problems through reasoning on very large databases. In such circumstances, knowledge-based systems are susceptible to 'knowledge explosion' (Hayes-Roth *et al.*, 1978), a combined explosion of all of the possible behaviors of these systems. At the stage of knowledge representation, structuring data by means of high-level descriptors is a common way of reducing this combinatory complexity. This method is called 'knowledge factorization' (Bobrow and Winograd, 1977) and leads to the building of **knowledge representation languages** based either on predicate logic, or on semantic networks such as scripts, frames, demons, or scenarios. The languages resulting from the graphic approach are aimed at reinforcing data semantics, but they lose all operational capability when used to describe semantic networks associated with very large databases. The logic approach, however, is much more suitable for handling data semantics using the relational data model.

In knowledge manipulation the performance of problem-solving processes depends most strongly on the nondeterminism of choices made by inference engines at each step of a resolution: which subproblems to solve, which procedure to activate, and whether to use backtracking control after a failure. These choices are made so as to give complete coverage of a search space according to a strategy which is specific to each inference engine, fixed, and domain-independent.

An alternative approach to this control problem in expert systems is to help experts to express their own stategies by means of domain-dependent meta-knowledge. The description of control strategies requires a logic programming meta-language which must cover the features of a **decision specification language** for management purposes (Ernst, 1985).

This control paradigm is meant to make the control structure accessible to expert system designers; it assumes that uncertainty factors affecting the judgmental knowledge of experts are taken into account. Fuzzy logic is currently used by most researchers trying to integrate uncertainty into expert systems. In particular, the **possibility theory** proposed by Zadeh (1978) is used in two areas of research:

- *Fuzzy inference mechanisms.* Among the first expert systems of this type was the system used by Mamdani (1976) to control industrial processes; this has been followed by many others, especially in the medical field.

- *Fuzzy databases.* The best-known research teams working in this area are led by Umano in Japan, Kandel in the USA, and Prade in France. These authors all try to make fuzzy logic mechanisms consistent with the relational data model (see, e.g. Umano *et al.*, 1979; Zemankova-Leech and Kandel, 1984; Prade and Testemale, 1984).

Database systems

The work on AI described above has been paralleled by attempts to match the deductive capabilities of inference engines with the interpretive capabilities of database management systems (DBMSs). As shown by Demolombe (see Chapter 3), this leads to two different approaches for building deductive systems (Gallaire, 1983):

- A *systems-oriented approach* which either extends inference engines with the features of relational database systems, or reinforces traditional DBMSs with logical capabilities, permitting external views or integrity constraints to be defined while also optimizing access to the storage structure of databases.

- A *language-oriented approach* which takes advantage of the external consistency of logic programming languages and relational languages in order to combine PROLOG and relational DBMS capabilities.

In any case, the most widely accepted approach to building deductive database systems is to adopt an architecture which guarantees the independence of deductive and interpretive mechanisms.

2.2 Management functions

As expert systems are now spreading to every field of human activity, the main question faced by managers is to gauge the roles that expert systems could play in business administration. According to the definition given at the beginning of the chapter, they are mainly decision-support systems which can be consulted by managers to solve specific problems.

The integration of these new management assistants into organizations raises problems related to their role as devices used to transfer expert knowledge. At a first level, this problem can be viewed in terms of information processing extended to transformation mechanisms of information into decisions. Beyond this cybernetic approach to management expert systems, the problem has to be analyzed in terms of the dependence of organizations upon their experts. This analysis must be based on two observations:

- the growing role of experts in industrial economies, characterized by the specialization and complexity of tasks,
- the increase of informal power generated by expert knowledge, which might disturb the established power hierarchy.

In this approach to expert knowledge transfer in organizations, management expert systems are mechanisms coupling information and decision-making. So, the pragmatics of decision-making introduced above provide a practical way of handling the role of decision-support systems as organizational, coordinating, and control tools (Ernst, 1981).

2.2.1 Organization function

Organization can be roughly defined as the art of allocating resources to activities subject to goals. The first step in an organizational process is to define structures, particularly the **competence range** of each decision-maker, according to a taxonomy of decision problems. This step can be successfully carried out by an expert system which reduces management problems to subproblems.

In AI it is essential to understand a problem before structuring a decision process. The process of competence segmentation in organizations is subject to the following constraints:

- a preliminary **diagnosis of problems** justifying the use of an expert system in order to support a specific management function,
- a preliminary definition of the **validity domain** of the management expert system.

The problem of diagnosis will be dealt with below.

The validity domain of an expert system is seldom carefully defined by knowledge engineers. By definition, expert systems are devoted to solving specific problems; moreover, their performance decreases abruptly when they are used for problems outside their validity domain, as the knowledge base is then lacking some of the expert reasoning that is needed to build a solution process (Hayes-Roth *et al.*, 1983). Consequently, the validity domain of an expert system must be defined by strictly specifying the problems that the system can be called upon for consultation.

2.2.2 Coordination function

The complexity of a management system can be handled by taking into account the interdependences between decision-makers. Coordination problems are directly linked to the number of these interdependences. All managers deal with coordination tasks, which are intended to maintain the consistency of decisions made at a lower level. The integration of managerial behavior in a management system depends on coordination principles originally formulated by Mesarovic *et al.* (1970):

- *predicting interactions* between tasks when their interdependence is unavoidable, or undesirable,

- *decoupling interactions* for possibly independent tasks.

The first principle is based on the decision-maker's ability to anticipate actions intended at a lower level (Cyert and March, 1970). An expert system can effectively support this coordination task by exploring the space of possible actions that is consistent with the current state of the database and the behavioral model of decision-makers embedded in the knowledge base. With the support of an expert system, a manager is able to explore the whole solution space of a problem, without being limited to the first acceptable solution, as is generally the case when no decision-support system is available (Keen and Scott Morton, 1978).

According to the second principle, the efficiency of a coordination process depends on the consistency of results, obtained at a lower level, of tasks assigned by upper-level managers. A decision structure with decoupled activities is more suitable for decentralized organizations; in this case, an expert system is used to control the consistency of decisions made by several managers involved in the same decision process. In a knowledge base, **consistency constraints** are expressed by meta-rules used as decision rules by the expert system in order to assign a space of possible solutions to a given problem.

Whatever the coordination principle of a management system, the explanatory function of an expert system plays an important role in integrating decision processes. An expert system has the capability of justifying the validity of a solution process according to the structure of managerial reasoning, and provides explanations of the choices made at each step of the process and the decision rules that led to these choices.

These explanations must provide more than a mere reasoning track or solution plan; they must effectively convey to users the natural expertise from which a formal representation was encoded in a knowledge base. The mapping made by the explanation system must make clear to users the methods of the experts whose experience the system contains.

Coordination principles in a management system take the form of various procedures: plan procedures, hierarchical procedures, or self-coordination procedures (Kieser and Kubicek, 1975). They all require a distribution of knowledge among managers involved in the resolution of common problems. Such knowledge sharing can be profitably achieved by an expert system providing information, advice, and explanations to decision-makers; the practical results of such coordination are a reinforcement of managers' expertise and motivation to cooperate, and a reduction in the number of meetings and a shortening of decision cycles.

2.2.3 Control function

In the firm, managers control activities that fall within their range of competence. While doing so, they use subjective or objective decision rules specific to each class of problem. With their technical capabilities, expert systems can provide support for the usual procedures of management control, the main steps of which are:

(1) *Performance assessment.* An expert system works interactively; it therefore offers decision-makers the possibility of dynamically altering their management chart.

(2) *Variance analysis.* The deductive capability of an expert system allows managers to analyze causal relationships between performance indicators established at step 1.

(3) *Selection of actions.* Managers select the most satisfactory solution from the solution space generated by an expert system.

Complete automation of the decision process shown in Figure 2.1 would imply modifying the state of the database in the course of a single solution, which would require the use of **nonmonotonic reasoning**. These dynamic updates of the database change the premises used in the previous steps of the decision process, and can generate solutions inconsistent with previous ones. However, this reasoning mode could be applied to management expert systems handling the time factor, which would mean reasoning on nonstatic databases.

2.3 Diagnosis of management problems

We may wonder which managerial functions, as briefly described above, would benefit most from the support in decision-making that expert systems can provide. First, we can say that management problems falling within the scope of expert systems are those requiring solution by unstructured, complex, or decentralized decision processes.

2.3.1 Unstructured processes

Programming languages used in AI are nondeterministic, in contrast to the deterministic, algorithm-oriented languages generally used in computer science. Thus we can define our first class of problems calling for an expert-system approach: those which are partially or totally unprogrammable by traditional languages.

For such problems, decision factors determining the paths followed at each step of the decision process are context-dependent: they result from judgmental knowledge based on the subjective rationalities of decision-makers. These problems can be solved efficiently only by interactively connecting a database describing the decision-making environment to a knowledge base containing expert knowledge.

2.3.2 Complex processes

The complexity of a decision process can be reduced to the combinatory complexity of the knowledge necessary to implement it. This complexity soon becomes inaccessible to human reasoning, particularly when a decision process requires the interaction of several decision units. Such interdependence raises coordination problems. As seen above, an expert system, by speeding up reasoning processes, proves to be an outstanding coordination device.

2.3.3 Decentralized processes

The solution of management problems in a firm can be decentralized, either by spatial dissemination of decision units, or by time constraints, especially when decision units face an uncertain environment. Then, in order to preserve the integration of the decision-making structure, managers must use two types of procedure:

- expertise transfer to operational decision units in order to broaden their competence range,
- reinforcement of performance assessment mechanisms in order to maintain the coherence of the management system.

The deduction and interpretation capabilities of expert systems have made them basic tools for management control, especially in decentralized firms.

2.4 Internal specifications

Expert systems will be seen and accepted as management assistants only if they are endowed with the internal specifications of decision-support systems. The internal structure of such an expert system requires three types of mechanism:

- coupling between inference engines and DBMSs, especially when decision-makers have to reason on very large databases,

- approximate reasoning, to handle the uncertainty of the cognitive environment of managers,

- controls to provide managers with languages to meet their specific needs.

These specifications are directly induced by management functions supported by expert systems and involve architecture issues, reasoning models, and decision specification languages.

2.4.1 Architecture of management expert systems

If a reasoning process requiring the use of a large amount of data is to function correctly, the internal specifications of the inference engine must be separated from those of the DBMS. This requirement brings an improved cooperation between deductive and interpretive mechanisms, as it allows for calls to a DBMS to be made during the solution process itself.

For language consistency reasons, the relational model approach greatly facilitates this cooperation. Nevertheless, it is necessary to strengthen this model at a semantic level in order to reduce distortions existing between terms used by experts to express their knowledge, and relations described in the conceptual schema of a database.

In the context of an expert system, relations are primitives used by experts to set up the definition rules (static knowledge) and decision rules (active knowledge) from which reasoning processes are built. A terminology is thus established which is specific to each class of user, and which evolves together with their thinking and actions. Semantic distortions between data and knowledge are inherent in the modeling of human reasoning, but cannot be preserved when coupling mechanisms between information and decision systems have to be automated.

In the context of the relational data model, knowledge representation is based on a **semantic differentiation** of relations described in a conceptual schema according to currently accepted general properties, chiefly aggregation, generalization (Smith and Smith, 1977), and manifestation (Bobrow and Winograd, 1977) properties. This semantic differentiation is made

- either by factorizing knowledge by means of meta-relations described with a logic programming meta-language (Ernst, 1985)
- or by deriving external views by means of inference rules managed by the expert system and acting as 'semantic postulates' (Carnap, 1965).

Both techniques lead to the building of deductive databases coupling expert systems with DBMSs. Also, they imply that irreducible relations be defined regarding their normality, while their meaning meets the needs of a deduction system. This approach is entirely different from traditional normalization methods (Delobel and Adiba, 1982) aimed at generating conceptual schemas through syntactic rules that are far from providing users with ensured meaningful relations.

2.4.2 Management reasoning models

The logic of a decision process in a firm requires that uncertainty processing be included in the internal specifications of expert systems. They must be capable of offering a set of possible solutions to decision-makers, by resorting to two uncertainty sources: the environment of decision-makers, and the assumptions they make in the course of their reasoning.

The choice of the **possibility theory** described by Zadeh (1978) for modeling human reasoning is explained by Dubois and Prade in Chapter 5, who show that this theory provides a unified approach for the conceptual framework of management expert systems, being both a semantic theory for imprecise knowledge representation and a decision theory for handling uncertainty in decision-makers' judgments (Ernst, 1982).

From a merely epistemological point of view, a possibility *is not* a probability. The role of management expert systems is to support managers' reasoning within a space of research which is possibilistic in nature. To illustrate the difference between probability and possibility, Zadeh (1978) gives the following example:

'Consider the statement "Hans ate X eggs for breakfast," with X taking values in $U = \{1,2,3,4,...\}$. We may associate a possibility distribution with X by interpreting $\pi_X(u)$ as the degree of ease with

Table 2.2 The possibility and probability distributions associated with X.

u	1	2	3	4	5	6	7	8
$\pi_X(u)$	1	1	1	1	0.8	0.6	0.4	0.2
$P_X(u)$	0.1	0.8	0.1	0	0	0	0	0

which Hans can eat u eggs. We may also associate a probability distribution with X by interpreting $P_X(u)$ as the probability of Hans eating u eggs for breakfast. Assuming that we employ some explicit or implicit criterion for assessing the degree of ease with which Hans can eat u eggs for breakfast, the values of $\pi_X(u)$ and $P_X(u)$ might be as shown in Table 2.2.

'We observe that, whereas the possibility that Hans may eat 3 eggs for breakfast is 1, the probability that he may do so might be quite small, e.g., 0.1. Thus, a high degree of possibility does not imply a high degree of probability, nor does a low degree of probability imply a low degree of possibility. However, if an event is impossible, it is bound to be improbable.'

This heuristic connection between possibilities and probabilities may be stated in the form of what is called by Zadeh **the possibility/probability consistency principle**: what is possible may be improbable, and what is impossible is necessarily improbable.

The paradigm of decision-making in business is possibilistic in nature: decision-makers refer to a possibility space defined as possible worlds or possible courses of actions, before selecting one of them. This possibilistic paradigm is justified below by Yager in Chapter 6.

2.4.3 Decision specification languages

From a theoretical point of view, expressing the active knowledge of experts belongs to the realm of language pragmatics (Ernst, 1985); it consists in defining how experts utilize static knowledge proper to their cognitive environment. The pragmatics of a knowledge representation language imply a specification of possible situations where a database is exploited.

The architecture of management expert systems, as outlined above, can be profitably implemented by reducing the pragmatics of a knowledge representation language to a **control meta-language** (Gallaire and Lasserre, 1979). The meta-language interpreter operates as a control structure for the expert system inference engine.

Many authors (see e.g., Davis, 1976; Hayes, 1977; Weyhrauch, 1980) have set forth the advantages of this control approach in expert systems: high descriptive capability resulting from the use of meta-primitives, strong controlling power due to the diversification of search strategies, independence of logic, and control in resolution processes.

It is important to know whether such a control meta-language can meet the requirements of a decision specification language. This implies that resolution strategies likely to be expressed through a meta-language accurately describe the behaviors of decision-makers. More precisely, a meta-language has to be consistent with approximate reasoning models characterizing the logic of decision processes in the firm (Ernst, 1985). Only an experimental approach of the control issue can ensure the validation of decision specification languages which in the future will be associated with management expert systems.

2.5 Conclusion

Management expert systems represent the first application of AI in business management. In this chapter we have explored the capabilities of expert systems for supporting decision-making in the firm. We have shown that the design and implementation of management expert systems are subject to three constraints:

(1) integration of the relational database approach into the resolution of knowledge representation and manipulation problems,

(2) formalization of reasoning models in accordance with the logic of decision processes,

(3) building of decision specification languages expressing the specific rationalities of managers.

These conditions will allow decision-support systems to skip from information processing requirements to the logic of management thinking. Such systems will therefore act as necessary management assistants in more and more complex organizations faced with an increasingly unstable environment.

References

Anthony, R.N. (1965). *Planning and Control Systems: A Framework for Analysis.* Cambridge, MA: Graduate School of Business Administration, Harvard University

Bobrow, D. and Winograd, T. (1977). 'An overview of KRL, a knowledge representation language' *Cogn. Sci.*, **1**, 3–46

Carnap, R. (1965). *Meaning and Necessity*. Chicago: University of Chicago Press

Cyert, R.M. and March, J.G. (1970). *Processus de Décision dans l'Entreprise*. Paris: Dunod

Davis, R. (1976). 'Applications of meta-level knowledge to the construction, maintenance and use of large knowledge bases', PhD Thesis, Stanford University

Delobel, C. and Adiba, M. (1982). *Bases de Données et Systèmes Relationnels*. Paris: Dunod

Ernst, C. (1981). 'Les processus de coordination et de communication dans l'entreprise: Une analyse structurale' *Mélanges Pierre Vigreux*. Toulouse: Institut d'Administration des Entreprises

Ernst, C. (1982). 'An approach to management expert systems using fuzzy logic', In *Fuzzy Set and Possibility Theory* (R. Yager; Ed.). Oxford: Pergamon Press, 196–203

Ernst, C. (1985). 'Un métalangage de programmation logique orienté vers le contrôle sémantique de systèmes experts de gestion', Thèse d'Etat, Université Paul Sabatier, Toulouse

Gallaire, H. (1983). 'PROLOG et bases de données', Lannion, Journées PROLOG, CNET

Gallaire, H. and Lasserre, C. (1979). 'Controlling knowledge deduction in a declarative approach' In Proc. 6th IJCAI, Tokyo

Hayes, P.J. (1977). 'In defense of logic' In Proc. 5th IJCAI, Cambridge

Hayes-Roth, F., Waterman, D.A. *et al.* (1978). 'Principles of pattern-directed inference systems' In *Pattern-Directed Inference Systems* (D.A. Waterman and F. Hayes-Roth; Eds). New York: Academic Press, 577–601

Hayes-Roth, F., Waterman, D.A. and Lenat, D.B.; Eds (1983). *Building Expert Systems*. Reading, MA: Addison-Wesley

Keen, P.G. and Scott Morton, M.S. (1978). *Decision Support Systems*. Reading, MA: Addison-Wesley

Kieser, A. and Kubicek, H. (1975). 'An organizational concept for the design of management information systems' In *Information Systems and Organizational Structure* (E. Grochla and Z. Szyperski; Eds). de Gruyter, 163–185

Mamdani, E.H. (1976). 'Applications of fuzzy logic to approximate reasoning using linguistic synthesis' In Proc. 6th Int. Symp. on 'Multiple-valued logic', IEEE76. CH 111–4C, 196–202

Mesarovic, M.D., Macko, D. *et al.* (1970). *Theory of Hierarchical Multi-Level Systems*. New York: Academic Press

Pitrat, J. (1984). 'La genèse des systèmes experts', *Bull. Liaison Recherche Inf. Autom.*, (97), 2–8

Prade, H. and Testemale, C. (1984). 'Generalizing database relational algebra for the treatment of incomplete/uncertain information and vague queries', *Inf. Sci.*, **34**, 115–143

Simon, H.A. (1960). *The New Science of Management Decision*. Harper & Row

Smith, J.M. and Smith, D.C.P. (1977). 'Database abstractions: Aggregation and generalization', *ACM Trans. Database Syst.*, **2**(2), 105–133

Tabatoni, P. and Jarniou, P. (1975). *Les Systèmes de Gestion, Politiques et Structures*. Paris: PUF

Umano, M., Mizumoto, M. *et al.* (1979). 'A system for fuzzy reasoning' In Proc. 6th IJCAI, Tokyo

Weyhrauch, R.W. (1980). 'Prolegomena to a theory of mechanized formal reasoning', *Artif. Intell.*, **13**, 133–170

Zadeh, L.A. (1978). 'Fuzzy sets as a basis for a theory of possibility', *Fuzzy Sets Syst.*, **1**, 3–28

Zemankova-Leech, M. and Kandel, A. (1984). *Fuzzy Relational Data Bases: A Key to Expert Systems*

3

Architecture of Management Expert Systems[†]

Robert Demolombe

3.1 Expert systems and database management systems

Until the end of the 1970s, the large amounts of data used for business management provided a description of the state of a firm or any other type of enterprise. For example, the data would make available knowledge of stock levels, standing orders, accounts, or personnel statements. Database management systems (DBMSs) were used to answer precise queries, such as how many orders there were for a product, or what were the wages of employees in a particular department.

Expert systems are used by managers for decision-making, or rather, to support the decision-making process. At first, operations research techniques that were tentatively used in this field often proved too rigid. However, it was soon realized that decisions are hardly ever made by systematically applying precise rules whose validity domain is well known, and that it is therefore necessary to use more flexible systems. This is why the expert system must run interactively with the user, in order to supply him or her with a number of related solutions rather than a single solution to a problem. These related solutions may sometimes point to the existence of related problems, more relevant than the problem that was first considered.

Let us consider an expert system for selecting a range of investment plans for portfolio management. The investor will be able to inquire about altering the proposed plan in order to get a higher return, even though the risks incurred might increase, or to see whether it is advisable to buy gold. After examining the available solutions, the investor will be able to specify the terms of the problem accordingly.

Although the expert system plays quite a different role to that of the

† This work was supported by the CEC as part of the ESPRIT project ESTEAM.

Table 3.1 The roles of expert systems and DBMSs.

Expert systems: Supporting decision-making
 Imprecise problems with multiple solutions
 Interactive research of related solutions

Database management systems: Recognizing situations
 Answering precise queries

DBMS, it is dependent on the DBMS as it requires access to all the relevant data before making a decision.

The roles of the two systems can be summarized as in Table 3.1.

3.2 General architecture of expert systems

Before considering the particular features of management-oriented expert systems, we shall look briefly at their typical architecture. Most systems are either built according to this architecture or follow it very closely (Guida and Somavilco, 1981; Hayes-Roth *et al.*, 1983; Rehak *et al.*, 1985).

Figure 3.1 illustrates the four main components of an expert system:

(1) A module supporting an **interactive dialogue** with users. Its role is twofold: to translate requests and replies from an external into an internal language, and to manage the dialogue (i.e., to connect each request with the context of all previous exchanges).

(2) A **problem-solving** module, which acts as an inference mechanism, making it possible to generate several solutions during the reasoning process, and as a reasoning mechanism, permitting efficient

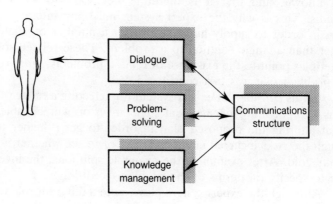

Figure 3.1 General architecture of an expert system.

operation of the inference mechanism as well as providing a justification for the proposed solutions.

(3) A **knowledge management** module, allowing access to and modification of knowledge, whether in the form of facts, rules, or even programs.

(4) A **communications structure**, supporting exchanges between the other three previous modules. This structure includes problems and subproblems to be or being solved, and problems solved with their solutions, as well as current reasoning.

3.3 Particular features of management expert systems

One of the main features of management expert systems, their proposal of several more or less related solutions through a dialogue with the user, has been mentioned above (see also Michaelson and Michie, 1983). Another important feature is that situations having to be modeled require a very large amount of data, stored in a database and managed by a DBMS. Thus questions relevant to this type of expert system concern interactions between the problem-solving module and the knowledge management module requiring a DBMS (Figure 3.2). These questions will be dealt with below.

These interactions give rise to an important requirement: we must define a method of extracting database subsets which are useful for solving each subproblem. ('Extracting' here means accessing information

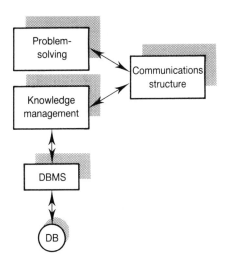

Figure 3.2 Interactions between expert system and DBMS.

stored on a disk and loading it in the main memory; the problem-solving module can operate efficiently only if data is stored in the main memory. 'Useful' means likely to be used for solving a subproblem or a related subproblem.)

Two questions arise:

- a question of *semantics*: how can we define the subset of useful information for solving a given problem?
- a question of *efficiency*: at what level of detail do we have to call the DBMS in the process of reducing problems into subproblems in order to minimize disk access?

3.4 Definition of useful information to be extracted from a database

The knowledge management block can be considered in turn as an expert system (Novak and Szablowski, 1984) directed to generate queries to the DBMS, whose answers provide the useful subset of information for solving a subproblem. The expert system needs to know the various classes of rule presented below.

The first class of rule is meant to link a problem with related problems whose solutions might be interesting enough to be proposed as alternatives. They have the following form:

> IF a given context and a given type of problem is to be solved
> THEN it is beneficial to provide also the solution to another type of problem.

Or, in a more concise form:

> Context and Type 1 problem → Type 2 problem   (1)

The context must allow the reasons or motivations leading to the problem-solving move to be described. To return to our example of portfolio management, the context must enable the user to know whether the client wishes to make an investment in order to buy a house ten years later, or a car three years later, or to deposit his money in a bank to advantage, or to pay less tax.

The second class of rule defines information types that are useful for the solution of a given type of problem. Here, 'type of information' and 'type of problem' can be described by means of keywords referring to topics, in the same way as documents and requests are described for information retrieval. These rules describe the nature of information in the database at a more abstract level and have the following form:

IF a given type of problem has to be solved
THEN it is useful to have this type of information available.

Or, in a more concise form:

Type of problem → Type of information   (2)

The third class of rule allows a relationship to be set up between each type of elementary information, corresponding for example to a keyword, and a query expressed in the DBMS language; the set of information of the given type is provided by the answer to this query. These rules have the following form:

IF such a type of elementary information is to be provided
THEN such a query has to be asked.

Or, in a more concise form:

Type of elementary information → Question.   (3)

Finally, the expert system must be able to access knowledge structuring the various types of information, in the same way as a thesaurus builds a structure upon keywords for information retrieval.

Together with rules (1), (2), and (3), which we call **retrieval rules**, combined with the information described above, a **query generation** module produces a set of queries for a given subproblem. The answers are given in the form of a set of relationships which will have to be translated into the language used by the communications structure to represent knowledge (Figure 3.3).

This architecture must be modified if the knowledge contains rules as well as facts. These rules are not of the same nature as the retrieval rules used to produce queries; they express semantic links between predicates representing facts in the database. When they are limited in number, they can be generated directly by the problem-solving module; when they are very numerous, data structures must be available to store them, as well as specific access methods. They are therefore handled by the knowledge management module.

There is, then, a clear need for a component that we call a **knowledge base management system** (KBMS). The KBMS manages a rule base and requires a DBMS to manage the database. The KBMS can serve to search for a subset of useful rules for the solution of a subproblem, and provide them as answers in the same way that a DBMS provides data, but without combining them. The KBMS can also use the rule base and the database to deduce new facts; in order to do so, it must include an inference mechanism, as in what are known as deductive databases (Figure 3.4).

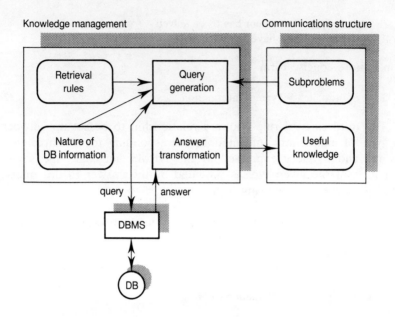

Figure 3.3   Detailed architecture of the knowledge management module.

So far, we have not yet touched upon the major problem of selecting a language to describe types of problems and types of information. The nature of the information contained in the database has to be described in this language. The database schema already provides a clear description of its contents, in the form of relations, attributes, and domains. This, however, is not sufficient: a notion of **semantic proximity** between these elements must also be expressed. As long as the database schema remains unchanged, this description is said to be **static**, whereas every time a subproblem appears in the communications structure its description has to be generated **dynamically** as a type of problem. This task may be quite difficult to achieve, depending on the language used to describe problems in the communications structure.

3.5 Efficiency of exchanges with a DBMS or KBMS

The methods used by the problem-solving module are generally designed under the implicit assumption that data having to be accessed during a solution process is stored in the main memory. If this assumption has to be verified in the context we are dealing with, then all useful information should be extracted from the database or knowledge base and stored in the main memory before the problem-solving process is started.

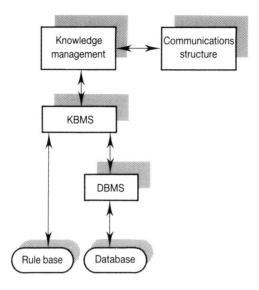

Figure 3.4 Architecture of a knowledge base management system.

This solution is quite suitable when the amount of information does not exceed the size of the main memory, which is very unlikely. Indeed, the more general the problem considered, the more difficult it is to delineate accurately the subset of useful information. For example, if a problem P can be decomposed into two subproblems, P_1 and P_2, the corresponding subsets of information to be extracted (I, I_1 and I_2) are such that the union of I_1 and I_2 is smaller than I; as P_1 and P_2 are simpler, it is easier to guess which information will be useful (Figure 3.5). However, it can be necessary to access information J in the base, in order to know that P can be decomposed into P_1 and P_2; in this case, the access to J is essential.

Before reducing the volume of information loaded in memory, it is necessary first to decompose a problem into subproblems; only then can access to the base be started. This reasoning could be carried to extremes, by postponing access until very precise information is needed. But the frequency of calls to the DBMS may be very high which could lead to a significant overhead (query analysis, optimization, and so on), and a large number of input/output transactions. This would unduly slow down the problem-solving mechanism.

This point will be illustrated by the following example. Neglecting the semantic problem, it is assumed that the problems to be solved are expressed in PROLOG. Let us consider the relations

ST-HOLD(STOCKHOLDER, COMPANY)
CONT(HOLDING COMPANY, COMPANY)

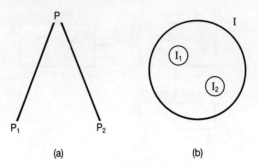

Figure 3.5   (a) Decomposition of a problem P into subproblems P_1 and P_2, and (b) corresponding useful information I, I_1, and I_2.

where ST-HOLD means that an institution holds stock in a company, and CONT means that a holding company has a controlling interest in another company. The rules below define CONT from ST-HOLD, and state that a company x has control over a company y if x is a stockholder of y or of a company controlling y:

CONT(x,y) ← ST-HOLD(x,y)
CONT(x,y) ← ST-HOLD(x,z) ∧ CONT(z,y)

Suppose we have to solve the problem of finding which companies IPM controls. This problem is translated into the expression:

P: CONT(IPM,x)

It can be decomposed into two subproblems:

P1: ST-HOLD(IPM,x)
P2: ST-HOLD(IPM,z) ∧ CONT(z,y)

Let, for example, ITP be a solution of ST-HOLD(IPM,z); then, solving P2 is equivalent to solving

P3: CONT(ITP,y)

which can be decomposed into

P4: ST-HOLD(ITP,y)
P5: ST-HOLD(ITP,z) ∧ CONT(z,y)

The decomposition process recurs in the same way for all companies directly or indirectly controlled by IPM.

If data in the relation ST-HOLD is managed by a DBMS, useful data for solving P can be extracted in two different ways. The first is to select useful information for solving the general problem P. In this case the whole relation ST-HOLD has to be extracted, as the companies controlled by IPM are unknown when starting the process. There will be a single access to the database. The second is to dynamically select useful information during the solution process of P. We must first extract the companies in which IPM holds stock, then companies in which ITP holds stock, and so on; in this case there are as many calls to the DBMS as there are subproblems of the same form as P1, P4, ... However, the amount of data extracted after each call is much lower than in the first method.

Consequently a choice has to be made between making very few calls to the DBMS, or extracting subsets containing small amounts of data. The first alternative leads to the extraction of large subsets from the database; the second necessitates many calls to the DBMS, creating a large overhead.

3.6 Conclusion

We have seen that management expert systems raise specific questions related to the use of very large databases or knowledge bases, and to the fact that they support decision-making rather than provide solutions to definite problems. In terms of architecture, these constraints lead to the knowledge management module itself being designed as an expert system; the knowledge base of which makes it possible to generate queries whose answers are sent to the problem-solving module. The architecture outlined here is just a framework which has allowed us to emphasize some important problems whose solution has yet to be found:

- How to specify a language to describe the information structure of the base. The keyword concept corresponding to propositional calculus may not be sufficient to ensure the much-needed accuracy.

- How to define precisely the concept of semantic proximity and the procedures for implementing it.

- How to decide to what level a problem has to be decomposed into subproblems in order to optimize the activation of calls to the DBMS or KBMS.

References

Guida, G. and Somavilco, M. (1981). 'Multi-problem solving, knowledge representation and system architecture', *Inf. Process. Lett.*, **13**, (4)

Hayes-Roth, F., Waterman, D.A. and Lenat, D.B.; Eds (1983). *Building Expert Systems*. Reading, MA: Addison-Wesley

Marque-Pucheux, G., Martin-Gallausiaux, J. *et al.* (1983). 'Interfacing PROLOG and relational database management systems', ICOD-2 Workshop, Cambridge

Michaelsen, R. and Michie, D. (1983). 'Expert systems in business', *Datamation*, Nov. 1983

Novak, E.J. and Szablowski, B.F. (1984), 'Expert systems in scientific information exchange', *J. Inf. Sci.*, **8**

Rehak, D.R., Howard, H.C. *et al.* (1985). 'Architecture of an integrated knowledge based environment for structural engineering applications' In *Knowledge Engineering in Computer-Aided Design* (J.S. Gers; Ed.). Amsterdam: North-Holland

4

Expert Systems and Knowledge Representation Languages

Henri Farreny

4.1 The role of knowledge representation languages in expert systems

The concept of expert systems is based on a functional definition: they consist of software (perhaps even hardware in the near future) which assumes responsibility for intellectual activities in fields where human expertise is (1) insufficiently structured to constitute a precise, reliable, and complete working method that can be directly transposed onto a computer, and (2) subject to revision or addition. The following objectives can therefore be assigned to expert systems:

- *Easy acquisition of 'granules' of knowledge*, in other words to facilitate the most direct expression possible of these granules with respect to the forms used by experts.
- *Exploitation of the granules as a whole*, by combining and/or concatenating the granules in order to infer new pieces of knowledge such as judgments, plans, proofs, decisions, predictions, or new granules, and perhaps by accounting for the way in which the new pieces of knowledge have been inferred.
- *Easy revisability of the set of granules*: it must be easy to add or delete granules.

Within the basic structure of an expert system, a distinction is usually made between two components: the knowledge base and the inference engine. But there is always a third fundamental component: the knowledge representation language, which allows specialization or instantiation of a general system (empty knowledge base), or makes possible the evolution of an expert system that has already been defined. The knowledge representation language plays an essential role in attaining the objectives set out above. When this knowledge representation language is sufficiently evolved (in particular, lacking in constraints for the user and relatively flexible) the term **declarative programming** is used.

4.2 Many languages, but few comparisons between them[†]

Over the past ten years or so, several hundred expert systems have given rise to a literature which represents, among other things, a considerable wealth of experience with knowledge representation languages. However, little effort has been made to compare the properties of these languages.

First, experiments on processing a single problem by several different engines are very rare. With a few exceptions, they concern 'toy' problems. (However, it must be admitted that the same can be said of traditional programming languages.)

Secondly, in contrast to experiments with traditional programming languages, experiments on processing several problems by a single engine (i.e., changes of knowledge base) have been very few and far between. However, this has been done with the MYCIN/EMYCIN family (in particular PUFF, DART, LITHO, SECOFOR, PDS, and TOM) and the OPS family (in particular R1/XCON, XSEL, ACE, AIRPLAN, AI-SPEAR, and YES/MVS). Among the fifty or so inference engines built in France, only a few have given rise to multiple instances on actual applications. In addition to PROLOG, which can indeed be considered – and used – as a general system, SAM, SPHINX, PROTIS (the original authors have achieved three implementations for each of these systems, all in the medical field), and SNARK (seven instances in various fields, by different teams) should be mentioned.

Thirdly, now that expertise is developing one might expect to see experiments on the evolution or updating of a knowledge base with respect to a single problem (or a group of related problems), but these are still relatively rare. The case of R1/XCON (800 rules in 1980, 1000 in 1981, 1500 in 1982, 2500 in 1983, 3250 in 1984, and 7000 in 1985) is an exception.

When one considers the current state of research, general comparisons or even simple classifications of languages associated with expert systems hardly seem attainable. Consequently, this chapter deals only with the characteristics by which languages may be differentiated. (The differences between languages are of course linked with certain differences between engines, a subject not covered here.)

[†] References to all the systems mentioned in this chapter are listed on p. 62.

4.3 Expert knowledge categories

As well as facts and rules, the languages associated with expert systems often propose – sometimes impose – other categories of knowledge. This section describes these categories and gives examples.

4.3.1 Facts

'Facts' is a broad category, covering a great variety of expressions, and interpretations of these expressions. Generally, it is agreed that facts are assertional knowledge granules which may be used to condition and then exploit operational knowledge, and which can be created or destroyed by the exploitation of operational knowledge.

In some systems different categories of fact can be distinguished according to the way in which they are handled. For example, in systems that are capable of planning actions, there are *facts* (established), *problems* (facts to be established), and *plans*. Examples of facts are given in Figure 4.1.

In SNARK, a triplet of 'constants', with the form:

    object   attribute   value

Two examples:

    round-11   nb-subscribers 110
    $7   nature   lichen

(i.e., the nature of object $7 is lichen).

In ARGOS-II, any list of constants. Two examples:

    (tool-3 in (case (5 10)) aspect (blue metal))

    (go-to (shop (10 12)))

In PROLOG-II, a 'literal' (predicative functional term) with 'variables'. An example:

    reduction (add,0,x,x);

(i.e., addition of 0 and x is reduced to x)

Figure 4.1   Examples of facts.

In SNARK:

```
BASIC-ROUND(G) = (BR)
GROUP(IR) = NO
NB-NEIGHBORS(BR) = (NB)
NB-NEIGHBORS(IR) < (NB)
→
BASIC-ROUND(G) ← (IR)
```

In PROLOG-II:

```
possible-forms ("r"."e"."y".x.q,broyer
                ind-pres(‹"e"."i".x.q.x.q›
                       ‹type-s-4,type-p-2›,i-pres).
                ind-imp ("y".x.q,type-1,i-imp).
                ind-ps:("Y".x.q,type-1,i-fs).nil)
                ind-fs("e"."i".x.q,type-1,i-fs).nil)
        →       in(x,"o"."u".nil)
                does-not-begin("o"."v"."n"."e".nil,x.q);
```

Figure 4.2 Examples of rules; in both cases the trigger part precedes the separator →.

4.3.2 Rules

Rules are operational granules of knowledge. The *trigger* part of a rule describes the triggering conditions of the rule in terms of more or less completely defined facts (the term **associative writing** of triggers is used); the *body* part describes the operations to be performed in the event of triggering. (The designations *body* and *trigger* or *head*, used for the two parts of a rule, depend on the procedural interpretation.) Depending on the system, there are several ways to describe the triggers and the body of rules. Often a distinction can be made between a sublanguage for the triggers and a sublanguage for the body of rules. Examples of rules are given in Figure 4.2.

4.3.3 Languages for triggers

Trigger languages play an essential role in making the 'associative writing' of rules more flexible, thus facilitating **declarative programming**: the use of definitions, independent of each other, of operational granules of knowledge. Each system conforms to a **compatibility model** between the facts and the elements, known as *patterns* or *filters*, that make up the

In OURCIN:

    IF MULTIMODAL VARIABLES...THEN...

              pattern

In SNARK:

    BASIC-ROUND (G) = (BR)... → ...

          pattern

(G) and (BR) are variables.

In PROLOG:

    P(x,f(y),g(a),a) → ...

        pattern

x and y are variables.

Figure 4.3   Examples of trigger parts.

triggers. The rule triggers for OURCIN, SNARK, and PROLOG are given in Figure 4.3.

In OURCIN, a pattern can only be compatible with a fact that is absolutely identical (character by character), in which case the reference compatibility model is identity, or with a fact consisting of words declared as being synonyms of words in the pattern, and words declared as being nonsignificant. For example, the pattern MULTIMODAL VARIABLES is compatible with the fact MULTIMODAL TYPE UNKNOWNS if UNKNOWNS is synonymous with VARIABLES and if TYPE is a nonsignificant word.

In SNARK, as in most inference engines, the compatibility model is **semi-unification** (i.e., a specific case of 'unification' as used in predicative logic). The SNARK rules, but not the facts, may explicitly include variables. In Figure 4.2 the symbols (G) and (BR) are variable identifiers which are compatible with any constant identifier or, as is generally the case, with any expression without variables.

In PROLOG, the compatibility model is full unification. Variables are permitted in facts as well as in rules. For example, the pattern in Figure 4.3 is compatible with a fact such as P(h(u),v,g(w)); where u, v, and w are variables.

In most so-called systems 'with variables', such as OPS 5, ARGOS-II, SNARK, or TANGO the rules only explicitly permit

Rule name		(r9
Trigger	F1	(take >x)
(three	F2	(<x part >y *)
patterns)	F3	ABSENT (<y * radioactive state *))
		(
	C1	(EXECUTE (point-in-part (<y)(>z)))
Body	C2	(REPLACEPB (go-to <z)(approach <x))
	C3	(RECORD
		(PLAN (grasp (<X)))
		(UPDATE
		(MODIFY (robot *)(taken<x))))))

Figure 4.4 A rule in ARGOS-II. The prefix > denotes variables in a capture situation; the prefix < in <x restores the last value captured by x; keywords of the language are in capital letters.

variables, but not facts. However, the compatibility models used by these systems are not always reduced to semi-unification. Thus, in ARGOS-II the trigger language provides, in addition to several types of variable, a range of matching operators, matching functions, and specific matching rules (known as 'theorems'). A few simple examples are given below.

Patterns F2 and F3 in Figure 4.4 use the *filtration operator* *, also known as the 'absorption operator', in a simple manner. This operator can appear anywhere in a pattern; it is compatible with any sequence, even an empty one, of ARGOS lists or atoms. It is possible to perform logic operations (e.g., negation, disjunction, or conjunction) on patterns or pattern elements. For example, in pattern F3 the ABSENT operator requires that no fact from the base be compatible with the element of the following pattern.

Procedures can be evaluated during matching. For example, if the variable x has already captured the list (blue white red), the pattern ((&class<x)>y) will be compatible with the fact ((white blue red)france) because (1) variable <x restores the list blue white red, (2) operator & initiates the procedure for classification in alphabetical order class and returns the list (white blue red), and (3) the variable >y is compatible with (and y captures) the value france.

A capture variable can be assigned a value other than the element matched by this variable. For example, the pattern (?(FONCRES>x price)) is compatible with the fact sand matter: the matching operator ? absorbs matter, whereas >x is compatible with any expression; during matching, x captures the price of sand (e.g., not-expensive) and not sand itself, as the FONCRES matching function initiates the price procedure on the argument matched by >x (i.e., sand) and assigns the result to x.

Normally, in ARGOS-II a rule can be triggered only if its trigger is recognized as being compatible with the current status of facts and problems. Sometimes it is practical for the user to endow the system with 'theorems' which virtually extend the base of facts when matching. For example, let theorem T be

((? blue) ← (?(& similar to blue)))

If a rule pattern is (blue block) and this pattern is incompatible with the fact base, the ARGOS engine should reject the rule; nevertheless, it will look beforehand in the 'theorem base' for a possible means of making the matching more flexible. Here the previous theorem T leads to the initiation of the 'similar' procedure on the argument blue (i.e., the result azure); the pattern (blue block) will now be replaced by (azure block) and a new comparison with the fact base will be attempted. The theorems lend themselves to recursion.

In some systems, such as MYCIN and its descendants, the compatibility between the trigger and the fact base is not reduced to only taking the values: absolute incompatibility or absolute compatibility, but rather the **degree of compatibility** is evaluated (for example a number between 0 and 1).

When fact categories are provided for, the triggers can refer to one or the other of them. For example, the first pattern (F1) in Figure 4.4 refers to the 'problems' base, whereas the following patterns (F2 and F3) refer to the fact base itself. From the point of view of the writer of the rule, pattern F1 characterizes the general *opportuneness* of the rule, whereas F2 and F3 characterize the subsidiary *applicability* conditions.

4.3.4 Languages for rule bodies

It is conventional to define rule trigger effects as transformations of the fact base. However, it seems more appropriate to distinguish between three types of effect, by comparing the three classical types of programming language instruction:

- *processing instructions*: effects on the knowledge base,
- *input/output instructions*: external communications,
- *control instructions*: effects on the engine operation process.

The effects on the knowledge base concern the fact base in the first instance. Usually languages propose primitives for the *elaboration* of existing facts and the *insertion* of new facts, or even for *deletion* in the fact base. In TANGO, for example, new facts must be added explicitly, but the engine, under its own control, can delete a fact if there is an addition to an object–attribute couple already present. Sometimes the

---

```
(($AND (SAME CNTXT PELVIC-ABSCESS)
   (RULES-OBJECTS EXIST (MENTIONING CONTXT PREMISE
   ENTEROBACTERIACEAE)SET1)
   (RULES-OBJECTS EXIST (MENTIONING CONTXT PREMISE RODS-GRAM+)
   SET2))
CONCATENATE-LIST SET1 BEFORE SET2 MEASURE 0.4)
```

Figure 4.5   A MYCIN meta-rule.

language allows recourse to matching primitives, similar to those available for writing triggers, for designating facts, groups or parts of facts (Figure 4.4) associatively. When the fact base is structured in subbases (e.g., facts, problems, plans, etc.) specific primitives are available.

Sometimes (e.g., with PAS-II, ADVISE, or ARGOS-II) primitives also allow modification of the rule base or, more generally, any part of the knowledge base. Rules capable of modifying the status of the rule base are usually classified as meta-rules (see Section 4.3.5).

Some languages propose primitives for sending messages, for consulting the environment (user, database, sensors, etc.) or, more generally, for initiating procedures external to the inference engine and the knowledge base (e.g., the EXECUTE primitive in Figure 4.4).

Some languages (e.g., ARGOS-II, SNARK, or ALOUETTE) have primitives that act directly on the inference engine behavior – for example, 'quit current base cycle, stop engine.' In ARGOS-II a (RETURN ‹patterns›) type of primitive causes a return until a previous cycle, such as the fact base associated with this cycle, is found which is compatible with ‹patterns›.

4.3.5 Meta-rules – or rules about rules

Meta-rules are granules of operational knowledge which define the ways and means of using the rules; in other words, they are rules about rules. In theory, meta-rules are called by associative access and so, like rules, they include a trigger and a body.

Figure 4.5 shows a MYCIN meta-rule. The second and third trigger patterns refer to the rule base, designated by RULES-OBJECTS. The rule is interpreted as: 'in the event of pelvic abscess, if rules mentioning ENTEROBACTERIACEAE in their premise or others mentioning RODS-GRAM+ exist, then classify the former before the latter.' In MYCIN there are primitives for writing the bodies of the meta-rules which classify a group of rules with respect to others or for fixing the 'utility' of certain rules.

In other systems (such as ARGOS-II or SNARK) the meta-rule

Identifier

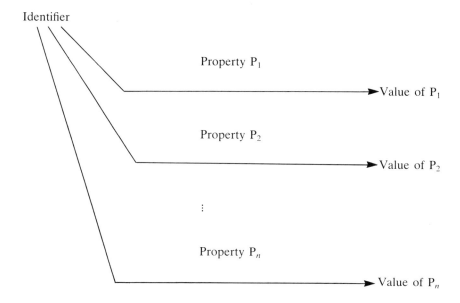

Property P_1

Value of P_1

Property P_2

Value of P_2

$\vdots$

Property P_n

Value of P_n

Figure 4.6 A simple assertional/operational object structure.

bodies can call on rule inhibition or validation primitives that are designated associatively. In ARGOS, inhibition or validation can if necessary be 'set' when the meta-rule is triggered, without immediate execution; patterns are associated with the setting primitives in the body of the meta-rule, and inhibition or validation will subsequently be executed automatically if the fact base becomes compatible with the patterns.

4.3.6 Assertional/operational objects

In some systems (e.g. MYCIN and its derivatives, CENTAUR, MOLGEN, and TROPICAID 2) the user can structure the assertional (facts) and/or operational (rules, procedures) knowledge in the form of significant conglomerations in the application field. In other contexts, different variants with varying degrees of complexity have been proposed, from *frames* (Minsky, 1975) to *objects* of 'object languages' such as SMALLTALK, and including *scripts* (Schank and Abelson, 1977) and *prototypes* (Bobrow and Winograd, 1977). These variants are designated here collectively as **assertional/operational objects**. A common, simple assertional/operational object is shown in Figure 4.6.

This structure combines a varying number of triplets of the form identifier–property–value in a single entity, for a single identifier. The property values can be of various types: constants, messages, procedures

IDENT

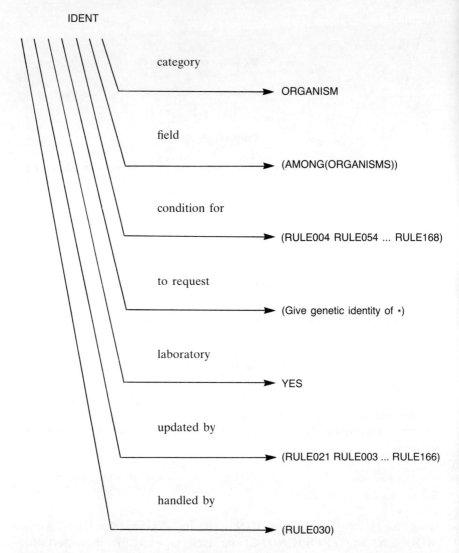

category

→ ORGANISM

field

→ (AMONG(ORGANISMS))

condition for

→ (RULE004 RULE054 ... RULE168)

to request

→ (Give genetic identity of *)

laboratory

→ YES

updated by

→ (RULE021 RULE003 ... RULE166)

handled by

→ (RULE030)

Figure 4.7   A MYCIN assertional/operational object.

to be activated, and so on. In MYCIN significant conglomerations are called 'clinical parameters' and 'context types.' An example of the 'clinical parameter' family is shown in Figure 4.7. The value of the 'category' property is the constant ORGANISM. The value of the 'field' property is a call of the AMONG procedure, whose argument is obtained by evaluating the expression (ORGANISMS). The 'updated by' property designates a list of rules to be triggered to evaluate the clinical parameter IDENT (the identity of a pathogenic agent).

If EMYCIN is to be used in a specialist application, the provision of such conglomerations is not only possible but mandatory, so the objects, properties, and values assignable to the field must be determined. It is important to emphasize that the definition of assertional/operational objects, such as 'clinical parameters' and 'context types', will take up a large part of the effort put into building the knowledge base, in addition to the definition of the expert rules.

Some assertional/operational objects can be designed, when exploiting the system, as specific cases of more general and predefined objects. When MYCIN is running the engine generates structured objects called *contexts*, and specific cases of other objects called *context types*. The assertional/operational objects can be organized in networks in which the values of certain properties act as pointers to antecedent, or consequent objects. For example, the value of the 'category' property in Figure 4.7 indicates a link between the IDENT and ORGANISM objects. The network structure can be exploited so that an object inherits the properties of the antecedent objects and so simplifies the representation of each object taken separately.

4.3.7 Procedures

Procedures are pieces of operational knowledge that the experts have considered should naturally be designated explicitly, and not by associative writing (the procedures are known and called by their names and not by their application conditions). If it is known that a certain piece of knowledge, precisely determined and definitely present in the system, must be called on without there being any alternative possibilities, then associative writing would effectively not be justifiable.

Some languages (e.g., ARGOS-II or TANGO) permit the introduction of procedures calls in the rules or meta-rules, in either the body or the trigger part (procedures implemented during pattern matching). It is also common to be able to use procedures in the writing of assertional/operational objects. For example, the AMONG procedure in Figure 4.7 is considered in the calculation of the value attached to the 'field' property of the IDENT object. This technique is known as *procedural attachment*.

4.3.8 Demons

Demons are pieces of operational knowledge generally described in associative writing, like rules or meta-rules, without being subject to the same basic cycles. These pieces of operational knowledge are automatically and immediately exploited as soon as certain events concerning the fact base (or sometimes other parts of the knowledge base) occur, such as additions, deletions, or consultations. The use of demons tends to increase the so-called 'reactivity' of expert systems.

The user controls the demons by special directions introduced into the rule body, as would be done with an interrupt system in the context of computer architecture. A demon can be 'enabled' or 'disabled,' conditionally or unconditionally. When an event of the type associated with the demon occurs, the demon, if enabled, performs a task related to a predefined type. Here, however, in contrast to the conventional use of interrupts, the events (as pure programs) likely to cause 'interrupts' are described associatively.

For example, in the body of a rule described in ARGOS-II, a demon can be defined by an expression of the form (DEFINE-DEMON add (lab-result >x)(EDIT <x available)). This demon, when active, edits a message each time a fact compatible with the pattern (lab-result >x) is added to the fact base (by the execution of any other piece of operational knowledge, a rule for example). If the fact added is (lab-result hemoculture), for example, >x will capture the hemoculture value which will then be restored by the symbol <x, hence the message (hemoculture available).

4.3.9 Use of variables

Some expert systems handle expressions of facts and rules that do not include any variables; an example is OURCIN (Figure 4.3). More commonly the languages associated with expert systems allow the presence of variables in the rules, but not in the facts (examples are PAS-II, MYCIN, OPS 5, ARGOS-II, SNARK, TANGO, and ALOUETTE). Generally the variables present in the rule triggers are implicitly universally quantified. For example, the rule in SNARK in Figure 4.2 must be interpreted as:

> 'whatever the particular values that can be substituted for the variables (G), (BR), (IR), and (NB) in order to satisfy the BASIC-ROUND(G) = (BR),   GROUP(IR) = NO,   NB-NEIGHBORS(BR) = (NB), and NB-NEIGHBORS(IR)<(NB) conditions while taking into account the fact base, the value (IR) can be assigned to BASIC-ROUND of (G).'

In a more general way, a rule such as DEC(x) → COR(x) is interpreted as:

> 'whatever the particular value of x making trigger DEC(x) compatible with the fact base, the instructions defined in the body of rule COR(x) can be run.'

Certain systems permit representation of the existential quantification. In

SNARK, for example, the rule MAN(X) = YES → CREATE(Y) FATHER-OF(X) ← (Y) is a representation of 'for any man x, a y exists such that y is the father of x.'

Among inference engines, PROLOG stands apart for various reasons, in particular because the use of variables is allowed in expressions used as rules, just as it is in expressions used as facts. All the variables present in the PROLOG expression are universally quantified. For example, A(x):– B(x)C(x) and C(y):– D(y) are rules that can be interpreted as: 'whatever x, in order to establish A(x), it is sufficient to establish B(x) and C(x); whereas, whatever y, in order to establish C(y), it is sufficient to establish D(y).' Another example is B(z):– is a fact that can be interpreted as: 'whatever z, B(z) is established.' D(a):– is a fact that can be interpreted as: 'D(a) is established.' :–A(u) is a problem that can be interpreted as: 'whatever u, A(u) is not established'; i.e., u must be found such that A(u) be established.

The use of variables enables several knowledge expressions to be condensed into one; this is sometimes called *knowledge factorization*.

4.3.10 Capacity for representing uncertain or imprecise knowledge

In fields where efforts are being made to develop expert systems, knowledge (facts and rules) processed or inferred quite often involve uncertainty or imprecision. Among the expert systems that can exploit uncertain or imprecise knowledge are MYCIN (and all its derivatives: PUFF, HEADMED, DART, SECOFOR, LITHO, PDS, TOM, etc.), PROSPECTOR, GARI, SAM, SPHINX, PROTIS, PLANT/ds (and its derivatives PLANT/dc and BABY), SNARK/SUPERIKON, ELFIN, SPII, TROPICAID 2, DIABETO, MANAGER, CRIQUET, and MEPRA. Examples of rules from three of these systems are given in Figure 4.8.

A fact is uncertain when it contains an assertion that cannot definitely be declared true or false, even though it must take one truth value or the other. An example is 'the cause of the illness is, perhaps, pseudomonas,' in which the uncertainty is indicated by 'perhaps.' A rule is uncertain when it produces uncertain conclusions even when the premise is certain. An example is 'if the patient has such and such a positively identified symptom, it is then likely that he has such and such a positively identified illness,' in which the uncertainty is suggested by 'likely.' A fact is imprecise if it contains incompletely identified objects. An example is 'the patient has a temperature of approximately 39.5°C, in which the imprecision is signified by 'approximately.' A rule is imprecise if it implicates imprecise facts as premise or conclusion, for example 'if the patient's temperature is high, he must be given a large spoonful of

In HEADMED:

if: 1) the diagnosis envisaged is: major depression, and
      2) the intensity of this depression is: moderate or slight, and
      3) the present mental state of the patient is: psychotic, and
      4) there has been no previous psychiatric problem recently
then: highly suggestive evidence (0.8) exists that the appropriate
      treatment category is: antipsychotic.

In LITHO:

if: 1) one or several flats exist on FDC curve, and
      2) one or several flats exist on CNL curve, and
      3) one or several flats exist on BHC curve, and
      4) the global porosity of the area is less than 10%
then: highly suggestive evidence exists (0.5) that the geological
      formation of the area is globally compressed.

In SPII:

if: the intelligence test mark, approximately speaking, is between 10 and 14, and
      the level in English, approximately speaking, is between 6 and 10
then: the test results are considered mediocre.

Figure 4.8   Rules involving uncertainty or imprecision.

such and such a medicine.' In Chapter 5, Dubois and Prade give further
details of the relationship between uncertainty and imprecision, and their
representation and processing.

In practice, the language of an expert system which can process
uncertain or imprecise facts or rules must provide for conventions and
primitives so that the user can assign a degree of uncertainty or a field of
imprecision to the knowledge being transmitted (facts only for ordinary
users, rules for experts). For example, in order to represent uncertainty,
the ordinary user can assign a number to the facts (in MYCIN and
PROSPECTOR) and the expert can assign one or two numbers to the
rules (one in MYCIN, two in PROSPECTOR). In MYCIN, the
attenuation coefficient of a rule with the form 'P implies Q' represents the
certainty that 'Q is true' when 'P is true' is certain. In PROSPECTOR the
sufficiency factor indicates at which point it is sufficient that 'P is true' be
certain for 'Q is true' to be certain, whereas the *necessity factor* indicates
at which point it is necessary that 'P is true' be certain for 'Q is true' to be
certain.

4.4 Declarative or incremental programming?

It is commonly emphasized that the principles of expert systems facilitate the progressive development and updating of knowledge bases according to a so-called **declarative** or **incremental programming** style. This means that, because (1) the rule triggers are written in terms of patterns, (2) the rules do not call other rules, and (3) the rules are separate from the engine, it should be easy to add or delete rules from the rule base of an expert system. If the fact base goes through a state compatible with the triggers of the new rules, it will be possible to trigger these rules, without the author of the additions having to specify that such and such new rule will be called by such and such another rule. If the fact base goes through a state which would have triggered rules now deleted it is possible that this state will now trigger other rules, unforeseen by the author of the deletions. Under these conditions several experts can contribute to updating a knowledge base more or less independently. This is in contrast to what happens with a traditional program: when the programmer deletes a procedure, he makes certain that none of the remaining procedures continues to call the deleted procedure (if this is not done the resulting program may stop short); if the programmer adds a procedure, he usually places calls for this procedure in other procedures in order for it to be usable.

The user should not have too high an expectation of the gain in flexibility resulting from the organization and operating principles of expert systems. Too much trust in declarative or incremental programming may result in disappointment, for the knowledge gleaned from the experts is manifested only as conventions, inference modes, and strategies (for the exploitation of these modes) integrated in the engines; these conventions, modes, and strategies, which are largely unknown to the experts supplying the knowledge base, do not always enable the engines to exploit the available knowledge to the full. This point of view can be developed further by briefly examining three problems.

4.4.1 Insensitivity to the order of rules? Rules in bulk?

There is some controversy over an engine's ability to exploit rules provided in bulk. An engine will tolerate rules in any order if, whatever the problem for which there is available a set of rules leading to a solution, the use of any permutation of that set of rules leads to the same solution (or possibly to a solution that is recognized as being in some way equivalent). Often an engine will not tolerate rules in bulk. One such is MYCIN which, although it orders the rules received under its own control, can provide markedly differing results, depending on the order in which certain rules (so-called 'self-referencing' rules) are acquired. Other systems (PROLOG or ARGOS, for example) may or may not loop on a same set of rules, depending on the order of these rules, as a result of their rule selection strategy. For the user, the degree of evolution of the knowledge expression language is effectively higher as it does not have to deal with ordering the rules.

When the language is particularly simple (e.g., if the rules are only logic propositions, without any variables, of the form $P \rightarrow Q$) it is possible to build engines that tolerate rules in any order. Of course, there are particular sets of rules that are order-independent for all engines; see for example the 'commutative production systems' proposed by Nilsson (1980).

4.4.2 Interpretation of knowledge with possible dependences

Consider, for example, the two rules

IF P THEN(0.5)Q,   IF Q THEN(1.)T

The numbers indicate attenuation coefficients, which are interpreted and exploited in the MYCIN manner. Let us suppose that we are certain of proposition P. According to R1, if P is certain, a *certainty factor* of 0.5 can be associated with Q. According to R2, if the certainty factor associated with Q is 0.5, the certainty factor of 0.5*1. = 0.5 can be associated with T.

We now suppose that a third rule R3 exists:

IF P THEN(0.6)T

According to R3, since P is certain, the certainty factor 1.*0.6 = 0.6 can be associated with T. Let a MYCIN-type engine blindly combine the two reasoning lines (the application of R1 and then R2 on the one hand and R3 on the other), without noticing that they both depend on P, and assign the factor 0.6 + 0.5 − 0.6*0.5 = 0.8 to T. The pieces of knowledge declared by the authors of the three rules are not *a priori* redundant or contradictory; each reflects an original element of knowledge compatible with the other two. Yet the reasoning line corresponding to the concatenation R1, R2 must be set aside as it is based on exactly the same piece of knowledge (that P is certain) as is the reasoning line corresponding to the application of R3; whereas R3 provides direct information about the relationship between the certainty of T and that of P.

4.4.3 Detection of inconsistencies between pieces of knowledge

Consider the three propositional logic rules

IF C THEN not D,   IF A THEN D or E,   IF B THEN not E

If A and B are found to be simultaneously true, the possible addition of the rule

IF A and B THEN C

will allow contradictory conclusions to be drawn. It would be desirable to detect the appearance of such inconsistencies.

The evolution of pieces of knowledge in systems provided with approximate reasoning capabilities leads to similar difficulties. Let us take the example in Section 4.4.2 (rules R1 and R2) and assume that an expert now introduces the rule R3′ IF P THEN(n)T into the base. If n is greater than 0.5 the reasoning line corresponding to the application of R3′ is not *a priori* inconsistent with the one corresponding to R1,R2 (nevertheless, to conclude on T it would be legitimate to retain the R3′ reasoning line and ignore the R1,R2 line, because both lines depend on P and R3′ is more direct). However, if n is less than 0.5 the two reasoning lines are quite contradictory. This type of inconsistency is not detected by MYCIN or similar systems.

4.5 Conclusion

According to Feigenbaum and McCorduck (1983),

'. . . knowledge is power. Power does not lie in the inference procedure. . . . Practically any inference method will do the job. Power rests in knowledge. . . .'

Indeed, from a computer science point of view at least, knowledge does not exist without a language, and a knowledge representation language does not exist without an engine capable of interpreting this language. So the study of the properties of the languages, and of the properties of the associated engines, is a prerequisite for the full exploitation of expert knowledge. The important questions to be asked about knowledge representation languages are what can be expressed with existing languages (and how), what cannot be expressed, what must be expressed explicitly, and what risks are run when a particular expression is used.

Expert systems combined with references

ACE   (Vesonder *et al.*, 1983)
ADVISE   (Michalski and Baskin, 1983)
AIRPLAN   (Masui *et al.*, 1983)
AI-SPEAR   (Billmers and Swartwout, 1984)
ALOUETTE   (Mulet-Marquis and Gondran, 1984)
ARGOS-II   (Farreny, 1980; Picardat, 1985)
BABY   (Michalski and Baskin, 1983)
CASNET   (Weiss *et al.*, 1978)
CENTAUR   (Aikins *et al.*, 1983)
CRIQUET   (Vignard, 1984)
DART   (Bennett and Hollander, 1981)
DIABETO   (Buisson *et al.*, 1985)
ELFIN   (Martin-Clouaire, 1984)
EMYCIN   (Van Melle, 1980)
GARI   (Descottes, 1981)
HEADMED   (Helser *et al.*, 1978)
LITHO   (Bonnet *et al.*, 1982)
MANAGER   (Ernst, 1985)
MEPRA   (Lefevre, 1984)
MOLGEN   (Friedland, 1979)
MYCIN   (Shortliffe, 1976; Buchanan and Shortliffe, 1984)
OPS 5   (Forgy, 1980)
OURCIN   (Demonchaux and Quinqueton, 1984)
PAS-II   (Waterman, 1975)
PDS   (Fox *et al.*, 1983)
PLANT/dc   (Michalski and Baskin, 1983)
PLANT/ds   (Michalski *et al.*, 1982)
PROLOG II   (Colmerauer, 1982)
PROSPECTOR   (Duda *et al.*, 1979)
PROTIS   (Soula *et al.*, 1983)
PUFF   (Aikins *et al.*, 1983)
R1/XCON   (McDermott, 1982)
SAM   (Gascuelo, 1981)
SECOFOR   (Courteille *et al.*, 1983)
SNARK   (Lauriere, 1984; Vialatte, 1985)
SPHINX   (Fieschi, 1984)
SPII-1   (Martin-Clouaire and Prade, 1985)
SUPERIKON   (Lagrange and Renaud, 1984)
TANGO   (Rousset, 1983)
TOM   (Cognitech, 1984)
TROPICAID 2   (Auvert *et al.*, 1984)
XSEL   (McDermott, 1982)
YES/MVS   (Griesmer *et al.*, 1984)

References

Aikins, J.S., Kunz, J.C. Shortliffe, E.H. and Fallat, R.J. (1983). 'An expert system for interpretation of pulmonary function data', *Computers Biomed. Res.*, (16), 199–208

Auvert, B., Van Look, F., Le Thi Huong Du, Aegerter, P., Gilbos, V., Emmanuelli, X., Bosseau, J.F., Boutin, P., Landre, M.F. and Philippe, A.M. (1984). 'Conception d'un système général d'aide à la décision médicale pour les infirmiers des pays en voie de développement' In Proc. Conf. on 'Information and medecine', Marseille

Bennett, J.S., Hollander, C.R. (1981). 'DART: An expert system for computer fault diagnosis' In Proc. 7th IJCAI, Vancouver, 843–845

Billmers, M.A. and Swartwout, M.W. (1984). 'AI-SPEAR: Computer system failure analysis tool' In Proc. ECAI 84, Pisa, 65–73

Bobrow, D. and Winograd, T. (1977). 'KRL: Another perspective', *Cogn. Sci.*, (3), 29–42

Bonnet, A., Harry, J. and Ganascia, J.G. (1982). 'LITHO: Un système expert inférant la géologie du sous-sol', *TSI*, **1**, (5), 393–402

Buchanan, B.G. and Shortliffe, E.H. (1984). *Rule-Based Expert Systems: The MYCIN Experiments of the Stanford Heuristic Programming Project*. Reading, MA: Addison-Wesley

Buisson, J.C., Farreny, H. and Prade, H. (1985). 'Un système-expert en diabétologie accessible par minitel' In Proc. 5th Conf. on 'Expert systems', Avignon, ADI-AFCET

Sté Cognitech (1984). 'Démonstration d'un système-expert en diagnostic et traitement des maladies et accidents culturaux de la tomate' In Proc. 4th Conf. on 'Expert systems', Avignon, ADI-AFCET

Colmerauer, A. (1982). 'PROLOG II, manuel de référence et modèle théorique', GIA, Faculté des Sciences de Luminy, Marseille

Corteille, J.M., Fabre, M. and Hollander, C.R. (1983). 'An advanced solution: The drilling advisor SECOFOR' In Proc. 58th Annual Technical Conf., San Francisco, CA

Demonchaux, E. and Quinqueton, J. (1984). 'OURCIN: Un langage iteratif en logique propositionnelle', *Bull. Liaison Recherche Inf. Autom.*, (94)

Descottes, Y. (1981). 'Représentation et exploitation de connaissances 'experts' en génération de plans d'actions', Thèse de Troisième Cycle, Institut National Polytechnique de Grenoble

Duda, R., Gashnig, J. and Hart, P. (1981). 'Model design in the PROSPECTOR consultant system for mineral exploration' In *Expert Systems in the Micro-Electronic Age* (D. Michie; Ed.). Edinburgh: Edinburgh University Press, 153–167

Ernst, C. (1985). 'Un métalanguage de programmation logique orienté vers le contrôle sémantique de systèmes experts de gestion', Thèse d'Etat, Université Paul Sabatier, Toulouse

Farreny, H. (1980). 'Un système pour l'expression et la résolution de problèmes orienté vers le contrôle de robots', Thèse d'Etat, Université Toulouse III

Farreny, H. (1985). *Systèmes-Experts: Principes et Exemples*. CEPADUES Editions

64   Management Expert Systems

Feigenbaum, E.A. (1984). 'Knowledge engineering: The applied side' In *Intelligent Systems, the Unprecedented Opportunity* (J.E. Hayes and D. Michie; Eds) 37–55

Feigenbaum, E.A. and McCorduck, M. (1983). *The Fifth Generation*. Reading, MA: Addison-Wesley

Fieschi, M. (1984). *Intelligence Artificielle en Médecine*. Paris: Masson

Forgy, C.L. (1980). 'The OPS 5 user's manual', Technical Report, Department of Computer Science, Carnegie–Mellon University

Fox, M.S., Lowenfeld, S. and Kleinosky, P. (1983). 'Techniques for sensor-based diagnosis' In Proc. 8th IJCAI, Karlsruhe, 158–163

Friedland, P. (1979). 'Knowledge-based experiment design in molecular genetics' In Proc. 6th IJCAI, Tokyo, 285–287

Gascuel, O. (1981). 'Un système expert dans le domaine médical', Thèse de Troisième Cycle, Université Paris VI

Griesmer, J.H., Hong, S.G., Karnaugh, M., Kastner, J.K., Schor, M.I., Ennis, R.L., Klein, D.A., Milliken, K.R. and Van Woerkom, H.M. (1984). 'YES/VMS: A continuous real time expert system' In Proc. AAAI 84, 130–136

Helser, J.F., Brooks, R.E. and Ballard, J.P. (1978). 'Progress report: Computerized psycho-pharmacology advisor' In Proc. Int. Collegium 'Neuropsychopharmacologicum', Vienna

Lagrange, M.S. and Renaud, M. (1984). 'SUPERIKON: Un essai de cumul de six expertises en iconographie: Erudition ou trivialité', Document de Travail No. 6, CRA and LISCH Laboratories, CNRS, Paris

Lauriere, J.L. (1984). 'Un langage déclaritif: SNARK' Report, Institut de Programmation Université Paris VI

Lefevre, J.M. (1984). 'Systèmes-experts: l'Avalanche', *Micro Robots*, (13), 11–16

McDermott, J. (1982). 'R1: A rule-based configurer of computer systems', *Artif. Intell.*, **19**, (1), 39–88

McDermott, J. (1982). 'XSEL: A computer salesperson's assistant' In *Machine Intelligence*, Vol. 10 (J.E. Hayes, D. Michie and Y.H. Pao; Eds). Chichester: Ellis Horwood

Martin-Clouaire, R. (1984). 'ELFIN: Une approche système-expert et théorie des possibilités appliquée en géologie pétrolière', Thèse de Troisième Cycle, Université Paul Sabatier, Toulouse

Martin-Clouaire, R. and Prade, H. (1986). 'SPII-1: A simple inference engine capable of accommodating imprecision and uncertainty' In *Computer-Assisted Decision Making* (G. Mitra; Ed.). Amsterdam: Noth-Holland, 117–131

Masui, S., McDermott, J. and Sobel, A. (1983). 'Decision-making in time-critical situations' In Proc. 8th IJCAI, Karlsruhe, 233–235

Michalski, R.S. and Baskin, A.B. (1983). 'Integrating multiple knowledge representations and learning capabilities in an expert system: The ADVISE system' In Proc. 8th IJCAI, Karlsruhe, 256–258

Michalski, R.S., Davis, J.H., Bisht, V.S. and Sinclair, J.B. (1982). 'PLANT/ds: An expert consulting system for the diagnosis of soybean diseases' In Proc. ECAI 82, Orsay, 133–138

Minsky, M. (1975). 'A framework for representing knowledge' In *The Psychology of Computer Vision* (P.H. Winston; Ed.). New York: McGraw-Hill

Mulet-Marquis, D. and Gondran, M. (1984). 'Un langage pour les systèmes-experts: ALOUETTE' Report HI/4773-02, Electricité de France, Clamart

Nilsson, N. (1980). *Principles of Artificial Intelligence*. Palo Alto, CA: Tioga

Picardat, J.F. (1985). 'Manuel ARGOS-II' Report LSI, Université Paul Sabatier, Toulouse

Rousset, M.C. (1983). 'TANGO, moteur d'inférences pour une classe de systèmes-experts avec variables', Thèse de Troisième Cycle, Université de Paris-Sud, Orsay

Schank, R. and Abelson, R. (1977). *Scripts, Plans, Goals and Understanding*. Lawrence Erlbaum

Shortliffe, E.H. (1976). *Computer-Based Medical Consultations: MYCIN*. New York: Elsevier

Soula, G., Vialettes, B. and San Marco, J.L. (1983). 'PROTIS: A fuzzy deduction-rule system: Application to the treatment of diabetes' In Proc. MEDINFO 83, Amsterdam, 533–536

Van Melle, W. (1980). 'A domain-independent system that aids in constructing knowledge-based consultation programs', PhD Dissertation, Computer Science Department, Stanford University

Vesonder, G.T., Stolfo, S.J., Zielinski, J.E., Miller, F.D. and Copp, D.H. (1983). 'ACE: An expert system for telephone cable maintenance' In Proc. 8th IJCAI, Karlsruhe, 116–121

Vialatte, M. (1985). Thèse soutenue sur SNARK 2, Université Paris VI

Vignard, P. (1984). 'CRIQUET: Un logiciel de base pour élaborer des systèmes-experts' In Proc. Int. Colloquium on 'Artificial intelligence', Marseille, 81–88

Waterman, D.A. (1975). 'Adaptive production systems' In Proc. 4th IJCAI, Tblisi, 296–303

Waterman, D.A. and Hayes-Roth, F.; Eds (1978). *Pattern-Directed Inference Systems*. New York: Academic Press

Weiss, S.M., Kulikovski, C.A., Amarel, S. and Safir, A. (1978). 'A model-based method for computer-aided mechanical decision-making', *Artif. Intell.*, **11**, (1/2), 145–172

5

Processing of Imprecision and Uncertainty in Expert System Reasoning Models

Didier Dubois and Henri Prade

5.1 Introduction

The human knowledge we seek to represent in the knowledge base of an expert system is often tainted with uncertainty and imprecision. **Uncertainty** refers to the truth or falsity of propositions representing factual or operational pieces of knowledge (rules of the type 'if ⟨conditions⟩ then ⟨conclusions⟩'); truth or falsity that has not been definitely established considering the conformity of these pieces of knowledge with respect to the information available concerning the reality. Uncertainty is modeled by assigning one or two numbers to a proposition as a measure of the confidence in the truth of this proposition. The choice between one and two numbers depends on an *a priori* hypothesis on the links between the degree of confidence in a piece of information and the degree of doubt about it. The degree of doubt is equivalent to the degree of confidence in the contrary piece of information.

Imprecision has to do with the content of a piece of information, one which includes vague predicates or quantifiers. The fact that the words used to express the piece of knowledge do not necessarily have a unique and precise interpretation, but cover a set of values of subjacent parameters whose limits are often known only approximately (as they may be assigned slightly different values by different experts), is then taken into account. A fact such as 'it will *probably* rain *a lot* tomorrow' includes a judgment (*probably*) of an imprecisely specified fact. If we wish to consider the meaning behind this fact, to go beyond the symbols that comprise it, then we must have some representation of the quantity of rain we expect to observe, and we must make a numerical evaluation of the likelihood of the fact.

Recent developments in the **theory of fuzzy sets** and **possibility**

theory enable imprecision and uncertainty to be processed within the same framework. This unity in the framework makes it possible to identify, at a given level of knowledge, a link between the imprecision and the uncertainty of the statements that can be formulated as follows: If an expert has to be precise, he will weight his judgments with confidence coefficients. But if he is allowed a certain degree of 'fuzziness,' he will be more assured in his statements, and he may sometimes be able to avoid the use of uncertainty coefficients. Many existing expert systems do not take imprecision into account explicitly, and instead use uncertainty coefficients, more or less empirically, in order to moderate knowledge.

If the pieces of knowledge handled during reasoning processes are likely to be imprecise or uncertain, the processes themselves may be valid, or may be only plausible. With a valid mode of reasoning and with premises that are certain it is guaranteed that conclusions that are certain will be obtained, whereas with a plausible mode of reasoning, such as reasoning by analogy, the conclusion reached cannot generally be taken as being certain, even if the premises are.

The framework proposed for taking into account imprecise and uncertain aspects of knowledge goes well beyond that of probability theory, which has certain disadvantages as far as the representation of subjective judgments is concerned. These disadvantages are discussed in the following section, where the formal framework for modeling the uncertain and the imprecise is presented and briefly discussed. The notions introduced are applied to various mechanizable reasoning modes within the framework of production rule systems. Associative access by fuzzy pattern-matching, deduction by generalized modus ponens, propagation of uncertainty coefficients, and the problems of information combination are mentioned in particular. This chapter can be considered as an extension of two of Prade's papers (Prade, 1984a; 1985a), which it completes and synthesizes.

5.2 A unified framework for the representation of uncertainty and imprecision

5.2.1 The limits of the probabilistic model

The facts and rules that are to be represented can be considered as logic propositions p forming a finite set $\mathcal{P}$. These propositions are assumed to be non-vague; i.e., they can be only true or false and their set can be seen as a list of possible events. Let us suppose that uncertainty in these propositions is represented by a probability measure P, which is an application of $\mathcal{P}$ in the interval $[0, 1]$, such that

$$P(\varnothing) = 0, \qquad P(\mathbf{1}) = 1 \tag{1}$$

$$\text{if } p \wedge q = \varnothing, \text{ then } P(p \vee q) = P(p) + P(q) \tag{2}$$

where $\varnothing$ represents the impossible event and $\mathbf{1}$ the event that is always realized; $p \wedge q = \varnothing$ means that p and q are two incompatible, mutually exclusive propositions. It should be noted that $P(p)$ represents the probability of p being true, but not the degree of truth of p (which, when the propositions have a clearly marked meaning – as is assumed here – equals 0 (false) or 1 (true)). A consequence of axioms (1) and (2) is that $P(p) + P(\neg p) = 1$, where $P(\neg p)$ is the probability of p being false. If an expert cannot decide in favor of p or $\neg p$ (non-p), the only option, within this framework, is to write $P(p) = P(\neg p) = \frac{1}{2}$. But if the choice is instead between three mutually exclusive propositions p, q, and r, where $\neg p = q \vee r$ and $q \wedge r = \varnothing$, the expert's indecision is now expressed by the probabilities $P(p) = P(q) = P(r) = \frac{1}{3}$, which is paradoxical in the case of total ignorance as it implies that $P(\neg p) = \frac{2}{3} > P(p)$. Furthermore, if it is accepted that $P(p) = \frac{1}{2}$ this would not eliminate the paradox. When the expert says he knows nothing of p and $\neg p$, he means that he does not know the value of $P(p)$ or of $P(\neg p)$; i.e., that he knows only, in the extreme case, that $P(p) \in [0, 1]$ and that $P(\neg p) \in [0, 1]$. This cannot be taken directly into account if we remain within the framework of probability theory, according to which it is impossible to know nothing or not enough (limits on the probability values). Nothing indicates that the knowledge of experts, in the absence of statistical data that may be inaccessible, is sufficiently developed to be amenable to purely probabilistic modeling.

We denote by $P_*(p)$ and $P^*(p)$ the lower and upper delimiters of the probability value $P(p)$. It is then easily seen that the only constraints on these values are $P_*(p) + P_*(\neg p) \leq 1$ and $P^*(p) + P^*(\neg p) \geq 1$. This underlines the fact that the introduction of imprecision into the probability value enables the paradox of total ignorance to be resolved.

Another disadvantage of working with probabilities is that it is necessary to list an *exhaustive* set of *mutually exclusive* alternatives which will constitute the so-called elementary propositions, $p_1, p_2, \ldots, p_n$, which are such that $p_i \wedge p_j = \varnothing$, $\forall i$, $\forall j$, and that $\forall i$, no proposition $p \in P$ exists outside of $\varnothing$ and p_i, which is such that $p \wedge \neg p_i = \varnothing$ (i.e., $\varnothing$ and p_i are the only propositions that are incompatible with $\neg p_i$). Any proposition $p \in P$ is then expressed in the form of a disjunction

$$\bigvee_{i \in I} p_i$$

of elementary propositions. The specification of the probability measurement passes through the enumeration of p_i s, and the adjunction of weights $m_i = P(p_i)$, such that

$$\sum_{i=1}^{n} m_i = 1$$

Nothing proves that the set of facts provided by the expert is either exhaustive or composed of mutually exclusive elements, and capable of being considered as being sufficiently *precise*, in the sense that they cannot be broken down nontrivially into the union of two propositions that would be (more) basic. Nor is it obvious that he should be tied down to this possibly utopic discipline.

Furthermore, the calculation of probabilities often leads in practice to axioms of independence between the facts handled, to formulae such as $P(p \wedge q) = P(p).P(q)$, which bring us back to hypotheses of the 'aleatory compensation of errors' type. There is no justification for such hypotheses in the context of expert knowledge. All that can be shown, on a general level, is that $P(p \wedge q) \leq \min(P(p), P(q))$.

In fact the use of probabilities, in other than frequentist and combinatory contexts, has been justified only within the framework of betting behavior theory, where $P(p)$ represents the stake placed on the proposition p; the normalization formula $P(p) + P(\neg p) = 1$ would be interpreted as indicating that the sum remaining in play is wagered on 'non-p'. But it would be difficult to defend the idea that experts should be treated as gamblers as far as the knowledge they provide is concerned. After all, we are dealing with a reference model whose application is justified only in a specific context such as gaming or financial decision-making. What is more, the total ignorance paradox is not resolved as the betting behavior model assumes that the gamblers are experienced, and not beginners: $P(p) = \frac{1}{2}$ means that p is considered as having as much chance of occurring as non-p. If not it would be a prudent attitude towards the bet that does not reflect the knowledge of the gambler. With the exception of betting behavior theory, all attempts to justify the additivity of degrees of confidence on purely qualitative and subjective bases seem to have failed (Fine, 1973).

A further disadvantage of probabilistic calculation is of a more practical nature. It is clear that not much reliance can be placed on numerical values of uncertainty coefficients provided by the expert. It is also clear that the calculation rules of probability theory tend to lead to greater errors (there are sums and products), so much so that a propagation string that is too long can reduce the meaning of the coefficients obtained to nothing, if an error calculation reveals too great a deterioration of the intervals delimiting the coefficients.

5.2.2 The possibilistic model

Consider the set $\mathcal{P}$ of propositions. Let g be an application of $\mathcal{P}$ in $[0, 1]$ which evaluates the **degree of confidence** $g(p)$ for each proposition p in the statement 'p is true.' It should be remembered that 'p implies q' means that $p \rightarrow q \triangleq \neg p \vee q = \mathbf{1}$. A minimum condition for the confidence measurement g being coherent with this notion is:

$$\text{if } p \rightarrow q\mathbf{1}, \text{ then } g(p) \leq g(q) \tag{3}$$

since q will be true at least each time that p is. Furthermore, it is accepted that $g(\varnothing) = 0$ and $g(\mathbf{1}) = 1$. Given this general framework, the procedures for building functions g satisfying Equation (3) must be defined. In order to do this it is necessary to limit oneself to *calculable* subsets of confidence measures. There are two ways of doing this (Dubois and Prade, 1988).

First the axiom (2) may be extended by postulating the existence of a combination operation $*$ such that

$$\text{if } p \wedge q = \varnothing, \text{ then } g(p \vee q) = g(p) * g(q) \tag{4}$$

The $*$ operations which are possible candidates have been examined by the authors (Dubois and Prade, 1982). It should be noted that, as a consequence of (3),

$$g(p \vee q) \geq \max(g(p), g(q)) \tag{5}$$

always holds. Here we examine the limiting cases of $\prod$ functions such that the equality in (5) is verified; $\prod$ is then called a **possibility measure** (Zadeh, 1978). This name is justified by the following construction of a possibility function $\prod_t$, based on a proposition $t \in P$ that is held to be true:

$$\prod_t (p) = \begin{cases} 1, & \text{if } p \wedge t \neq \varnothing \quad (\text{i.e., if } t \nrightarrow \neg p) \\ 0, & \text{otherwise} \end{cases} \tag{6}$$

Given that t is true, $\prod_t(p) = 1$ clearly means that 'p is possibly true.' More generally, the $\prod$ functions can be built from a set $I = \{p_1, ..., p_k\}$ of elementary propositions and values $\pi_i = \prod(p_i)$, $i = 1, k$, such that $\max_{i=1,k} \pi_i = 1$. In this case it can be shown that

$$\forall p \in \mathcal{P}, \prod(p) = \max \{\pi_i \mid p \wedge p_i \neq \varnothing\} \tag{7}$$

defines a possibility measure, and conversely that $\forall \prod$, a set of elementary propositions I exists such that (7) is satisfied. It should be noted that $\prod(p)+\prod(\neg p)\geq 1$. Furthermore, $\max(\prod(p),\prod(\neg p))=1$; i.e., of the two contrary propositions, at least one is possibly true. The quantity

$$N(p) = 1 - \prod(\neg p) \tag{8}$$

evaluates at which point $\neg p$ is impossible (i.e., at which point it is certain that p is true). The function N, known as the **necessity function**, verifies (3), and $N(p \wedge q)=\min(N(p),N(q))$ always holds.

So two numbers are associated with each proposition p: a measure of necessity $N(p)$ and a measure of possibility $\prod(p)$. These functions are not subject, as the probability measures are, to the total ignorance paradox; this can easily be modeled by

$$N(p) = 0, \quad \forall p \neq \mathbf{1}, \qquad \prod(p) = 1, \quad \forall p \neq \varnothing$$

The second way of defining a confidence measure in an operational manner is to divide the certainty into weights $m(p)$ assigned to elements of a subset $\mathcal{F}$ of $\mathcal{P}$ known as the *set of focal propositions*. These propositions are the subject of the expert's knowledge. There are no restrictions on $\mathcal{F}$, other than that it cannot be empty and that

$$\forall p \in \mathcal{F}, m(p) > 0, \qquad \varnothing \notin \mathcal{F}, \qquad \sum\{m(p) \mid p \in \mathcal{F}\} = 1 \tag{9}$$

where $\sum\{\ \}$ represents the sum of elements of the set described between $\{\ \}$.

The notion of probability is generalized in the sense that m is a probability assignment when $\mathcal{F}$ contains only elementary propositions. But we are no longer bound to enumerating the elementary propositions; there is no longer the problem of exhaustivity. The weight assigned to total ignorance will be $m(\mathbf{1})$, in particular, if $\mathbf{1}\in\mathcal{F}$. In order to evaluate the truth of a proposition p, given $\mathcal{F}$ and m, two sets of focal propositions are considered:

$$\text{Pos}(p) = \{q \in \mathcal{F} \mid p \wedge q \neq \varnothing\} = \qquad \text{the set of focal propositions that are not incompatible with } p$$

$$\text{Nec}(p) = \{q \in \mathcal{F} \mid q \rightarrow p = 1\} = \qquad \text{the set of focal propositions that imply the truth of } p$$

We are then led to define a degree of credibility $\text{Cr}(p)$ and a degree of plausibility $\text{Pl}(p)$ for p (Shafer, 1976):

$$\text{Cr}(p = \sum\{m(q) \mid q\in\text{Nec}(p)\}, \qquad \text{Pl}(p) = \sum\{m(q) \mid q\in\text{Pos}(p)\} \tag{10}$$

Since $Nec(p) \subseteq Pos(p)$, then $Cr(p) \leq Pl(p)$. The degree of plausibility takes into account the knowledge that makes p possible; the degree of credibility accounts for the knowledge that makes p certain. $Pl(p) = 1 - Cr(\neg p)$ is verified, i.e. the degree of plausibility of p expresses the lack of credibility of non-p, or it is the complement of unity of a degree of doubt with respect to p. In other words, p is somewhat credible only insofar as the opposite proposition is not very plausible.

If the knowledge provided by the experts is coherent; i.e., if $\mathcal{F}$ is a chain $\{q_1, q_2, ..., q_k\}$ such that $\forall i = 1, k - 1, q_i \to q_{i+1} = \mathbf{1}$, then $Pl = \prod$ and $Cr = N$, i.e., degrees of possibility and necessity are found. This condition means that the pieces of information provided by the experts are naturally arranged in their order of precision, as they correspond to nested sets of values $A_1 \subseteq A_2 \subseteq \cdots \subseteq A_k$, if each proposition q_i is seen as a statement of the type 'the variable X takes its value from A_i' or, more briefly, 'X is A_i.'

Furthermore, if, for each focal proposition q_i, an elementary proposition p_i is chosen such that $p_i \to q_i = \mathbf{1}$, and a probability measure is defined such that $\forall i = 1, k, P(p_i) = m(q_i)$, each probability measure constructed in this way will be limited by $P_*(p) = Cr(p)$ for the lower bound and by $P^*(p) = Pl(p)$ for the upper bound. Thus a modeling framework including probabilities as specific cases has been correctly defined, enabling a meaning to be given to vague propositions. Furthermore, it has been possible to propose a quantitative mathematical model of the possible and the necessary, or, more generally, for the plausible and the credible.

5.2.3 The representation of imprecision in a possibilistic model

Let X be a variable taking its value from a set S. Propositions of the type $p = {}'X$ is $\{s\}$', where s is an element of S, constitute a set of elementary propositions. These propositions are precise with respect to S since they assign a value to X which is completely determined in S. By identifying $\mathcal{P}$ with the set of parts of S, a proposition $p \in \mathcal{P}$ will be imprecise insofar as it is not elementary. Within this framework, any possibility measure $\prod$ on $\mathcal{P}$ evaluating the uncertain nature of propositions of $\mathcal{P}$ can be interpreted as a *vague* proposition of the type 'X is A,' where A is a fuzzy subset of S with the characteristic function μ_A defined by

$$\forall s, \mu_A(s) = \prod(p), \text{ where } p = {}'X \text{ is } \{s\}'$$
$$\stackrel{\triangle}{=} \pi_X(s) \tag{11}$$

Here π_X is said to be the possibility distribution of the variable X.

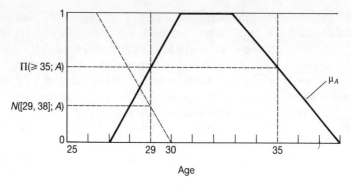

Figure 5.1   The possibility distribution $\pi_{\text{age(John)}} = \mu_A$.

Conversely, any vague proposition $\bar{p}$ of the type 'X is A' (e.g., X is *big*), where A is a fuzzy set of possible values of X, brings us back to the statement of a set of mutually exclusive elementary propositions weighted by their respective degree of possibility, or to the statement of a set of coherent focal propositions each weighted with a part of certainty that can be seen as a degree of probability.

Let us consider an example. It is known (for certain) that John is *about* 30 to 33 years old and that he is certainly no younger than 27 and no older than 38. This imprecise information can be represented by a possibility distribution $\pi_{\text{age(John)}} = \mu_A$, as shown in Figure 5.1. It is then easy to calculate the possibility and the necessity of John's age being situated in a subset F of S from the formulae

$$\Pi(F; A) = \sup_{s \in F} \mu_A(s) \tag{12}$$

$$N(F; A) = \inf_{s \notin F} \{1 - \mu_A(s)\} \tag{13}$$

which results directly from (7) and (8) with $p = $'$X$ is F' where $X = \text{age(John)}$, $p_i = $'$X$ is $\{s_i\}$' from (11), and by generalizing (7) to infinite sets (by replacing 'max' with 'sup'). Thus the possibility and the necessity of John being over 35 years old are respectively equal – in our example – to Π (≥ 35; A) $\simeq 0.6$ and to N (≥ 35; A) $= 0$; whereas for the proposition 'John is between 29 and 38 years old' to be evaluated, these quantities are equal to $\Pi([29,38]); A) = 1$ and $N([29,38]; A) \simeq 0.3$ (see Figure 5.1). It is important to note that these values are purely indicative, insofar as a precise identification of the possibility distribution μ_A is not possible or makes no sense in general. However, the values of $\Pi(F;A)$ and $N(F;A)$ are not very sensitive to slight variations of μ_A. What is important, above all, is the identification of the regions where $\mu_A = 1$ or $\mu_A = 0$; in the other regions of S, degrees of possibilities are assigned which must become greater as the associated values considered become increasingly possible for the variable X.

5.3 Processing of imprecision and uncertainty in reasoning

5.3.1 General reasoning scheme

Many reasoning schemes, in particular those implemented in production rule systems, can have the general form

First premise (p,q)

Second premise p'

Conclusion q'

where the first premise (p,q) expresses a connection (which may or may not be a causal relation) between propositions p and q, whereas the second premise consists of a proposition p' which 'recalls' p in a certain way; the conclusion q', which recalls q in a similar way, is then inferred. It is clear that the validity of such an inference depends on the nature of the comparison between p and p' and on the nature of the relationship between p and q. The scheme above covers valid forms of reasoning such as modus ponens (if p implies q and if p is true, then q is true) as well as plausible forms of reasoning such as reasoning by analogy (q' is to q as p' is to p).

In the following section we examine reasoning by analogy in greater detail, before dealing in Section 5.3.3 with the extension of modus ponens to imprecise propositions. We continue in Section 5.3.4 with an examination of uncertain facts and rules, and we show in Section 5.3.5 how uncertainty coefficients are combined.

5.3.2 Reasoning by analogy and fuzzy pattern matching

In reasoning by analogy, three propositions p, p', and q are considered as being true, and from them a fourth proposition q', which is to q what p' is to p, is inferred. This can be expressed in the form of the following diagram:

$$(p, \quad q)$$
$$\Phi \uparrow \quad \downarrow \Phi^{-1}$$
$$p' \quad q'$$

where the function Φ is assumed to link the contents of p' and p by matching aspects which are identical and associating aspects which are homologous but different. For example, if p describes a situation S, and q

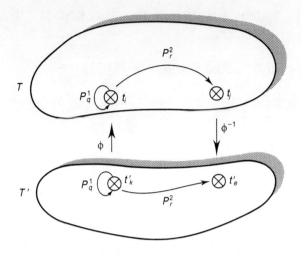

Figure 5.2   The analogy between T and T'.

an action A to be performed in situation S, the action A' that may have to be performed in situation S', which recalls S in certain aspects, is the action A, modified by taking into account the difference between S and S' so as to adapt A to S'; i.e., $q' = \Phi^{-1}(q)$.

In order to explain what is meant by analogy, let us formalize the problem, as it is proposed by Farreny and Prade (1982) and Prade (1984b). Two systems T and T', each defined by the collection of its elements and the collection of predicates known to have been satisfied by these elements, will be declared analogous in the sense of Φ if a bijection Φ exists between the elements t_i of T and the elements t'_k of T' such that if n elements of T satisfy an n-ary predicate P_r^n, their homologues – in the sense of Φ – in T' satisfy the same predicate (or at least a similar predicate). It is the identity (or at least the 'semantic' resemblance between the predicates satisfied by the elements of the two systems) that leads to these elements being placed in correspondence through Φ, and which thus validates the analogy defined by Φ; this placing in correspondence is not necessarily unique. The analogy between T and T' is shown schematically in Figure 5.2.

Reasoning by analogy, then, consists in inferring that if a new predicate (which has not been used to establish the analogy) is satisfied by elements of T, then this predicate should also be satisfied by the elements of T', homologous in the sense of Φ.

A reasoning-by-analogy formalization has been proposed and implemented recently by Bourelly *et al.* (1983). The model is based on the following scheme:

The information A concerning the system T resembles the information C concerning the system T'

NOW   The information B concerning T depends on the information A concerning T

THEREFORE   The information D concerning T', which resembles B, is inferred

For example:

A Marseilles is situated on the coast and at a middle latitude

B Marseilles' climate is temperate

C Rome is situated on the coast and at a middle latitude

THEREFORE D Rome's climate is temperate

It should be noted that the inference will be valid insofar as it is assumed that the climate of European towns depends only on their geographical situation and their latitude.

The predicates satisfied by the elements of each of the two systems can be fuzzy (a predicate such as *big* is fuzzy insofar as, even in a given context, the elements considered as 'big' do not constitute a precisely bounded set, as 'big' covers a range of sizes). The similarity between the predicates of two systems, which is the basis of the analogy, can be more or less great, in particular if these predicates are fuzzy.

Possibility theory enables the evaluation of the resemblance between two predicates A and A' within the same universe of discourse. It is a **semantic matching**, taking into account their representation in the form of possibility distributions (Cayrol *et al.*, 1982); matching based on a pure identity of symbols proves to be insufficient in this framework. Two measurements $\prod(A;A')$ and $N(A;A')$ of conformity of A with A' are defined by

$$\prod(A;A') = \sup_{s \in S} \min(\mu_A(s),\ \mu_{A'}(s)) \qquad (14)$$

$$N(A;A') = 1 - \prod(\overline{A};A') = \inf_{s \in S} \max(\mu_A(s),\ 1 - \mu_{A'}(s)) \qquad (15)$$

where $\mu_{\overline{A}}=1-\mu_A$ is the characteristic function of the complement A, and $\prod(A;A')$ and $N(A;A')$ are evaluations of possibility and necessity which generalize (12) and (13) in the case of vague propositions of the type 'X is A.'

These evaluations will enable the following example to be processed:

The town T is *beside* the sea and at a *middle* latitude

The climate of T is *temperate*

The town T' is *not very far* from the sea and is at a *middle* latitude

What can be said about the climate of T'?

The confidence in the result of an inference by analogy will depend on the validity of the analogy (i.e., on the degrees of similarity between the predicates which preside over its establishment and the certainty that the predicates, even if identical, mean the same thing in the different propositions), on the extent of the analogy, and lastly of course on the degree of interdependence between the predicate bearing the inference and the predicates that have been used to establish the analogy. In the example above, it seems possible to reach a conclusion about the climate of T', given the similarity of the predicates, whose meaning is sufficiently specific (not too vague), and because of the dependence (which is not expressed in the premises) between the climate on the one hand and the location and the latitude on the other. When such a dependence or relationship is explicitly taken into account in the reasoning, we have arrived at the framework of generalized modus ponens.

5.3.3 Imprecise rules and generalized modus ponens

A production rule system including a fact base and a rule base are likely to be tainted with uncertainty or imprecision. For simplicity, we assume the facts to be of the type 'X is A,' where A is a subset of elements of S, possibly fuzzy or possibly reduced to a precise value. The rules are of the type 'if ⟨condition⟩ then ⟨conclusion⟩,' where '⟨condition⟩' is a fact of the type 'X is A',' and '⟨conclusion⟩' is either a fact of the type 'Y is B'' or a procedure triggering order.

Let us first examine a single rule. An imprecise rule will be of the type 'if X is A, then Y is B,' where A and B are fuzzy sets on reference frames S and T, respectively. This rule is seen as a causal link of S to T, expressed in the form of a conditional possibility distribution $\pi_{Y|X}$ on $T \times S$. If π_X is a possibility distribution on S, then $\pi_{Y|X}$ induces the distribution π_Y on T such that (Dubois and Prade, 1985a)

$$\pi_Y(t) = \sup_s \min (\pi_X(s), \pi_{Y|X}(t,s)) \tag{16}$$

This is in fact the calculation of the possibility of the fuzzy event $A \times \{t\}$, where $\pi_X = \mu_A$, in the sense of the possibility measure induced by $\pi_{Y|X}$. The rule 'if X is A, then Y is B' implicitly defines a conditional possibility distribution $\pi_{Y|X}$ by placing $\pi_X = \mu_A$, $\pi_Y = \mu_B$ in (16).

The greatest solution $\hat{\pi}_{Y|X}$ of (16) (in the sense of the inclusion $F \subseteq G \leftrightarrow \mu_F \leq \mu_G$) is then defined by

$$\hat{\pi}_{Y|X}(t,s) = \mu_A(s) \rightarrow \mu_B(t) = \begin{cases} 1, & \mu_A(s) \leq \mu_B(t) \\ \mu_B(t), & \text{otherwise} \end{cases} \tag{17}$$

An inference pattern is then obtained, known as **generalized modus ponens** (Zadeh, 1979), by considering a fact of the form 'X is A'':

X is A'
If X is A, then Y is B
$\qquad\qquad Y$ is B'

where B' is calculated by applying (16):

$$\mu_{B'}(t) = \sup_s \min (\mu_{A'}(s), \pi_{Y|X}(t,s)) \tag{18}$$

In this pattern, what is known of the general law of dependence between X and Y is applied to the fact 'X is A',' whereas in reasoning by analogy two singular situations are compared, in the absence of the applicable general law. This scheme has the following properties:

$\forall A,\ B' \supseteq B\ (\mu_{B'} \geq \mu_B)$

if $A' \subseteq A\ (\mu_{A'} \leq \mu_A)$, then $B'=B$

$\forall A',\ \forall t,\ \mu_{B'}(t) \geq \alpha, \qquad \alpha = \sup_s \{\mu_{A'}(s) \mid \mu_A(s) = 0\} \tag{19}$

So it can be seen that this pattern never provides conclusions more precise than B, but it does manage to draw nontrivial conclusions when A' differs slightly from A (contrary to classical modus ponens, which may be derived from the present pattern as a particular case). This characteristic is satisfying as it is not obvious that an imprecise fact will always coincide with the condition part of one of the production rules. Fortunately, the system is not always thwarted when this happens.

The inequalities in (19) mean that a uniform level of indetermination appears if a significant part of A' is not included in A, which seems intuitively natural. In particular, if $A' = \bar{A}$ or if, more generally, there exists $s \in S$, $\mu_{A'}(s) = 1$, and $\mu_A(s) = 0$, then $B' = T$ (total indetermination). So, if it is known that A' is *near* (but appreciably different from) A in the sense of a certain metric, then generalized modus ponens is not capable of deducing from 'X is A'' and from 'if X is A, then Y is B' that 'Y is B',' where B' is 'near' B; this can be done only if there is available complementary information about the continuity and monotonicity of the behavior of the causal link between X and Y in the vicinity of (A,B) (Dubois and Prade, 1983/84). For example, starting with the rule 'if the tomato is red, then it is ripe' and with the fact 'the tomato is very red,' then generalized modus ponens does not lead to the conclusion that 'the tomato is very ripe'; this conclusion can be reached only if it is known that the degree of ripeness increases with the redness of the fruit.

Furthermore, it may be verified that from fuzzy rules of the type 'if X is A, then Y is B' and 'if Y is B', then Z is C,' a fuzzy rule 'if X is A, then Z is C' can be built provided $B \subseteq B'$ (Dubois and Prade, 1985a), and will lead directly, by generalized modus ponens, to the same result for Z as is given by the cascade application of the two rules.

Let us now suppose that there are n rules 'if X is A_i, then Y is B_i,' $i = 1,n$, for describing a causal link btween X and Y. Each rule i is represented by a fuzzy set $A_i \rightarrow B_i$ whose characteristic function is $\mu_{A_i} \rightarrow \mu_{B_i}$ (see (17)), and the set of rules can be represented by the intersection

$$\bigcap_i (A_i \rightarrow B_i)$$

where $\cap$ is to be interpreted as the 'minimum' operation. This result is proved elsewhere (Dubois and Prade, 1985a). The generalized modus ponens is then expressed in the case of several rules by

$$\forall t, \ \mu_{B'}(t) = \sup_s \ \min \ (\mu_{A'}(s), \ \min_{i=1,n} \ (\mu_{A_i}(s) \rightarrow \mu_{B_i}(t))) \tag{20}$$

The reader should consult Dubois and Prade (1985a) for a more detailed study of generalized modus ponens.

5.3.4 Uncertain facts and rules

An uncertain fact $p = $ 'X is A,' where A is a crisp subset of S, is assumed to be assigned with a degree of necessity $N(p)$ and of possibility $\Pi(p)$ such that $\max(\Pi(p), \ 1 - N(p)) = 1$ (normalization). According to the approach suggested by Martin-Clouaire and Prade (1986), this uncertain fact is interpreted as an imprecise fact $\bar{p} = $ 'X is $\hat{A}$' with

$$\mu_{\hat{A}}(s) = \begin{cases} \Pi(p), & s \in A \\ 1 - N(p), & s \notin A \end{cases} \tag{21}$$

A rule 'if p, then q' is uncertain if it is not absolutely certain that q is true when p is true. The approach proposed by Martin-Clouaire and Prade (1985) will be followed here, and this uncertainty will be quantified by means of two numbers: $N(p \rightarrow q)$, expressing at which point it is sufficient that p be true for q to be true, and $N(q \rightarrow p) = N(\neg p \rightarrow \neg q)$, expressing at which point it is necessary that p be true for q to be true. This idea generalizes the notion of a necessary and sufficient condition, and is used in different forms in certain expert systems such as PROSPECTOR (Duda *et al.*, 1981) or PROTIS (Soula *et al.*, 1983); here N is a measure of necessity, so it is assumed that two numbers a and a' are available such that

$$N(p \rightarrow q) \geq a > 0, \qquad N(q \rightarrow p) \geq a' > 0 \qquad (22)$$

The rule 'if p, then q' with $p = $ 'X is A,' $q = $ 'Y is B,' $A \subseteq S$, $B \subseteq T$, is then seen as an imprecise rule, defining a conditional possibility distribution $\hat{\pi}_{Y|X}$, as previously, on $T \times S$, built by applying (21) to propositions $p \rightarrow q$ and $q \rightarrow p$; it gives

$$\hat{\pi}_{Y|X}(t, s) \quad \begin{cases} \leq 1 - a, & s \in A, t \notin B \\ \leq 1 - a', & s \notin A, t \in B \\ = 1, & \text{otherwise} \end{cases}$$

In this case if the uncertain fact p is such that $N(p) \geq b$ and $\prod(p) \leq b'$, then by using (18) with $A' = \hat{A}$ defined by (21) we may deduce that

$$\mu_{B'}(t) = \begin{cases} \prod(q) \leq \max(b', 1 - a'), & t \in B \\ \prod(\neg q) \leq 1 - \min(a,b), & t \notin B \end{cases} \qquad (23)$$

Or $N(q) \geq \min(a,b)$. It should be noted that the normalization condition $\max(\prod(p), 1 - N(p)) = 1$ is transmitted to $N(q)$ and $\prod(q)$.

This result can be obtained directly by applying the possibility calculation rules ($\prod(p \vee q) = \max(\prod(p), \prod(q))$) for calculating $N(q)$ and $\prod(q)$ from $N(p \rightarrow q)$, $N(q \rightarrow p)$, $N(p)$, and $\prod(p)$ (Dubois and Prade, 1988). There are other reasoning patterns, based on material implication – as here – or on the notion of conditioning, within the framework of possibility theory (Dubois and Prade, 1987; Prade, 1985a). This type of possibilistic approach to the uncertain can be mechanized in the form of an easy matrix calculation that can be used in a quantitative approach to reasoning by default (Farreny and Prade, 1984; 1986).

When the facts and the condition parts of rules are vague, and a rule to be triggered is to be chosen, it is possible to extend the classical matching procedures (Winston, 1977) so as to accommodate the vagueness, which implies that the condition part of a rule will be unlikely to coincide exactly with the vague proposition that constitutes a fact. Given a set of rules of the type 'if X is A_i, then ⟨action i⟩,' the measurements ($\prod(A_i;A')$; $N(A_i;A')$) defined by (14) and (15) can be used to select the rule which is most appropriate to 'X is A'' or to detect the possible insufficiency of the set of rules. $\prod(A;A')$ estimates the possibility of conformity between rule and fact, and measures at which point the fact and the ⟨conditions⟩ part of the fuzzy rule can have a common interpretation. In particular, $\Pi(A;A') = 1$ indicates that the fact and the rule are coherent, but nothing stops the fact from being coherent with other rules; $\Pi(A;A') = 0$ indicates that the rule and the fact are incompatible. $N(A;A')$ indicates at which point the fact is a special case of the conditions part of the rule. In particular, if $\mu_{A'} \leq \mu_A$ then $N(A;A') \geq 0.5$, whereas $N(A;A') = 0$ indicates that the fact does not conform with the rule. We still have the natural condition $\Pi(A;A') \geq N(A;A')$.

The factors $\Pi(A;A')$ and $N(A;A')$ can be used as uncertainty coefficients $\Pi(\bar{p})$ and $N(\bar{p})$ associated with the condition part $\bar{p}$ of a rule 'if $\bar{p}$, then q' whose condition part is simultaneously fuzzy and uncertain, resulting in the application of (23). This approach is adopted in the SPII-2 inference engine (Martin-Clouaire and Prade, 1986) for processing these hybrid rules.

5.3.5 Combination of uncertainty coefficients

If there are several rules of the type 'if p_i, then q,' $i = 1,n$, there arises a set of uncertainty coefficients reflecting the uncertain nature of q, $\{(c_i, c'_i),\ i = 1,n\}$ with $N_i(q) = c_i$ and $\Pi_i(q) = c'_i$. Let us then use the combination of these values to build the two numbers $N(q)$ and $\Pi(q)$. Two approaches can be considered.

First within the framework of fuzzy sets (Zadeh, 1965), each pair can be seen as a fuzzy set F_i on $\{q, \neg q\}$ such that $\mu_{F_i}(q) = \Pi_i(q)$ and $\mu_{F_i}(\neg q) = 1 - N_i(q)$; $N(q)$ and $\Pi(q)$ are then defined by the fuzzy set

$$F = \bigcap_i F_i, \qquad \mu_F = \min \mu_{F_i}$$

The possibility normalization condition requires that $\max(\mu_F(q),\mu_F(\neg q)) = 1$, which leads to the formulae (Martin-Clouaire and Prade, 1985; Dubois and Prade, 1988)

$$N(q) = 1 - \frac{1 - \max_i c_i}{\max(\min_i(1 - c_i), \min_i c'_i)} \tag{24}$$

$$\Pi(q) = \frac{\min_i c'_i}{\max(\min_i(1 - c_i), \min_i c'_i)} \tag{25}$$

Secondly within the framework of the Shafer (1976) theory, possibility measures can be combined by means of the Dempster rule (Dempster, 1967). First it should be noted that $\Pi_i(q)$ and $N_i(q)$ data are equivalent to the probability assignment data m_i such that

$$m_i(q) = c_i, \qquad m_i(1) = 1 - c_i, \qquad c_i > 0, \qquad c'_i = 1$$
$$m_i(\neg q) = 1 - c'_i, \qquad m_i(1) = c'_i, \qquad c_i = 0, \qquad c'_i \leq 1$$

and $\Pi_i(q)$ and $N_i(q)$ are then found by applying (10). The Dempster rule consists in supposing that the sources $i = 1,n$ are independent so as to be able to combine the m_i by

$$\forall p \in \mathcal{P} = \{\varnothing, q, \neg q, 1\}, \quad m(p) = \sum \{\prod_{i=1}^{n} m_i(p_i) \mid p_1 \wedge p_2 \cdots \wedge p_n = p\}$$

followed by a normalization deleting the term $m(\varnothing)$:

$$\overline{m}(p) = \frac{m(p)}{(1 - m(\varnothing))}$$

For coherent sources $(c_i > 0, \forall i)$ the term $m(\varnothing)$ does not exist and for $n = 2$ in particular it is found that

$$\overline{m}(q) = N(q) = c_1 + c_2 - c_1 c_2 \tag{26}$$

This formula is used in MYCIN (Shortliffe and Buchanan, 1975).

The disadvantage of this second approach lies in the great sensitivity of the results to the value of the coefficients c_i and c_i' (Dubois and Prade, 1985b). Furthermore, the reinforcing effect of coherent sources, as it appears in (26), is not always justified; the possibilistic approach does not suppose this effect.

The combination of uncertainty coefficients poses certain fundamental questions whatever approach is chosen: Is combination advisable with conflicting sources, some favoring q and others favoring $\neg q$? Is normalization justifiable? Sometimes combination gives counterintuitive results, as shown by the following example. The following information is available:

Fact:	X_0 satisfies property A
Rule 1 (certain):	All those that satisfy property A satisfy property B
Rule 2 (uncertain):	Nearly all those that satisfy property B satisfy property C
Rule 3 (uncertain):	*Most* of those that satisfy property A do not satisfy property C

This situation is shown schematically in Figure 5.3. If only rules 1 and 2 are used, we deduce that X_0 probably satisfies C (as it certainly satisfies B). If rule 3 is applied directly, we conclude that X_0 probably does not satisfy C! However, the three rules taken together are not necessarily inconsistent. In fact, it is sufficient that the exceptions to rule 2 occur only among those elements that satisfy properties A and B for there to be no

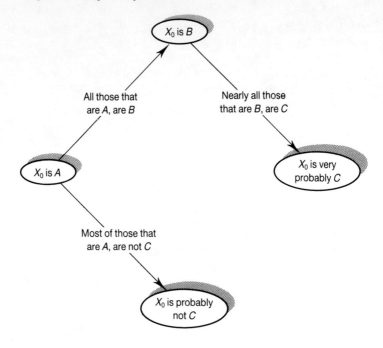

Figure 5.3 Example of apparently inconsistent results obtained by combining uncertainty coefficients.

inconsistency. Rule 3 is more specific, and the conclusion drawn from it should be preferred to the conclusion drawn from rules 1 and 2 in cascade. So in this case there should be no combination; only the conclusion obtained using rule 3 is to be taken into account. If we did not have rule 3, rules 1 and 2 could then be legitimately used to draw some (uncertain) conclusion about X_0; however, as Zadeh (1984) pointed out, using rules 1 and 2 in no case can the general rule 'nearly all those that satisfy property A satisfy property C' be derived.

Most other reasoning problems arise through uncertain pieces of information having to be taken into account (Dubois *et al.*, 1985); these problems are generally independent of the approach chosen for representing the uncertainty. In general, they must be managed at the level of inference control, as above, so as to establish whether or not to combine.

5.4 A brief review of some existing systems

Until fairly recently there were only a few approximate inference systems based on possibility theory. Most of those that do exist use only some of the results presented in this chapter. By exploiting one of Zadeh's ideas

(Zadeh, 1973), a form of generalized modus ponens was used for the first treatment of fuzzy rules by Mamdani (1977) who applied it to the control of continuous industrial processes (see also Sugeno, 1985). Generalized modus ponens has been used in other forms in medical diagnosis by Lesmo et al. (1983), Adlassnig and Kolarz (1982), Soula and Sanchez (1982), and Buisson et al. (1986), in management assisted decision making systems by Whalen and Schott (1983) and Ernst (1985), in petroleum geology – the ELFIN system (Martin-Clouaire, 1984) – based on the SPII-1 engine (Martin-Clouaire and Prade, 1986), and more recently in production management. The OPAL system for job-shop scheduling (Bensana et al., 1986) is able to integrate two kinds of knowledge about the production process: theoretical knowledge (using scheduling theory) which deals with time constraints propagation, and practical knowledge (provided by the shop-floor manager) about specific technological constraints which must be satisfied. The latter constraints are not usually taken into account at a theoretical level, because they vary from one case to another and are often pervaded with vagueness as they take the form of pieces of advice expressed in natural language. This knowledge is implemented in a set of fuzzy decision rules about the opportunity of an operation preceding another on a machine. These fuzzy rules compete with one another, and a fuzzy voting procedure is implemented to evaluate the best-supported decisions. Possibility theory could also find application to relational databases, for the representation of incomplete or imprecise pieces of knowledge (Baldwin and Zhou, 1984; Prade and Testemale, 1984).

Reasoning schemes with uncertain rules have been implemented by Soula et al. (1983) and Fieschi (1984) in the PROTIS and SPHINX medical expert systems, and by Tong et al. (1983) in a documentary research system. Little work has been done on rules that are fuzzy and uncertain at the same time. Ishizuka et al. (1981) have treated imprecise and uncertain pieces of information in a civil engineering production rule expert system, the SPERIL system; these authors evaluate uncertainty by means of credibility functions, in the Shafer sense, applied to fuzzy events (Ishizuka et al., 1982). Martin-Clouaire and Prade (1985; 1986) have proposed a unified imprecision and uncertainty treatment within the framework of possibility theory, with a view to applications to expert systems. Similarly, the TAIGER inference engine (Farenny et al., 1986) is able to handle not only uncertain rules, but also imprecise and uncertain factual pieces of knowledge about the values of logical or numerical variables. The system is being tested on knowledge bases in financial analysis. The possibilistic representation of uncertainty which is used is quite similar to that in MYCIN, but the chaining and combination operations of the possibility theory approach differ somewhat from the empirical choice (obtained as distorted probabilistic laws) made in MYCIN. TAIGER manipulates numerical values tainted with imprecision and uncertainty, while inference engines like the one in MYCIN treat uncertain rules and facts only. TAIGER maintains a representation of imprecise or uncertain facts in terms of possibility distributions, while the uncertainty of a rule is modeled by attaching the numbers appearing in a 2×2 matrix representation of the rule. TAIGER works in backward chaining. SPII-1 and TAIGER are currently implemented on micro-computers. Other inference systems based on fuzzy logic are described by Prade and Negoita (1986).

References

Adlassnig, K.P. and Kolarz, G. (1982). 'CADIAG-2: Computer-assisted medical diagnosis using fuzzy subsets' In *Approximate Reasoning in Decision Analysis* (M.M. Gupta and E. Sanchez; Eds). Amsterdam: North-Holland, 219–247

Baldwin, J.F. and Zhou, S.Q. (1984). 'A fuzzy relational inference language', *Fuzzy Sets Syst.*, **14**, 155–174

Bensana, E., Correge, M., Bel, G. and Dubois, D. (1986). 'An expert system approach to industrial job shop scheduling' In Proc. Int. Conf. on 'Robotics and automation', San Francisco, CA, IEEE, 1645–1650

Bourelly, L., Chouraqui, E. and Ricard, M. (1983). 'Formalisation of an approximate reasoning: The analogical reasoning' In Proc. Int. Symp. on 'Fuzzy information, knowledge representation and decision analysis', Marseille, IFAC, 135–141

Buisson, J.C., Farreny, H. and Prade, H. (1986). 'The development of a medical expert system and the treatment of imprecision in the framework of possibility theory', *Inf. Sci.*, **37**, 211–226

Cayrol, M., Farreny, H. and Prade, H. (1982). 'Fuzzy pattern matching' *Kybernetes*, 11, 103–116

Dempster, A.P. (1967). 'Upper and lower probabilities induced by a multi-valued mapping' *Ann. Math. Statist.*, **38**, 325–339

Dubois, D., Farreny, H. and Prade, H. (1985). 'Sur divers problèmes inhérents à l'automatisation des raisonnements de sens commun' In Proc. 5th Congr. on 'Pattern recognition and artificial intelligence', Grenoble, AFCET, 321–328

Dubois, D. and Prade, H. (1982). 'A class of fuzzy measures based on triangular norms', *Int. J. Gen. Syst.*, **8**, 43–61

Dubois, D. and Prade, H. (1983/84). 'On distances between fuzzy points and their use for plausible reasoning' In Proc. Int. Conf. on 'Cybernetics and society', Bombay and New Delhi, IEEE, 300–303

Dubois, D. and Prade, H. (1985a). 'The generalized modus ponens under sup–min composition: A theoretical study' In *Approximate Reasoning in Expert Systems* (M.M. Gupta et al.; Eds). Amsterdam: North-Holland, 217–232

Dubois, D. and Prade, H. (1985b). 'Combination and propagation of uncertainty with belief functions: A reexamination' In Proc. 9th IJCAI, Los Angeles, CA, 111–113

Dubois, D. and Prade, H. (1988). *Possibility Theory: An Approach to Computerized Processing of Uncertainty*. New York: Plenum Press

Duda, R., Gashnig, J. and Hart P. (1981). 'Model design in the PROSPECTOR consultant system for mineral exploration' In *Expert Systems in the Micro-Electronic Age* (D. Michie; Ed.). Edinburgh: Edinburgh University Press 153–167

Ernst, C. (1985). 'Un métalangage de programmation logique orienté vers le contrôle sémantique de systèmes experts de gestion', Thèse d'Etat, Université Paul Sabatier, Toulouse

Farreny, H. and Prade, H. (1982). 'About flexible matching and its use in analogical reasoning' In Proc. ECAI 82, Orsay, 43–47

Farreny, H. and Prade, H. (1984). A possibility-theory-based approach to default and inexact reasoning', *Commun. Cogn.*, **17**, (4), 85–99

Farreny, H. and Prade, H. (1986). 'Default and inexact reasoning with possibility degrees', *IEEE Trans. Syst. Man Cybernet.*, **SMC-16**, 270–276

Farreny, H., Prade, H. and Wyss, E. (1986). 'Approximate reasoning in a rule-based expert system using possibility theory: A case study' In *Information Processing 86* (H.J. Kugler; Ed.). Amsterdam: North-Holland, 407–413

Fieschi, M. (1984). *Intelligence Artificielle en Médecine: Des Systèmes Experts*. Paris: Masson

Fine, T. (1973). *Theories of Probability*. New York: Academic Press

Ishizuka, M., Fu, K.S. and Yao, J.T.P. (1981). 'Inexact inference for rule-based damage assessment of existing structures' In Proc. 7th IJCAI, Vancouver, 837–842

Ishizuka, M., Fu, K.S. and Yao, J.T.P. (1982) 'Inference procedures with uncertainty for problem reduction method', *Inf. Sci.*, **28**, 179–206

Lesmo, L., Saitta, L. and Torasso, P. (1983). 'Fuzzy production rules: A learning methodology' In *Advances in Fuzzy Sets, Possibility Theory and Applications* (P.P. Wang; Ed.). New York: Plenum Press, 181–198

Mamdani, E.H. (1977). 'Application of fuzzy logic to approximate reasoning using linguistic systems' *IEEE Trans. Computers*, **COM-26**, 1182–1191

Martin-Clouaire, R. (1984). 'ELFIN: Une approche système-expert et théorie des possibilités appliquée en géologie pétrolière', Thèse de Troisième Cycle, Université Paul Sabatier, Toulouse

Martin-Clouaire, R. and Prade, H. (1985) 'On the problems of representation and propagation of uncertainty in expert systems', *Int. J. Man–Machine Studies*, **22**, 251–264

Martin-Clouaire, R. and Prade, H. (1986). 'SPII-1: A simple inference engine capable of accommodating imprecision and uncertainty' In *Computer-Assisted Decision Making* (G. Mitra; Ed.). Amsterdam: North-Holland, 117–131

Prade, H. (1984a). 'Modèles de raisonnement approché pour les systèmes experts' In Proc. 4th Congr. on 'Pattern recognition and artificial intelligence', Paris, AFCET, 355–373

Prade, H. (1984b). 'Analogie et flou', BUSEFAL No. 18, LSI, Université Paul Sabatier, Toulouse, 83–91

Prade, H. (1984c). 'A fuzzy-set-based approach to analogical, default and other kinds of plausible reasoning' In Proc. 6th Int. Congr. on 'Cybernetics and systems', Paris, 187–192

Prade, H. (1985a). 'A computational approach to approximate and plausible reasoning, with applications to expert systems', *IEEE Trans. Pattern Analysis Machine Intell.*, **PAMI-7**, 260–283 (with corrections in **PAMI-7**, 747–748)

Prade, H. (1985b). 'Reasoning with fuzzy default values' In Proc. 15th Int. Symp. on 'Multiple-valued logic', Kinston, Ontario, IEEE, 191–197

Prade, H. and Negoita, C.V.; Eds (1986). *Fuzzy Logic in Knowledge Engineering*. Cologne: Verlag TÜV Rheinland

Prade, H. and Testemale, C. (1984). 'Generalizing database relational algebra for the treatment of incomplete/uncertain information and vague queries', *Inf. Sci.*, **34**, 115–143

Shafer, G. (1976). *A Mathematical Theory of Evidence*. Princeton, NJ: Princeton University Press

Shortliffe, E.H. and Buchanan, B.G. (1975) 'A model of inexact reasoning in medicine', *Math. Biosci.*, **23**, 351–379

Soula, G. and Sanchez, E. (1982). 'Soft deduction rules in medical diagnosis processes' In *Approximate Reasoning in Decision Analysis* (M.M. Gupta and E. Sanchez; Eds). Amsterdam: North-Holland, 77–88

Soula, G., Vialettes, B. and San Marco, J.L. (1983). 'PROTIS: A fuzzy deduction-rule system: Application to the treatment of diabetes' In Proc. MEDINFO 83, Amsterdam, 533–536

Sugeno, M.; Ed. (1985). *Industrial Applications of Fuzzy Control*. Amsterdam: North-Holland

Tong, R.M., Shapiro, D.G., Dean, J.S. and McCune, B.P. (1983). 'A comparison of uncertainty calculi in an expert system for information retrieval' In Proc. 8th IJCAI, Karlsruhe, 194–197

Whalen, T. and Schott, B. (1983). 'Issues in fuzzy production systems' *Int. J. Man–Machine Studies*, **19**, 57–71

Winston, P.H. (1977). *Artificial Intelligence*. Reading, MA: Addison-Wesley

Zadeh, L.A. (1965). 'Fuzzy sets', *Inf. Control*, **8**, 338–353

Zadeh, L.A. (1973). 'Outline of a new approach to the analysis of complex systems and decision processes', *IEEE Trans. Syst. Man Cybernet.*, **SMC-3**, 28–44

Zadeh, L.A. (1978). 'Fuzzy sets as a basis for a theory of possibility', *Fuzzy Sets Syst.*, **1**, 3–28

Zadeh, L.A. (1979). 'A theory of approximate reasoning' In *Machine Intelligence*, Vol. 9 (J.E. Hayes *et al.*; Eds). Elsevier, 149–194

Zadeh, L.A. (1984). 'A theory of commonsense knowledge' In *Aspects of Vagueness* (H.J. Skala, S. Termini and E. Trillas; Eds). Dordrecht: Reidel, 257–295

6

A Diagnosis Method for Decision-Making[†]

Ronald R. Yager

6.1 Introduction

The author has developed a diagnosis system which takes as its input a set of symptoms and gives as its output a set of possible diagnoses (Yager, 1985a); the motivation for developing this system was the work of Nau, Reggia, and co-workers (Reggia *et al.*, 1983; 1985). In this chapter is described an extension of this system to include an expert component that takes the diagnosis set and indicates an appropriate action. This new additional component is made up of two units. The first unit, the problem-solving unit, takes the set of possible diagnoses and provides a set of potential solutions. The second unit selects from the set of potential solutions a prescribed action.

The additional component provides the novelty and generality of allowing a mixture of probabilistic and possibilistic uncertainty as well as nonmonotonicity. In particular, the system can now allow for uncertainty between a diagnosis and a set of possible effective solutions. We also include in the action selection unit a rule based on the principle 'do the easiest thing first.' This simplicity principle requires the implementation of a hierarchical default rule which in turn induces nonmonotonicity; the principle of implementing first the easiest of any potential solutions is one which many experts follow. Expert systems that realistically follow the way experts do things must have a structure for realizing this highly nonmonotonic rule. Figure 6.1 is a schematic illustration of the system. In this chapter we concentrate on the portion of the system enclosed in the dashed lines, units B and C. The complete system as depicted would be dynamic in the sense that if a prescribed action did not provide a cure to

[†] This research was supported in part by grants from the National Science Foundation and the Air Force Office of Scientific Research.

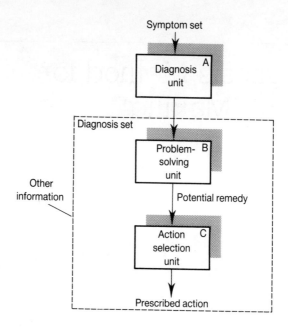

Figure 6.1   Schematic illustration of the system.

the symptoms it would at least provide additional information to all the units to be used in the selection of a second treatment.

The problem-solving unit consists of a knowledge base constructed of rules which relate dysfunctions to possible effective solutions. In our system we allow for uncertainty in the association between dysfunctions and the success of solutions. The output of this unit is information about potential solutions, based upon the diagnosis input. The representation of the knowledge base in B as well as the inference mechanisms used in B draws heavily on previous work on a general theory of reasoning with uncertainty (Yager, 1985b; 1986a, b; 1988). In particular, we use as a basic knowledge structure a possibility–probability granule which allows for the representation of possibilistic, probabilistic, and usuality-type uncertainty.

The action selection unit takes as its input the set of potential solutions, together with any information about actions already tried; its output is information about the chosen solution, called the action. A central feature of the unit is a knowledge base that embodies our default simplicity principle of 'doing the easiest thing first.' The concept allows for appropriate definition. The representation and inference mechanism for this selection draws heavily on previous work on the representation of default rules (Yager, 1986c; 1987).

6.2 Problem-Solving Unit

The central feature of the problem-solving unit is the representation of information relating the association between diagnosis and potential solutions. It is assumed that there exists some uncertainty in these associations. In order to represent the uncertain information which may appear in the problem-solving unit, we use the representation scheme known as the general theory of uncertainty (Yager, 1985b; 1986a, b; 1988). We now briefly describe the necessary ideas from this theory which we shall find useful.

We assume that U is a variable which takes a value in the set Y. A canonical statement is of the form

U is A

where A is a fuzzy subset of Y. The purpose of a canonical statement is to indicate that for each $y \in Y$, $A(y)$ indicates the possibility that the value of V is y. In a general sense, a canonical statement is a reflection of the fact that the value of V must satisfy some property denoted by A. For example, if U is a person's temperature, then a canonical statement would be

U is high

A basic probability assignment (BPA) on Y is a mapping

m: $I^Y \rightarrow [0,1]$

in which the fuzzy sets A_1, ..., A_q for which

$m(A_j) > 0$

are called the focal elements of m. The focal elements must be normal, in that if A_j is a focal element then there must exist at least one $y \in Y$ such that $A_j(y) = 1$.

In addition, a basic probability assignment function m must satisfy

$$\sum_{\substack{\text{focal} \\ \text{elements}}} m(A_j) = 1$$

A possibility–probability (PP) granule is a statement of the form

U is m

where m is a BPA on X. If $A_1, \ldots, A_q$ are the focal elements of m with weights $m(A_j) = a_j$, then the purpose of a PP granule

$$V \text{ is } m$$

is to represent the information that a_j is the probability that 'V is A_j' is the appropriate canonical statement representing our knowledge about V.

PP granules allow various types of knowledge to be represented in a unified way. For example, if our knowledge about U is in terms of a pure probability distribution on Y with prob $(U = y_j) = p_j$, then

$$A_j = \{y_j\}, \qquad m(A_j) = p_j$$

If our knowledge is a simple canonical statement 'U is A,' then

$$m(A) = 1$$

If our knowledge is that 'usually U is A,' then

$$m(A) = \alpha, \qquad m(Y) = 1-\alpha$$

where α is close to unity. The value of α reflects how usual the occurrence of A is.

Now assume that V is another variable taking its value in the set X. A typical inference statement for representing our knowledge about the association between V and U is

$$\text{if } V \text{ is } B, \text{ then } U \text{ is } m$$

where B is a fuzzy subset of X and m is a PP granule on Y with focal elements $A_1, \ldots, A_q$ with weights $m(A_j) = a_j$. The effect of such a statement is to induce a PP granule with respect to the joint variable (V,U) such that

$$(V,U) \text{ is } m^*$$

where m^* is a BPA on $X \times Y$ with focal elements $H_1, \ldots, H_q$, where

$$H_j = B^- U A_j$$
$$H_j(x,y) = (1-B(x)) \vee A_j(y)$$

where $\vee$ indicates 'maximum' and $m(H_j) = m(A_j) = a_j$.

There are other possible implementations of H_i, such as $H_i(x,y) = 1 \wedge (1-B(x)) + A_i(y))$. However, when $B(x) \in \{0,1\}$, the case we shall be dealing with, all these different implementations become the same.

Let us assume that

$$(V,U) \text{ is } m_1^*, \qquad (V,U) \text{ is } m_2^*$$

are two independent propositions about the relationship of V and U, where H_i and G_j are the focal elements of m_1^* and m_2^*, respectively, and $m_1^*(H_i) = a_i$ and $m_2^*(G_j) = b_j$.

The effect of both these rules, their conjunction, is a proposition

$$(V,U) \text{ is } m^*$$

where

$$m^* = m_1^* \cap m_2^*$$

is obtained by Dempster's rule (Dempster, 1967; Shafter, 1976), as follows. For each normal $F \subset X \times Y$

$$m^*(F) = (1/(1-K)) * \sum_{\substack{\text{over } i,j \\ \text{such that} \\ H_i \cap G_j = F}} (a_i * b_j)$$

and where

$$K = \sum_{\substack{i,j \\ H_i \cap G_j, \text{ not} \\ \text{normal}}} a_i * b_j$$

Effectively, the focal elements of m^* are all the normal sets $F_{ij} = H_i \cap G_j$.

We note that if H_i and G_j are fuzzy subsets of $X \times Y$, then

$$F_{ij}(x,y) = H_i(x,y) \wedge G_j(x,y)$$

where $\wedge$ indicates 'minimum'. Repeated application of this rule allows us to calculate the effect of more than two propositions about the association of U and V.

Let us now assume $P_1, ..., P_q$ to be a set of propositions of the type just described relating V and U, and let

$$(V,U) \text{ is } m^*$$

be the effective PP granule representing all these associations. Assume $H_i, ..., H_K$ are the focal elements of m^* with weights $m^*(H_i) = a_i$.

Let our knowledge about V be contained in the canonical statement

$$V \text{ is } D$$

where D is a fuzzy subset of X. From these two pieces of knowledge we can infer that

U is m^+

where m^+ is a BPA on Y with focal elements B_i, $i = 1, ..., K$, $m^+(B_i) = a_i$ and

$B_i = \text{proj}_Y H_i \cap D$

that is,

$$B_i(y) = \max_{x \in X} [H_i(x,y) \wedge D(x)]$$

With this background we can now examine the workings of the problem-solving unit. Let $X = \{x_1, ..., x_q\}$ be a set of possible dysfunctions, and let V be the variable 'the diagnosed dysfunction,' the output of the diagnosis unit. Let $Y = \{y_1, ..., y_p\}$ be a set of actions, and let U be the variable 'effective or potential actions.'

The knowledge base in the problem-solving section consists of a set of q rules of the form

R_i: if V is D_i, then U is m_i, $i=1, ..., q$

where $D_i = \{x_i\}$ and m_i is a PP granule on Y with focal elements

A_{ij}, $j=1, ..., n(i)$, and $m_i(A_{ij}) = a_{ij}$

Thus for each dysfunction we have an associated rule that indicates the potential actions. Because of the structure of the BPA we can represent very complicated knowledge about actions which includes uncertainty in the effectiveness of an action.

By applying Dempster's rule to the set of rules $R_1, ..., R_q$, we obtain an overall representation of our knowledge base in this section as

(V,U) is m^*

where $m^* = m_1 \cap m_2 \cap \cdots \cap m_q$. The input to this section is the knowledge

V is D

where D is a fuzzy subset of X indicating the set of possible dysfunctions as obtained from the diagnosis unit; i.e., 'V is D' is the output of the diagnosis unit.

By applying the described inference mechanism, the output from this section is obtained as

U is m^+

where U indicates the 'effective actions' for the diagnosis. We note that our knowledge of U and m^+, may include various types of uncertainty.

The following discussion provides an understanding of the meaning of the assignment of a PP granule as the value of the effective action.

Let 'U is m' be a PP granule in which m is a BPA defined on the set Y with focal elements A_i, $i=1, \ldots, n$ and weights $m(A_i) = a_i$. Assume that B is any subset of Y and that $\text{prob}(B)$ indicates the probability that the effective action lies in the set B. Then

$\text{bel}(B) \leq \text{prob}(B) \leq \text{pl}(B)$

where $\text{pl}(B)$ is called the plausibility of B and is defined by

$$\text{pl}(B) = \sum_{i=1}^{n} \text{poss } (B/A_i) * m(A_i)$$

In the definition of $\text{pl}(B)$,

$$\text{poss } [B/A_i] = \max_{y \in Y}[B(y) \wedge A_i(y)]$$

and is called the possibility of B given B_i; $\text{bel}(B)$, called the belief of B, is defined as

$$\text{bel}(B) = \sum_{i=1}^{n} \text{cert } (B/A_i) * m(A_i)$$

where

$$\text{cert } [B/A_i] = 1 - \text{poss } [B^-/A_i]$$

Thus, if we have a diagnosis 'V is D' and a knowledge base '(V,U) is m^*,' and if this results in a solution U is m^+, then for each $y \in Y$

$$\text{bel}^+\{y\} \leq \text{prob}^+(y) \leq \text{pl}^+\{y\}$$

indicates the probability that y is the solution.

The following example illustrates the operations involved in manipulating the problem-solving unit.

Example

Let us assume that

$$X = \{d_1, d_2, d_3\}$$

is a set of potential diagnoses, and that

$$Y = \{a_1, a_2, a_3\}$$

is a set of solutions. Let V be the variable standing for the current diagnosis, and let U be the potential solutions.

Assume that the problem-solving unit consists of the following rules:

R_1:   if V is d_1, then U is m_1
R_2:   if V is d_2, then U is m_2
R_3:   if V is d_3, then U is m_3

Let m_1 be a BPA on Y with one focal element $A_1 = \{a_1\}$ and with $m_1(A_1) = 1$. Let m_2 be a BPA on Y with three focal elements,

$$A_1 = \{a_2\}, \qquad A_2 = \{a_1, a_3\}, \qquad A_3 = \{a_1, a_2, a_3\}$$

and with weights

$$m_2(A_1) = 0.5, \qquad m_2(A_2) = 0.3, \qquad m_2(A_3) = 0.2$$

Let m_3 be a BPA on Y with two focal elements,

$$A_1 = \{a_3\}, \qquad A_2 = \{a_1, a_2, a_3\}$$

where

$$m_3(A_1) = 0.7, \qquad m_3(A_2) = 0.3$$

We can represent each of these rules as a BPA on $X \times Y$ of the form

$$R_i: \quad (V,U) \text{ is } m_i^*$$

In particular, if m_i has focal element A_{ij}, then m_i^* has focal element B_{ij} on $X \times Y$ such that

$$B_{ij}(x,y) = (1 - D_i(x)) \vee A_{ij}(y)$$

Since $D_i = \{x_i\}$, it follows that

$$B_{ij}(x,y) = \begin{cases} 1, & x \neq x_i \\ A_{ij}(y), & x = x_i \end{cases}$$

Thus for rule 1, m_1^* has one focal element,

$$B_{11} = \begin{array}{c} \\ d_1 \\ d_2 \\ d_3 \end{array} \begin{array}{ccc} a_1 & a_2 & a_3 \\ \begin{bmatrix} 1 & 0 & 0 \\ 1 & 1 & 1 \\ 1 & 1 & 1 \end{bmatrix} \end{array}$$

and $m_1^*(B_{11}) = 1$.

For rule 2, m_2^* has three focal elements,

$$B_{21} = \begin{array}{c} \\ d_1 \\ d_2 \\ d_3 \end{array} \begin{array}{ccc} a_1 & a_2 & a_3 \\ \begin{bmatrix} 1 & 1 & 1 \\ 0 & 1 & 0 \\ 1 & 1 & 1 \end{bmatrix} \end{array}, \quad B_{22} = \begin{array}{c} \\ d_1 \\ d_2 \\ d_3 \end{array} \begin{array}{ccc} a_1 & a_2 & a_3 \\ \begin{bmatrix} 1 & 1 & 1 \\ 1 & 0 & 1 \\ 1 & 1 & 1 \end{bmatrix} \end{array},$$

$$B_{23} = \begin{array}{c} \\ d_1 \\ d_2 \\ d_3 \end{array} \begin{array}{ccc} a_1 & a_2 & a_3 \\ \begin{bmatrix} 1 & 1 & 1 \\ 1 & 1 & 1 \\ 1 & 1 & 1 \end{bmatrix} \end{array}$$

where

$$m_2^*(B_{21}) = 0.5, \qquad m_2^*(B_{22}) = 0.3, \qquad m_2^*(B_{23}) = 0.2$$

For rule 3, m_3^* has two focal elements,

$$B_{31} = \begin{array}{c} \\ d_1 \\ d_2 \\ d_3 \end{array} \begin{array}{ccc} a_1 & a_2 & a_3 \\ \begin{bmatrix} 1 & 1 & 1 \\ 1 & 1 & 1 \\ 0 & 0 & 1 \end{bmatrix} \end{array} \quad B_{32} = \begin{array}{c} \\ d_1 \\ d_2 \\ d_3 \end{array} \begin{array}{ccc} a_1 & a_2 & a_3 \\ \begin{bmatrix} 1 & 1 & 1 \\ 1 & 1 & 1 \\ 1 & 1 & 1 \end{bmatrix} \end{array}$$

where

$$m_3^* = 0.7, \qquad m_3^*(B_{32}) = 0.3$$

Using Dempster's rule, we can combine the three rules to give an overall BPA

$$(V, U) \text{ is } m$$

where

$$m = m_1 \cap m_2 \cap m_3$$

In this case m is also a BPA on $X \times Y$ with six focal elements,

$$H_1 = \begin{array}{c} d_1 \\ d_2 \\ d_3 \end{array} \begin{array}{ccc} a_1 & a_2 & a_3 \\ \left[\begin{array}{ccc} 1 & 0 & 0 \\ 0 & 1 & 0 \\ 1 & 1 & 1 \end{array}\right], \end{array} \qquad H_2 = \begin{array}{c} d_1 \\ d_2 \\ d_3 \end{array} \begin{array}{ccc} a_1 & a_2 & a_3 \\ \left[\begin{array}{ccc} 1 & 0 & 0 \\ 1 & 0 & 1 \\ 1 & 1 & 1 \end{array}\right] \end{array}$$

$$H_3 = \begin{array}{c} d_1 \\ d_2 \\ d_3 \end{array} \begin{array}{ccc} a_1 & a_2 & a_3 \\ \left[\begin{array}{ccc} 1 & 0 & 0 \\ 1 & 1 & 1 \\ 1 & 1 & 1 \end{array}\right], \end{array} \qquad H_4 = \begin{array}{c} d_1 \\ d_2 \\ d_3 \end{array} \begin{array}{ccc} a_1 & a_2 & a_3 \\ \left[\begin{array}{ccc} 1 & 0 & 0 \\ 0 & 1 & 0 \\ 0 & 0 & 1 \end{array}\right] \end{array}$$

$$H_5 = \begin{array}{c} d_1 \\ d_2 \\ d_3 \end{array} \begin{array}{ccc} a_1 & a_2 & a_3 \\ \left[\begin{array}{ccc} 1 & 0 & 0 \\ 1 & 0 & 1 \\ 0 & 0 & 1 \end{array}\right], \end{array} \qquad H_6 = \begin{array}{c} d_1 \\ d_2 \\ d_3 \end{array} \begin{array}{ccc} a_1 & a_2 & a_3 \\ \left[\begin{array}{ccc} 1 & 0 & 0 \\ 1 & 1 & 1 \\ 0 & 0 & 1 \end{array}\right] \end{array}$$

with weights

$$m(H_1) = 0.15, \qquad m(H_2) = 0.09, \qquad m(H_3) = 0.06$$
$$m(H_4) = 0.35, \qquad m(H_5) = 0.21, \qquad m(H_6) = 0.14$$

The above structure represents the knowledge base of the problem-solving unit.

If we input to this structure our knowledge of the diagnosis 'V is D,' where D is a fuzzy subset of X, we obtain a potential action

U is m^*

where m^* is a BPA on Y with focal elements G_i, $i = 1, ..., 6$, where

$$m^*(G_i) = m(H_i)$$

and

$$G_i(y) = \max_{x \in X} [D(x) \wedge H_i(x,y)]$$

We now look at the solution selection for a number of cases of diagnosis.

Case I

For $D = \{d_1\}$ the diagnosis is simply d_1, and

$$\forall i, G_i = \{a_i\}$$

Hence m^* has just one focal element $G = \{a_1\}$, with weight 1.

Case II

If the diagnosis is d_2 or d_3, $D = \{d_2, d_3\}$, then

$$G_1 = G_2 = G_3 = G_6 = \{a_1, a_2, a_3\}$$
$$G_4 = \{a_2, a_3\}, \qquad G_5 = \{a_1, a_3\}$$

Thus m^* has just three distinct focal elements, $G_1 = \{a_1, a_2, a_3\}$, $G_2 = \{a_2, a_3\}$, and $G_3 = \{a_1, a_3\}$, with weights $m^*(G_1) = 0.44$, $m^*(G_2) = 0.35$, and $m^*(G_3) = 0.21$.

Case III

If we allow D to be the fuzzy subset

$$D = \{0.7/d_1, 1/d_2, 0.3/d_3\}$$

then the distinct focal elements of m^* are

$$G_1 = \{0.7/d_1, 1/a_2, 0.3/a_3\}, \qquad G_2 = \{1/a_1, 0.3/a_2, 1/a_3\}$$
$$G_3 = \{1/a_1, 1/a_2, 1/a_3\}, \qquad G_4 = \{1/a_1, 0/a_2, 1/a_3\}$$

with weights

$$m^*(G_1) = 0.5, \qquad m^*(G_2) = 0.09, \qquad m^*(G_3) = 0.2, \qquad m^*(G_4) = 0.21$$

6.3 Action selection unit

The action selection unit takes as its primary input the effectiveness of the various solutions in the face of the diagnosis. That is, the input to this unit is the output of the problem-solving unit. It also can use additional knowledge as input, such as particular restrictions to certain actions, and actions already tried. The output of this unit is a prescribed action. At the heart of this selection unit is a knowledge base and inference mechanism which contains our knowledge of how we select the appropriate action from the set of possible actions.

The advantage of separating the process of action selection from the selection of potential actions allows us to store the more meaningful association between dysfunctions and solutions in the problem-solving unit, while keeping the more 'local' information in the selection unit. By local information we mean things like the competence of personnel to make decisions, or local expertise.

Here we consider one type of selection rule, the principle 'do the easiest thing first.' Essentially this rule says that we should first try the potential action that is easiest to implement; by 'easiest' we mean requiring the least effort, expense, or time, for example. From a theoretical point of view such an 'easiest first' rule provides an example of a hierarchical default rule. We shall use this framework for describing the implementation of such hierarchical rules.

Let Y be the set of actions that are within the framework of the problem; thus $y_i \in Y$ is an action. Let U be a variable corresponding to 'the potential effective actions based on the symptoms.' As indicated in Section 6.2, the output of the problem-solving unit is 'U is m^*,' where m^* is a possible problem granule on Y with focal elements G_1, G_2, ..., G_q, with assignments $m^*(G_i) = b_i$.

At this point we can include any special knowledge about the environment. For example, if we have already tried action y_i and it failed to work, we can add this, and we would then have

U is m^* and U is not $\{y_i\}$

When all these special data are included we are in a position to select an action to implement. Let W be a variable indicating the selected or implemented action. For clarification we let the set Z be the set from which we select the action. Thus in this case $z_i = y_i$, and thus Z and Y are effectively the same set. Thus W will be an element in Z (actually in Y).

The knowledge base in the action selection unit consists of our procedure for selecting the value of W based on our knowledge of U. As indicated, we shall be using the 'easiest first' rule to select our implemented action. The simplest manifestation of an 'easiest first' rule occurs when there exists a simple linear ordering on the elements of Z indicating their ease of implementation. Thus, without loss of generality, we may assume the elements of Z to be indexed in order of increasing difficulty of implementation. Thus $z_1 > z_2 > z_3 > ... > z_p$, where $z_i > z_j$ indicates that z_i is easier to implement than z_j.

A typical manifestation of this rule can be seen in the following matrix, where we consider only sets with three elements:

$$
\begin{array}{c c c c}
 & z_1 & z_2 & z_3 \\
\{y_1\} & 1 & 0 & 0 \\
\{y_2\} & 0 & 1 & 0 \\
\{y_3\} & 0 & 0 & 1 \\
\{y_1,y_2\} & 1 & 0 & 0 \\
\{y_1,y_3\} & 1 & 0 & 0 \\
\{y_2,y_3\} & 0 & 1 & 0 \\
\{y_1,y_2,y_3\} & 1 & 0 & 0
\end{array}
$$

This matrix indicates that if our knowledge of U is restricted to knowing that U is an element of one of the sets on the left, then we must implement the action with a '1' in the corresponding row. Thus, if we know that $U \in \{y_1, y_2\}$, we must implement z_1. The above matrix is an example of a hierarchical default rule in that we default to the easiest of the set of possible actions. The structure is nonmonotonic insofar as we know that $U \in \{y_1, y_3\}$, then it tells us to implement z_1. If, however, we were to obtain more information, allowing us to infer that $U \in \{y_3\}$, then we would be led to implement z_3.

The knowledge contained in such an 'easiest first' strategy can be captured by a set of production rules, one rule for each y_i. The hierarchical aspect of the 'easiest first' rule is explicitly seen in this representation. The knowledge base must consist of a set of rules, one for each y_i, of the form 'if y_i is a possible action suggested by U, and no easier actions are suggested by U, then implement z_i. Formally, we can express such a rule within the theory of approximate reasoning (Yager, 1987) as

R_i: If U is not G_i and U is 'E_i is possible,' then W is F_i

In this formulation

F_i = implement action $z_i = \{z_i\}$
$E_i = \{y_i\}$
$G_i = \{y_i, ..., y_{i-1}\}$, the set of actions preferable to y_i
    (note that $G_i = \varnothing$)

By the translation rules of the theory of approximate reasoning (Yager, 1987), each rule is translated into

(U, W) is S_i

where

$S_i = G_i U (E_i^+)^- U F_i$

Furthermore, the overall rule base can be represented as

(U, W) is S

where

$S = \bigcap_i S_i$

In the above definition E_i^+ is the translation of the statement 'E_i is possible.' As shown by Yager (1987), if E is a fuzzy subset of y then E^+ is a fuzzy subset of the power set of Y, such that for each fuzzy subset H of Y

$$E^+(H) = \text{poss } [H/E_i]$$
$$= \max_y [H(y) \wedge E_i(y)]$$

In our particular case

$$E = E_i = \{y_i\}$$

and therefore

$$E_i^+(H) = \max_y [H(y) \cap E_i(y)] = H(y_i)$$

Furthermore, since $(E^+)^-$ (which we shall denote by E^*) is the negation of E^+, then

$$E_i^*(H) = 1 - H(y_i)$$

Before we proceed, a technical issue which arises in problems involving these types of default rule must be addressed. Let us assume Y to be a set of objects; let A be a subset of Y and B a subset of the power set of Y. In some problems we have to find poss $[B/A]$. In order to do this, we consider A to be a fuzzy subset of the power set of Y, $A\circ$, such that

$$A\circ = \{\text{poss}[A]/A\}$$

where the membership grade of A in $A\circ$ is poss $[A] = \max_y [A(x)]$. Then

$$\text{poss}[B/A] = \text{poss}[B/A\circ] = \text{poss } [A] \wedge B(A)$$

We continue with our example by investigating the action selection unit. Let $y = \{a_1, a_2, a_3\}$ be the set of actions, and let $Z = \{b_1, b_2, b_3\}$ where $b_i = $ 'implement a_i.' We assume that $a_1 > a_2 > a_3$ indicates ease of implementation. The action selection unit can be represented by three rules:

R_1:   If 'U is $\{a_1\}$' is possible, then 'W is $\{b_1\}$'
R_2:   if 'U is not $\{a_1\}$ and U is $\{a_2\}$' is possible, then 'W is $\{b_2\}$'
R_3:   if 'U is not $\{a_1, a_2\}$' then 'W is $\{b_3\}$'

Formally, these rules are given as

$$S_1 = E_1^* \ U \ B_1, \qquad S_2 = L_2 \ U \ E_2^* \ U \ B_2, \qquad S_3 = L_3 \ U \ B_3$$

where

$$B_i = \{b_i\}, \quad i = 1, 2, 3, \qquad L_2 = \{a_1\}, \qquad L_3 = \{a_1, a_2\}$$

and E_i^* are fuzzy subsets of the power set of Y standing for not (E_i is possible), thus

$$E_i^* (H) = 1 - H(a_i)$$

The conjunction of these three rules gives us the knowledge base of the action selection unit:

$$S = S_1 \cap S_2 \cap S_3$$

and hence

$$S = (L_2 \cap E_1^*) \cup (L_3 \cap E_1^* \cap E_2^*) \cup (B_1 \cap L_2) \cup (B_1 \cap L_3 \cap E_2^*) \cup$$
$$(B_2 \cap E_1^* \cap L_3) \cup (B_3 \cap E_1^* \cap L_2) \cup (B_3 \cap E_1^* \cap E_2^*)$$

We assume the output of the problem-solving unit to be

$$U \text{ is } m^*$$

where m^* is a BPA with focal elements F_i and weights $m(F_i)$. In this case the selected action is

$$W \text{ is } m\circ$$

Where $m\circ$ is a BPA on Z with focal elements T_i, where

$$m\circ(T_i) = m^*(F_i), \qquad T_i = \text{proj}_Z (S \cap F_i)$$

Thus, if F_i is an arbitrary focal element of m^*, then T is an associated action selection where

$$T_i(z) = (\text{poss}[E_1^*/L_2 \cap F_i] \vee \text{poss}[E_2^* \cap E_1^*/L_3 \cap F_i]$$
$$\vee B_1(z))$$
$$\wedge (\text{poss}[E_2^*/L_3 \cap F_i] \vee \text{poss}[L_2/F_i]) \vee B_2(z)$$
$$\wedge \text{poss}(E_1^*/L_3 \cap F_i]$$
$$\vee B_3(z) \wedge (\text{poss}[E_1^*/L_2 \cap F_i] \vee \text{poss}[E_1^* \cap E_2^*/F_i])$$

Let us now apply this formulation to the three cases discussed in the previous example. We shall use the notation

$$L_2 \cap F_i = R_2, \qquad L_3 \cap F_i = R_3$$

Case I

'U is m^*,' where m^* has just one focal element:

$$F = \{a_i\} = E_i$$

In this case

$$R_2 = L_2 \cap F = \{a_1\} = E_1, \qquad R_3 = L_3 \cap F = \{a_1\} = E_1$$

hence

$$\text{poss } [E_1^*/R_2] = \text{poss } [E_1^*/E_1] = 1 \wedge (1-\text{poss}(E_1/E_1) = 0$$
$$\text{poss } [E_1^* \cap E_2^*/R_3] = \text{poss } [E_1^* \cap E_2^*/E_1] = 0$$
$$\text{poss } [L_2/F] = \text{poss } [E/E_1] = 1$$
$$\text{poss } [E_1^*/R_3] = \text{poss } [E_1^*/E_1] = 0$$
$$\text{poss } [E_1^* \cap E_2/F] = \text{poss } [E_1^* \cap E_2^*/E_1] = 0$$

Therefore

$$\begin{aligned} T(b) &= 0 \vee 0 \vee B_1(z) \wedge 1 \vee B_2(z) \wedge 0 \vee B_3(z) \wedge 0 \\ &= B_1(z) \end{aligned}$$

Hence $T = B_1$, and so

$$W \text{ is } B_1$$

Since $B_1 = \{b_1\}$, the decision is simply to implement action a_1.

Case II

'U is m^*,' with three focal elements:

$$F_1 = \{a_1, a_2, a_3\}, \qquad F_2 = \{a_2, a_3\}, \qquad F_3 = \{a_1, a_3\}$$

where

$$m(F_1) = 0.44, \qquad m(F_2) = 0.35, \qquad m(F_3) = 0.21$$

First consider F_1:

$R_2 = L_{22} \cap F_1 = \{a_1\}, \qquad R_3 = L_3 \cap F_1 = \{a_1, a_2\}$

$\mathrm{poss}[E_1^*/R_2] = \mathrm{poss}[E_1^*/E_1] = 0$

$\mathrm{poss}[E_2^* \cap E_1^*/R_3] = \mathrm{poss}[E_1^* \cap E_2^*/\{a_1, a_2\}] = 0$

$\mathrm{poss}[L_2/F_1] = 1$

$\mathrm{poss}[E_1^*/R_3] = \mathrm{poss}[E_1^*/\{a_1, a_2\}] = 1 \wedge (1 - \mathrm{poss}[E_1/\{a_1, a_2\}]) = 0$

$\mathrm{poss}[E_1 \wedge E_2^*/F_1] = \mathrm{poss}[E_1^* \wedge E_2/Y] = (1-\mathrm{poss}[E_1/Y]) \wedge (1-\mathrm{poss}[E_2/Y]) \wedge 1 = 0$

Hence $T_1(b) = B_1(b)$; i.e., $T_1 = B_1$.

For the second focal element $F_2 = \{a_2, a_3\}$,

$R_2 = L_2 \cap F_2 = \varnothing, \qquad F_3 = L_3 \cap F_2 = \{a_2\}$

$\mathrm{poss}\ [E_1^*/R_2] = \mathrm{poss}\ \{E_1^*/\varnothing\} = 0$

$\mathrm{poss}\ [E_2^* \cap E_1^*/R_3] = 0$

$\mathrm{poss}\ [L_2/F_2] = \varnothing$

$\mathrm{poss}\ [E_2^*/\{a_2\}] = 0$

$\mathrm{poss}\ [E_1^* \cap E_2^*/F_2] = 0$

$\mathrm{poss}\ [E_1^*/R_3] = \mathrm{poss}\ [E_1^*/a_2] = 1 \wedge (1-\mathrm{poss}(E_1/a_2)) = 1$

Hence $T_2(b) = B_2(b)$; i.e., $T_2 = B_2$.

Similarly, with $F_3 = \{a_1, a_3\}$ we can show that $T_3 = B_1$.

Thus our proposed decision is

W is $m\circ$

where $m\circ$ has two focal elements:

$B_1 = \{b_1\}, \qquad B_2 = \{b_2\}$

with weights

$m(B_1) = 0.65, \qquad m(B_2) = 0.35$

Therefore the appropriate decision is to select either b_1 or b_2, with 0.65 probability that we select b_1 and 0.35 probability that we select b_2.

Case III

The focal elements are

$F_1 = \{0.7/a, 1/a_2, 3/a_3\}, \qquad m(F_1) = 0.5$
$F_2 = \{1/a_1, 0.3/a_2, 1/a_3\}, \qquad m(F_2) = 0.09$
$F_3 = \{a_1, a_2, a_3\}, \qquad m(F_3) = 0.2$
$F_4 = \{a_1, a_3\}, \qquad m(F_4) = 0.21$

For F_1,

$$L_2 \cap F_1 = \{0.7/a_1\}, \quad L_3 \cap F_1 = \{0.7/a_1, \ 1/a_2\}$$
$$\text{poss}[E_1^*/L_2 \cap F_1] = 0.7 \wedge 0.3 = 0.3$$
$$\text{poss}[E_1^* \cap E_2^*/L_3 \cap F_1] = 0$$
$$\text{poss}[E_2^*/L_3 \cap F_1] = 0$$
$$\text{poss}[L_2/F_1] = 0.7$$
$$\text{poss}[E_1^*/L_3 \cap F_1] = 0.3$$
$$\text{poss}[E_1^*/L_2 \cap F_1] = 0.3$$
$$\text{poss}[E_1^* \cap E_2^*/F_1] = 0$$

Hence

$$T_1(b) = 0.3 \vee (0.7 \wedge B_1(b)) \vee (0.3 \ B_2(b) \vee 0.3 \wedge B_3(b))$$
$$T_1 = \{0.7/b_1, \ 0.3/b_2, \ 0.3/b_3\}$$

For F_2,

$$L_2 \cap F_2 = \{1/a_1\}, \quad L_3 \cap F_2 = \{1/a_1, \ 0.3/a_2\}$$
$$\text{poss}[E^*/L_2 \cap F_2] = 0$$
$$\text{poss}[E_1^* \cap E_2^*/L \cap F_2\} = 0$$
$$\text{poss}[E_2^*/L_3 \cap F_2] = 0.3$$
$$\text{poss}[L_2/F_2] = 1$$
$$\text{poss}[E_1^*/L_2 \cap F_2] = 0$$
$$\text{poss}[E^*/L_2 \cap F_1] = 0$$
$$\text{poss}[E_1^* \cap F_2^*/F_2] = 0$$

Hence $T_2(b) = B_1(b)$.

It can easily be shown that

$$T_3 = B_1, \quad T_4 = B_1$$

and therefore

W is m

where

$$T_1 = \{0.7/B_1, \ 0.3/b_2, \ 0.3/b_3\}, \quad m(\Pi) = 0.5$$
$$T_2 = \{b_1\}, \quad\quad\quad\quad\quad\quad\quad m(\Pi) = 0.5$$

In this case we select our action according to the performance of a random experiment in which

$$P(b_1) = 0.85, \quad P(b_2 \text{ or } b_3) = 0.15$$

6.4 Conclusion

Although the methodology of decision-making has been presented in the context of a management application, it is equally applicable to any problem in which one has to choose what action to take in the face of undesirable functioning of a system.

References

Dempster, A.P. (1967). 'Upper and lower probabilities induced by a multi-valued mapping', *Ann. Math. Statist.*, **38**, 325–339

Reggia, J., Nau, D. and Wang, P. (1983). 'Diagnostic expert systems based on a set covering model' *Int. J. Man–Machine Studies*, 437–460

Reggia, J., Nau, D., Wang, P. and Peng, Y. (1985). 'A formal model of diagnostic inference', *Inf. Sci.*, **37**, 227–285

Shafer, G. (1976). *A Mathematical Theory of Evidence*. Princeton, NJ: Princeton University Press

Yager, R.R. (1985a). 'Explanatory models in expert systems', *Int. J. Man–Machine Studies*, **23**, 539–549

Yager, R.R. (1985b). 'Reasoning with uncertainty for expert systems' In Proc. 9th IJCAI, Los Angeles, 1295–1297

Yager, R.R. (1986a). 'Toward a general theory of reasoning with uncertainty. Part I: Non-specificity and fuzziness', *Int. J. Intell. Syst.*, **1**, 45–67

Yager, R.R. (1986b). 'A general approach to decision making with evidential knowledge' In *Uncertainty in Artificial Intelligence* (L.H. Kanal and J.L. Lemmer; Eds). Amsterdam: North-Holland, 317–330

Yager, R.R. (1986c). 'Non-monotonic compatibility relations in the theory of evidence' Technical Report MII–615, Machine Intelligence Institute, Iona College, New Rochelle, NY

Yager, R.R. (1987). 'Using approximate reasoning to represent default knowledge', *J. Artif. Intell.*, **31**, 99–112

Yager, R.R. (1988). 'Toward a general theory of reasoning with uncertainty. Part II: Probability', *Int. J. Man–Machine Studies* (to appear)

Part II

Case Studies

7

FINEX: A PC-based Expert Support System for Financial Analysis[†]

Larry Kerschberg and John Dickinson

7.1 Introduction

The field of artificial intelligence (AI) has provided new and revolution-ary insights into the construction of knowledge-based systems. One particular class of knowledge-based system is the expert system, which embodies in a computer program the knowledge and problem-solving capabilities of a human expert. An expert's knowledge consists not only of public knowledge, found in articles and textbooks, but also private knowledge culled from years of experience in solving problems in the expert's area of expertise (Hayes-Roth et al., 1983).

In this chapter we address several important issues related to business expert systems. In particular, we present

- a taxonomy of expert systems based on their mode of development and their organizational role
- application domains for business expert systems
- a novel architecture for the implementation of business expert systems on personal computers (PCs)
- a prototype implementation of a PC-based business expert system that uses ratio analysis for the financial analysis of a company's financial statement.

The chapter is organized as follows. Section 7.2 presents a taxonomy of expert systems from an organizational viewpoint, and discusses the role of business expert systems. Section 7.3 discusses the role of PCs in knowledge-based systems for business decision-making. Section 7.4

[†] This chapter is published with special permission of Jean-Claude Rault, Chairman of the Annual International Conference on Expert Systems and their Applications, Avignon.

provides an example of a business expert system for the financial analysis of a business's income statement and balance sheet. Experience with knowledge engineering is presented, and an interactive knowledge acquisition technique is proposed. In Section 7.5 we present our conclusions and suggestions for future research.

7.2 A taxonomy of expert systems

Expert systems have been developed for scientific, industrial, medical, and business applications. In the scientific arena we can cite DENDRAL (Lindsay *et al.*, 1980) and MOLGEN (Stefik, 1981a,b). Industrial applications include XCON (O'Connor, 1984), the Dipmeter Advisor (Smith, 1984), and PROSPECTOR (Duda *et al.*, 1978; 1979; Duda and Reboh, 1984). Medical expert systems include MYCIN (Shortliffe, 1976), INTERNIST/CADUSEUS (Pople *et al.*, 1975), and PUFF (Kunz *et al.*, 1978). There are few business expert systems, however, but two examples are TAXADVISOR (Michaelson, 1982) and a proposed system for auditing (Dungan, 1982). The scarcity of business applications indicates that this area is somehow 'different' from the others. We wish to explore this notion by establishing a taxonomy for expert systems and showing how business applications fit into it.

An excellent taxonomy for ES was provided by Hayes-Roth *et al.* (1983). It focuses on the nature of the problem domain, the characteristics of the data, and the problem-solving approach; that is, the search technique and control strategy. Our taxonomy is different in that it focuses on organizational issues and the depth of knowledge contained in the system. It makes two main types of distinction:

- between internal and external expert systems,
- between advisory systems, expert systems, and expert support systems.

Thus our framework distinguishes between internally developed and externally acquired expert systems, as well as between the different roles systems play in the organization. Some systems are used in conjunction with knowledge workers to improve productivity, while others provide high-level expertise that is not available in the organization, thus playing the role of a true expert.

7.2.1 Internal and external expert systems

Here we discuss the nature of internal and external systems, their differences, and the characteristics of the knowledge they contain.

Internal expert systems

An internal expert system is designed, built, and maintained by a group within the organization. An example of such a system is the Dipmeter Advisor (Smith and Young, 1984). Some expert systems are developed for companies by third parties, but using the expertise of members of that company. The R1 system (McDermott, 1980), the precursor of XCON, was developed by McDermott at Carnegie–Mellon University in consultation with experts from Digital Equipment Corporation (DEC). The R1 system was taken over by DEC and became XCON. DEC now has an Intelligent Systems Technologies Group which manages the evolution of the knowledge base for XCON and other expert systems such as ISA (Intelligent Scheduling Assistant) and IMACS (Intelligent Management Assistant for Computer Systems Manufacturing) (O'Connor, 1984). Teknowledge, a company specializing in knowledge engineering and knowledge-based prototyping tools for the construction of expert systems, has built a Drilling Advisor for Elf-Aquitaine and a Sales Order expert for the NCR Corporation (Hayes-Roth, 1984).

These examples of third-party expert system development and subsequent technology transfer can be considered as internal expert systems because they are produced for a specific company and use the expertise contained within that company. The third-party companies provide the knowledge engineering expertise which is in such short supply and such high demand.

External expert systems

An external expert system is one that will be used by the 'general' public. For such systems the problem domain will be of interest to a large audience, the knowledge base will be quite stable and well accepted by that audience, and the expert knowledge used for problem-solving will be provided by an internationally recognized 'expert'.

There are very few external expert systems in the marketplace, although several prototypes such as PROSPECTOR can be classified in this category. PROSPECTOR was designed and built at SRI International and contains expert knowledge on geology. It predicted the presence of a large molybdenum ore deposit, valued in excess of $150 million, in an area that a mining company was using to dump spoil.

7.2.2 Advisory systems, expert systems, and expert support systems

Here we discuss how a knowledge-based system would be used within an organization. The systems examined vary in the degree and depth of the knowledge they contain, and in their role within the organization.

Advisory systems

Shank and Slade (1984) have introduced the notion of advisory systems. They argue that current expert systems have shortcomings which prevent them from being accepted in the business community. To overcome these shortcomings, they suggest that expert systems must evolve into advisory systems that have memory, and exhibit the following characteristics: they must

- learn from experience so that both favorable and unfavorable outcomes can be incorporated into an 'experiential memory' for use in future inferencing,
- understand the problem in the context of the user's environment,
- perceive the user's goals and be able to adapt to new users and situations.

Although several prototype programs such as POLITICS (Shank and Slade, 1984), AM (Lenat, 1982), and EURISKO (Lenat and Brown, 1984) do exhibit the characteristics of advisory systems, none is available on the market. AM and EURISKO are considered to be knowledge-based rather than expert systems.

Expert systems

In many companies an expert system is used to supplement the work of organizational experts. This allows the company to leverage its organizational expertise, without the expense of recruiting and training new experts. In some cases the expert system has become crucial to the operations of the company, as for example at DEC with its XCON system (Cherubini, 1984).

Expert support systems

Sometimes expert systems are used to complement the knowledge of human experts so they can 'work smarter.' This is the case in Japanese companies, where company policy and tradition dictate that skilled employees are retained for the whole of their working life. The Japanese companies are building knowledge-based systems that incorporate the knowledge of their senior-level engineers, and these systems are being used by others within the corporation to enhance their effectiveness and productivity. NEC's Wirex system is used to aid in the design of very-large-scale integrated circuits, and halves the design time.

   Expert support systems are the ones most likely to find their way into business organizations. They can provide checklists of items that a decision-maker might forget, a wealth of book knowledge that the

Table 7.1 Classification of expert systems.

	Internal	*External*
Advisory	POLITICS AM EURISKO	
Expert	XCON, ISA, IMACS Dipmeter Advisor MOLGEN Drilling Advisor	DENDRAL PROSPECTOR MYCIN PUFF
Expert support	Wirex	TAXADVISOR Office intelligence system

ordinary decision-maker might not be aware of, and knowledge-based interpretation capabilities. Many professionals in areas such as financial services, insurance, tax consulting, auditing, and law could make effective use of such systems.

Another business application system would be an office intelligence system that could acquire knowledge about the way an office functions, and could then provide advice on standard operating procedures and the flow of information.

Table 7.1 classifies the systems mentioned above within our framework.

7.3 The role of PCs in knowledge-based systems

The PC is becoming the standard businessman's workstation. The most useful tools in today's PC environment are

- spreadsheets for budgeting and planning,
- word-processing for memos and reports,
- database management systems for managing large collections of data,
- business graphics for the data presentation in decision-impelling format,
- communications software for access to online information services.

Information is interchanged among software tools by means of the data interchange format (DIF), a data representation standard for importing and exporting files between tools. A number of integrated packages provide menu-driven interfaces that automatically perform inter-tool data translation. These packages use data dictionaries or directories to manage data translation.

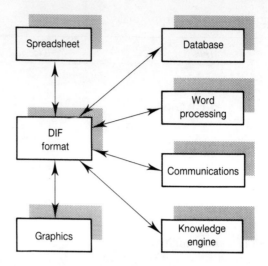

Figure 7.1 A loosely coupled architecture: PC tool integration via data interchange format.

We maintain that a new generation of knowledge-based tools for the PC is needed to increase organizational productivity. The first such tool – the main focus of this paper – will be an interface between a 'knowledge engine' and existing PC software tools. A number of expert system 'shells' and AI languages are available for PCs. In effecting this integration of knowledge-directed inferencing with the businessperson's view of data (e.g., spreadsheets and databases), knowledge engineers will be able to create novel decision-support systems.

The integration may be a **loose coupling** of PC tools (Figure 7.1), as exemplified by the FINEX architecture described in Section 7.4. We believe that future developments will lead to **tight coupling** of architectures, in which knowledge-based reasoning will play a central role.

In a tightly coupled architecture (Figure 7.2) the user agent (UA) will replace the simple DIF translation. The UA will be capable of learning about the user's environment, establishing the user's profile of preferred modes of interaction (e.g., commands or menus), and assist the user in taking full advantage of the system's resources and knowledge. The UA will help the user in defining the problem to be solved, and will suggest either a predefined expert support system, say for capital budgeting, or the appropriate tools and techniques for solving the problem.

In addition to problem-solving assistance, the UA would act as an information intermediary in accessing external online databases, and would thus play the role of an expert reference librarian for these information resources. The UA would have information on protocols and

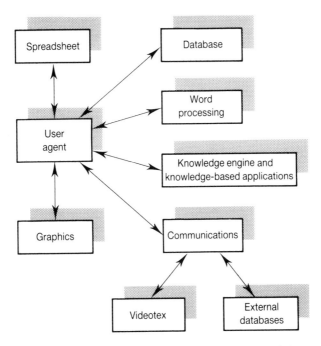

Figure 7.2 A tightly coupled architecture: the user-agent as advisory system.

passwords and, more importantly, the facilities to transform a user's request (stated perhaps in natural language) into appropriate retrieval statements for one or more target utilities. The transformation process would entail the use of local and remote thesauri and data dictionaries or directories.

The concept of a knowledge-based UA is in keeping with the evolution of knowledge-based tools for the PC environment. The goal is to provide knowledge-based access to organizational resources and expertise. Thus the UA could be developed in-house by the knowledge engineering group, or it could be acquired externally and adapted to the organization's needs. The UA falls into the category of an advisory system.

7.4 FINEX: an expert system for financial analysis

The financial analysis expert system FINEX has as its problem domain corporate ratio analysis in the petroleum wholesale industry. The expert source of knowledge is Professor Philip Cooley of the Department of Finance, University of South Carolina. The topic was chosen because it is a business application that fits into a rule-based scheme of decision-making, and requires expert knowledge for a meaningful interpretation. It is also attractive from the practitioner's viewpoint because it introduces the novel idea of the 'intelligent spreadsheet.' With the advent of the microcomputer and the advancements in and proliferation of spreadsheet software, a logical extension of the modeling capabilities of these spreadsheets is to include some type of inference mechanism that can apply expert knowledge to the day-to-day decisions made by business managers.

Ratio analysis has many applications, such as the evaluation of a company's financial situation for investment purposes, loan approvals, and bond ratings. Thus, this area of finance and the concept of the intelligent spreadsheet represents a business application of expert systems that could have widespread use as an external expert support system. We continue with a short introduction to ratio analysis, proceeding to describe the FINEX system architecture and its knowledge representation. We also provide some insights gained from the knowledge engineering process.

7.4.1 Ratio analysis of income statements and balance sheets

Ratio analysis is a method by which financial experts assess the strengths and weaknesses of a firm by looking at specific ratios of numerical data found on the firm's primary annual financial statement: the statement of income and balance sheet. The areas of the analysis can be broken down into four major categories, all of which have an impact on the firm's return on equity (ROE), the ultimate measure of financial success. These areas are profitability, asset management, debt management and liquidity. Figure 7.3 shows a taxonomy of the ratios used for this analysis.

Profitability, as measured by a profit margin (PM), is the measure of the firm's ability to make a profit. It is affected by the proportion of expenses incurred in the operation of the business as a percentage of the total sales. These expenses are measured by gross margin (GM) and operating expenses (OE) as percentages of sales.

Asset management, as measured by total asset turnover (TATO), is the measure of the firm's ability to handle its assets efficiently in operating the business. It is broken down into fixed asset turnover (FATO) and current asset turnover (CATO). CATO is then broken down into accounts receivable turnover (ARTO) and inventory turnover (ITO).

Debt management, as measured by the financial leverage multiplier (FLM), reflects the financial risk, or leverage, that a firm incurs as a result of external financing by debt. It is broken down into current debt/total assets (CD/TA) and long-term debt/total capitalization (LTD/TC).

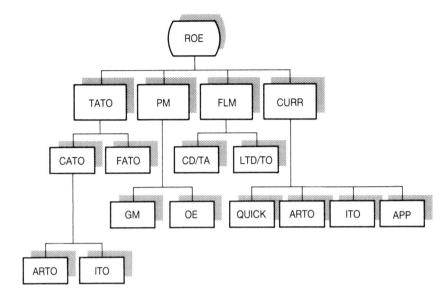

Figure 7.3 Taxonomy of ratios used in ratio analysis. ROE, return on equity; TATO, total asset turnover; CATO, current asset turnover; ARTO, accounts receivable turnover; ITO, inventory turnover; FATO, fixed asset turnover; PM, profit margin; GM, gross margin; OE, operating expenses; FLM, financial leverage multiplier; CD/TA, current debt/total assets; LTD/TC, long-term debt/total capitalization; CURR, current ratio; QUICK, quick ratio; APP, accounts payable period.

Liquidity, as measured by the current ratio (CURR), is a measure of the firm's ability to meet its short-term financial obligations. It is broken down into the quick ratio (QUICK), the accounts receivable turnover (ARTO), the inventory turnover (ITO), and the average accounts payable period (APP).

These four areas of financial analysis are considered collectively in assessing the overall financial strength of a firm. A model developed by the DuPont Corporation (Figure 7.4) shows the algebraic (e.g., numerical) relationships between these ratios and how they interact to give the final measure of strength, the ROE (called by DuPont 'return on net worth').

7.4.2 System architecture

A diagrammatical representation of the system is shown in Figure 7.5. It consists of three modules: the first is part of a Lotus 1-2-3 spreadsheet, the second is a BASIC program, and the third is a micro-PROLOG program. The target machine for FINEX is the IBM XT, running DOS 2.0 as the operating system. A hard disk is needed for this

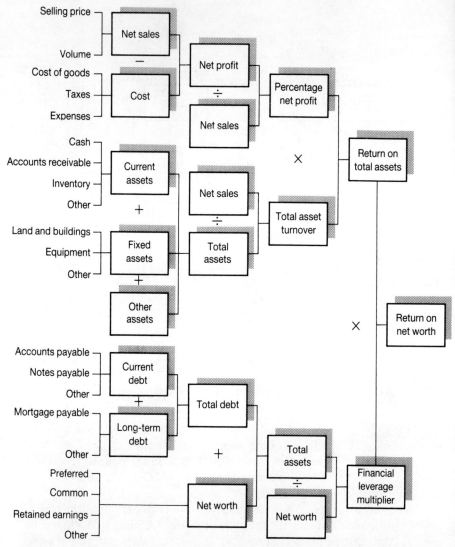

Figure 7.4 DuPont model of a firm's financial strength.

application mainly as a permanent residence for Lotus 1-2-3, but it is not a limiting requirement.

The FINEX system is initiated by invoking a DOS batch file named EXPERT.BAT, which acts as a driver for the system, calling each of the modules as the previous one is completed. The first module to be called is the spreadsheet program (Figure 7.6). The spreadsheet contains financial statements for Starr Oil Distributors; they are in a format consistent with the Petroleum Marketers' Educational Foundation yearly publication of industry ratios (Cooley, 1983b).

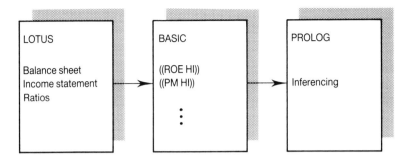

Figure 7.5 Overview of FINEX.

After the balance sheet and income statement figures for the firm are entered, the ratios are calculated and a Lotus program is executed that evaluates and classifies each of the ratios as OK, HIGH, or LOW, according to thresholds established by Cooley. The Lotus program writes beside each ratio the appropriate finding in a format that will later be acceptable to the micro-PROLOG program for inferencing.

The purpose of the spreadsheet is to provide a user-friendly means of data entry by giving the businessperson a tool with which they are familiar. The burden is then on the Lotus and BASIC programs to translate these raw data into a form that is acceptable for inferencing. It also allows the user to do a type of 'what if' questioning and receive an expert analysis of the effects of the 'what if.'

Once the ratios are calculated and evaluated, the spreadsheet is written out to a DIF file. This DIF allows data to be passed between many types of software packages such as Lotus, Visicalc, dBaseII, or any procedural language such as BASIC.

Once the spreadsheet is in DIF, the user exits Lotus, at which point the batch file resumes control, and in turn calls a BASIC program. The function of the BASIC program is to select from the DIF file the facts that need to be used by the micro-PROLOG program for inferencing. Since the facts have already been translated into a micro-PROLOG-compatible form by the Lotus program, the BASIC program must simply pick them off as it scans the DIF file and write them to a disk file. Figure 7.7 shows the output of the BASIC program.

When the BASIC program completes execution, the batch file resumes control and promptly calls micro-PROLOG. On booting-up, the micro-PROLOG program loads an interpreter (entitled SIMPLE, as it simplifies the user interface), the facts from the spreadsheet as passed through the BASIC program, and the knowledge base and inference program. At this point the system turns control back to the user and awaits a command to initiate action. Once the inferencing is completed

STARR OIL DISTRIBUTORS
BALANCE SHEET

ASSETS		LIABILITIES AND NET WORTH	
CURRENT ASSETS		CURRENT LIABILITIES	
CASH	$37	ACCOUNTS PAYABLE	$81
MARKETABLE		LTD – CURRENT	
SECURITIES	$10	PORTION	$14
RECEIVABLES, TRADE		NOTES PAYABLE	$12
(NET)	$102	OTHER CURRENT	
INVENTORY	$77	LIABILITIES	$24
OTHER CURRENT		TOTAL CURRENT	
ASSETS	$13	LIABILITIES	$131
TOTAL CURRENT ASSETS	$239	LONG-TERM DEBT	$56
FIXED ASSETS (NET)	$75	OTHER LONG-TERM	
ALL OTHER NONCURRENT		LIABILITIES	$3
ASSETS	$14	TOTAL LONG-TERM	
TOTAL NONCURRENT		LIABILITIES	$59
ASSETS	$89	TOTAL LIABILITIES	$190
TOTAL ASSETS	$328	NET WORTH	
		COMMON STOCK	$32
		OTHER EQUITY	
		ACCOUNT	$1
		RETAINED EARNINGS	$105
		TOTAL NET WORTH	$138
		TOTAL LIABILITIES AND	
		NET WORTH	$328

STARR OIL DISTRIBUTORS
INCOME STATEMENT

NET SALES	$5,736	RATIO ANALYSIS		
LESS COST OF GOODS SOLD	$4,982			
		Return on Equity	26.59%	((ROE HIGH))
GROSS PROFIT	$754	Profit Margin	0.64%	(PM OK)
OPERATING EXPENSES		Total Asset		
ADVERTISING AND		Turnover	17.49	((TATO HIGH))
PROMOTION	$13	Fin Lev Multiplier	2.38	((FLM OK))
CHIEF EXECUTIVE SALARY	$50	Current Ratio	1.82	((CURR HIGH))
OTHER SALARIES AND		Current Asset		
WAGES	$280	Turnover	24.00	((CATO HIGH))
DEPRECIATION	$49	Fixed Asset		
VEHICLE EXPENSE	$64	Turnover	64.45	((FATO HIGH))
LEASE AND RENTAL	$18	A/R T Over	56.24	((ARTO HIGH))
INSURANCE	$43	Inventory		
LICENSES, NON-INCOME		Turnover	74.49	((ITO HIGH))

TAXES	$40	Gross Margin	13.15% ((GM HIGH))
OTHER OPERATING		Operating Exp	
EXPENSES	$145	Percentage	12.23% ((OE HIGH)
	———	LTD/Total Cap	17.99% ((LTD OK))
TOTAL OPERATING		Current Debt/	
EXPENSES	$701	Tot Cap	39.94% ((CD CK))
NET OPERATING INCOME	$53	Quick Ratio	1.14 ((QUICK HIGH))
TOTAL NONOPERATING		A/P to Total	
INCOME	$42	Assets	24.70% ((APTA OK))

Figure 7.6   Lotus spreadsheet.

and micro-PROLOG is exited, the batch file completes its execution and returns control to the user.

7.4.3 Knowledge organization

The FINEX prototype provides two distinct modes of interaction:

- The *interpretation mode*, in which a report (an example of which is shown in Figure 7.8) is provided for the user. This report gives a high-level interpretation of the ratios and likely causes of certain problems.
- The *analysis mode*, in which an in-depth analysis of a particular problem is carried out by means of interactive knowledge acquisition and inferencing.

In the interpretation mode the system makes use of public knowledge, while the analysis mode uses expert knowledge. We now present the knowledge representation paradigm used by FINEX.

Interpretation mode

The knowledge representation for the interpretation mode is a collection of production rules of the form 'if X then Y.' This rule structure fits very well because of its structured form of cause and effect.

Figure 7.8 shows a sample session with the interpretation part of the inference module. The user initiates the inferencing by entering a Does(Analysis(go)) prompt into the system. Micro-PROLOG then responds with an overall explanation of the findings of the inference process, telling the user the standing of the company's ROE as well as each of the four major areas of evaluation, and tells the user how to obtain further explanations. The user can then direct the system into any one of the four areas for further explanation. The structure of the

```
((ROE HIGH))
((PM OK))
((TATO HIGH))
((FLM OK))
((CURR HIGH))
((CATO HIGH))
((FATO HIGH))
((ARTO HIGH))
((ITO HIGH))
((GM HIGH))
((OE HIGH))
((LTD OK))
((CD OK))
((QUICK HIGH))
((APTA OK))
ENDING PROGRAM...
```

Figure 7.7 Output of BASIC program.

explanations corresponds to the taxonomy shown in Figure 7.3, with each major area branching down into the detailed analysis of the specific ratios in each category. Figure 7.9 shows some sample rules for this module in English and in the micro-PROLOG implementation.

Analysis mode

Whereas the interpretation mode considers the ratios within each major taxonomic area separately, the analysis mode has private knowledge that can be used to ascertain the logical relationships between the concepts and the ratios of the taxonomy. This mode requires more information than is provided by the spreadsheet, and the system requests information from the user. The user may be an industry analyst privy to sensitive information, or a company officer who is trying to ascertain his firm's problems. The knowledge representation for this private knowledge is patterned after Hendrix's partitioned semantic nets (Hendrix, 1979) and the inference nets used in the PROSPECTOR system (Duda *et al.*, 1978).

Figures 7.10 and 7.11 show a conceptual representation of the logical relationships between a gross margin (GM) that is too low and other ratios that may reveal a reason for it being low. The factors shown here that may affect a firm's GM are competition (which has a direct effect on prices and credit policies), supplier prices, and the presence of wholesale resale of petroleum products. These interrelationships were discovered by the authors as the expert made comments on the explanation function of the GM based on his past experience in the oil wholesale market.

An Expert Financial Analyzer

A preliminary evaluation is given below. All
comparisons are made to industry averages as found
in the Petroleum Marketers' Educational Foundation's
annual publication of industry averages.

Return on Equity is high.
Profit Margin is average.
Total Asset Turnover is high.
The Financial Leverage Multiplier is average.
Current ratio is high.

These comparisons cover the major areas used to evaluate
a firm's financial strength. The ROE is a function of the
other four areas. To receive a more in depth explanation
of one of these areas, enter the appropriate command.

Does(xxxxx(explain))

where 'xxxxx' is PM, TATO, FLM, or CURR
YES
&.

Profit Margin is a measure of a firm's net income
as a percentage of sales. Two components of profit margin
are Cost of Goods Sold, as measured by Gross Margin, and
Operating Expenses. These two measures are now evaluated
for our firm.

Gross Margin

This firm's Gross Margin is higher than the industry
average. This is most likely due to lower supplier
costs or efficient purchasing practices such as
quantity discounts.

Enter Y to continue...y

Operating Expenses

Operating Expenses as a percentage of sales is
high for this firm as compared to the industry.
This is an indication that inefficiencies occur in the
production process. Some specific problems may be in
machinery downtime, job scheduling, or low personnel
productivity.
&.

Figure 7.8   Output of micro-PROLOG program.

Micro-PROLOG

Analysis(go) if XROE(x1) & XPM(x2) & XTATO(x3)) & XFLM(x4) & XCURR(x5)

XTATO(LOW) if TATO(LOW) & P("   ASSET MANAGEMENT") & PP( ) & PP( )
    & P("   This firm's asset management is poor. Total Asset ") & PP( ) &
    P("Turnover (TATO) is low and could be due either to ") & PP( ) & P("poor
    current asset management, or poor fixed asset ") & PP( ) &
    P("management.") & PP( ) & XCATO(x1) & XFATO(x2)

English

Initiate the session by Analysis(go) if each of the areas listed in the rule can be instantiated.

To instantiate XTATO(LOW), first instantiate TATO(LOW), display the given text on the screen, and instantiate the facts XCATO(x1) and XFATO(x2).

Figure 7.9   Example of a FINEX rule, in micro-PROLOG and in English.

Figure 7.10 shows schematically the effects of the previously mentioned factors on GM. The diagram is made up of source nodes, arcs, and target nodes. The description on a given arc belongs to the source node. For example, COMPETITION is a source node with arcs connecting it to the target nodes of PRICES and CREDIT. The descriptor HI belongs to COMPETITION, showing that competition is high for this firm. The arc connecting PRICES to GM is LOW, showing that the result of the high competition is low prices. Each of the node–arc pairs shows a relationship between the factors and the low GM.

Figure 7.11 is a detailed representation of the dialogue that would occur between FINEX and the user. To make the graph readable, the nodes have been labeled with abbreviations for facts (F), questions (Q), and conclusions (C). The beginning node is a fact (F1) that is resident within the knowledge base. From this fact the system sets out to determine from the user, by querying for additional information, the probable source of the problem. This scenario utilizes the ability of micro-PROLOG to add and delete facts (or conclusions) from the knowledge base as the inferencing process proceeds. By following the arcs through the question nodes, one is able to discern from the graph the conclusions that can be drawn from the user's responses. Based on the user's responses, the system adds or deletes facts from the knowledge base.

As an example, let us follow the graph through the first path to its conclusion. On finding the fact that the GM is low, the system asks the

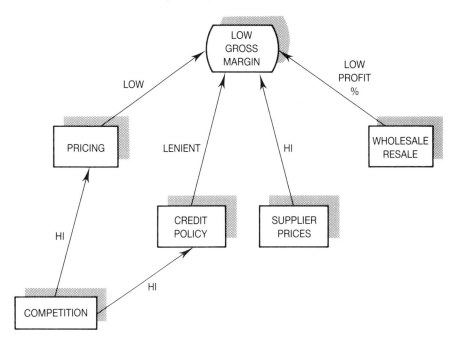

Figure 7.10   Schematic representation of relationship between gross margin and factors affecting it.

user if competition is stiff (Q1). If the user responds 'Yes,' the system inquires as to the effect of this high competition. (If the user responds 'No,' that path fails and the next path is chosen.) The system then asks the user whether prices have had to be lowered (Q1.1). If the user answers 'Yes,' the system adds to the knowledge base the fact that competition is causing the user to lower prices (C1.1).

The system then checks the knowledge base to see if accounts receivable turnover (ARTO) is low (Q1.2). If so, the system asks the user whether stiff competition is causing the firm to offer more lenient credit terms (Q1.2.1). If the user answers 'Yes,' the system adds to the knowledge base the fact that, since the competition is causing the user to offer more lenient credit terms, the size of the A/R balance is high, causing a lower ARTO and costing the user capital to fund the A/R (C1.2.1). The system then checks whether C1.1 and C1.2.1 are both in the knowledge base. If they are, then it adds a new fact saying that competition is causing a double strain on profits by lowering prices and causing the user to maintain high levels of A/R (C1.1–2), and deletes the other two facts (C1.1 and C1.2.1). The final step in such a dialogue, after all paths are traversed, is for the system to draw together all facts in the knowledge base and display a final analysis for the user.

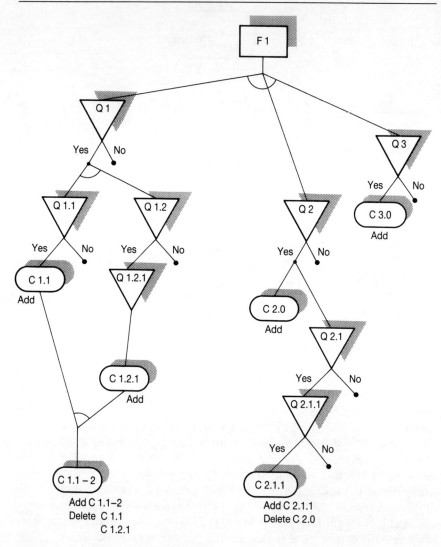

Facts

    F1   Gross Margin is LOW.

Questions

    Q1   'Is your competition stiff?'

    Q1.1   'Does the stiff competition require you to lower prices?'

    Q1.2   'Is your Accounts Receivable Turnover LOW?' (NOTE: this could also be ascertained from the fact-base.)

    Q1.2.1 'Your ARTO is LOW. Do you feel that this is due to your competition's causing you to offer more lenient credit terms?'

    Q2   'Have you been reselling goods to other wholesalers at a lower markup?'

Q2.1   'Is your Inventory Turnover LOW?' (NOTE: this could also be ascertained from the fact-base.)

Q2.1.1   'Your Inventory Turnover is LOW. Is this the reason you sold goods to other wholesalers?'

Q3   'Have the prices charged to you by your suppliers risen within the last year (as a percentage of sales)?'

Conclusions

C1.1   Competition has caused the firm to lower its prices, thereby lowering its Gross Margin.

C1.2.1   Competition has caused the firm to offer more lenient credit terms, raising its Accounts Receivable level and increasing the expense of funding A/R, thereby lowering its Gross Margin.

C1.1–2   Competition has caused a double squeeze on Gross Margin by causing the firm to lower its prices and fund higher levels of Accounts Receivable.

C2.0   The firm is reselling goods on the wholesale market at a lower price markup, thereby lowering its Gross Margin.

C2.1.1   Due to excess inventory, the firm is reselling goods on the wholesale market at a lower price markup, thereby lowering its Gross Margin.

C3.0   The firm has experienced higher Cost of Goods Sold due to higher supplier prices, thereby lowering its Gross Margin.

Figure 7.11   Example of FINEX–user dialogue.

This example shows the kinds of conclusion that can be drawn from the given question base, but, more importantly, demonstrates how this type of interaction between expert system and user can be used to maintain a dynamic knowledge base. This example also shows how large the number of interrelationships can quickly make the network of facts and inferences (or 'inference net,' (Hendrix, 1979)) very complex when the entire domain is considered. (Remember that this net is only for the effects of one 'subratio'.) The challenge in building the knowledge base in terms of an inference net is to achieve proper structuring of the expert's knowledge.

7.4.4 Knowledge engineering experience

Knowledge engineering is the process by which the knowledge engineer acquires the knowledge from the expert. It falls into two stages: the discovery of 'public' knowledge, and the discovery of 'private' knowledge (Hayes-Roth *et al.*, 1983).

Public knowledge is knowledge that can be gained from public sources such as textbooks or articles. (One of the authors had a special advantage in that he was in a corporate finance class taught by Cooley, and could quickly gain a working understanding of this public knowledge.) The role of the expert in this phase was to advise the knowledge engineer of recommended sources of public knowledge and answer any specific questions on this knowledge put by the engineer. It should be pointed out that this public knowledge, while supplying some knowledge about the domain, is not sufficient knowledge for an expert system. What makes an expert system truly 'expert' is the private knowledge or heuristics that the expert possesses and applies in actual analysis.

The process of acquiring private knowledge is an iterative process that requires close interaction between the expert and the knowledge engineer. The authors found it best to incorporate the public knowledge in a rough-and-ready prototype which could demonstrate the capabilities of the system to the expert. (Smith (1984) advocates this approach of rapid prototyping followed by successive refinements.) As the expert saw the system functioning, he was able to add to the private knowledge by commenting, many times in a matter-of-fact way, on rules of thumb that he had accumulated from his experience.

Once an adequate amount of private knowledge has been acquired from the expert, the engineer can then incorporate that knowledge into the system, and once again allow the expert to test it against his expertise. In capturing the hidden knowledge in these *ad hoc* sessions, it was found best to tape record the entire session, thus preserving the spontaneity of the meeting.

The expert suggested that as he conducts one-on-one analysis sessions in his consulting work, a more formal way of capturing this private knowledge might be to have mock analysis sessions with the engineer. This method would reveal the expert's strategy of analysis with a client, and would show his deductive reasoning at work. This method was used to structure the dialogue shown in Figure 7.11.

7.5 Conclusions and suggestions for future research

An organizational taxonomy for expert systems, in particular, business expert systems, has been presented. Future business applications are expected to fall into the 'expert support system' category, in which the system will work in conjunction with the decision-maker, supplying knowledge-based expertise for examinations of alternative strategies for business decisions.

External expert support systems are those that will be available off-the-shelf, and will be capable of adapting to the user's environment by means of sophisticated knowledge-acquisition interfces. Into this category falls the FINEX prototype system, a PC-based expert system for financial analysis which provides knowledge-based interpretation of ratios from a company's income statement and balance sheet. FINEX has a number of important features:

- It uses readily available data, and has been certified by public accounting firms. Such statements are available from information utilities such as DOW/JONES News Retrieval, and can be 'downloaded' to a PC.
- Ratio analysis is used in a variety of applications, including the screening of loan applications, stock market investment, and determining bond ratings.
- The concept of the 'intelligent spreadsheet,' the coupling of an electronic spreadsheet and a knowledge engine, is not only feasible but desirable. This approach extends the capabilities of the spreadsheet so that logical inferences may be performed.

Current trends in PC-based software point to the integration of software facilities such as spreadsheets, word-processing, database management, communications, and business graphics. We contend that the 'missing link' is the knowledge engine. This knowledge representation and inferencing capability will greatly increase the types of possible application, and we foresee many advances for external expert support systems in such areas as natural language interfaces to software tools, financial risk analysis, and online access to external knowledge utilities. A recently introduced software package, GURU from Micro Data Base Systems Co., provides an environment that allows the user to write rules that access both spreadsheets and databases to perform knowledge-directed problem-solving. Such advances will allow us to achieve the aim of incorporating AI in business expert system environments.

References

Brown, A. 'Wall Street on your spreadsheet', *Dowline*, (8)

Cherubini, Q. (1986). 'Knowledge base management systems working group' In *Proc. 1st Int. Workshop on Expert Database Systems* (L. Kerschberg; Ed.). Menlo Park, CA: Benjamin/Cummings

Cooley, P.L. (1983a). *How to Value an Oil Jobbership for Purchase or Sell.* Petroleum Marketers' Educational Foundation

Cooley, P.L. (1983b). *Financial Characteristics of Petroleum Marketers.* Petroleum Marketers' Educational Foundation

Deliyanni, A. and Kowalski, R.A. (1979). 'Logic and semantic networks' *Commun. ACM*, **2**, (3)

Duda, R.O., Hart, P.E., Konolige, K. and Reboh, R. (1979). 'A computer-based consultant for mineral exploration', Final Report, SRI International, Menlo Park, CA

Duda, R.O., Hart, P.E., Nilsson, N.J. and Sutherland, G.N. (1978). 'Semantic network representations in rule-based inference systems' In *Pattern-Directed Inference Systems* (D.A. Waterman and F. Hayes-Roth; Eds). New York: Academic Press

Duda, R.O. and Reboh, R. (1984). 'AI and decision making: The PROSPECTOR experience' In *Artificial Intelligence Applications for Business* (W. Reitman; Ed.). Norwood, NJ: Ablex, 111–147

Dungan, C. (1982). 'Auditor', PhD Dissertation, University of Illinois

Hayes-Roth, F. (1984). 'The industrialization of knowledge engineering' In *Artificial Intelligence Applications for Business* (W. Reitman; Ed.). Norwood, NJ: Ablex, 159–177

Hayes-Roth, F., Waterman, D.A. and Lenat, D.B.; Eds (1983). *Building Expert Systems*, Reading, MA: Addison-Wesley

Hendrix, G.G. (1979).'Encoding knowledge in partitioned networks' In *Associative Networks* (N. Findler; Ed.). New York: Academic Press

Keller, R. and Townsend, P. (1984). 'Knowledge-based systems' *Computerworld*, **18**, (49A)

Kowalski, R. (1979). *Logic for Problem Solving*. New York: Elsevier

Kunz, J.C., Fallat, R.J., McClung, D.H., Osborn, J.J., Votteri, R.A., Nii, H.P., Aikins, J.S., Fagan, L.M. and Feigenbaum, E.A. (1978). 'A physiological rule-based system for interpreting pulmonary function test results' Report HPP-78-19, Heuristic Programming Project, Computer Science Department, Stanford University

Lenat, D.B. (1982). 'On automated scientific theory formation: A case study using the AM program' In *Knowledge-Based Systems in Artificial Intelligence* (R. Davis and D.B. Lenat; Eds). New York: McGraw-Hill

Lenat, D.B. and Brown, J.S. (1984). 'Why AM and EURISKO appear to work', *Artif. Intell.*, **23**, (3), 269–294

Lindsay, R.D., Buchanan, B.G., Feigenbaum, E.A. and Lederberg, J. (1980). *Applications of Artificial Intelligence for Organic Chemistry: The DENDRAL Project*. New York: McGraw-Hill

McDermott, J. (1980). 'R1: An expert in the computer systems domain' In Proc. 1st Annual National Conf. on 'Artificial Intelligence', 269–271

Michaelson, R. (1982). 'TAXADVISOR', PhD Dissertation, University of Illinois

O'Connor, D.E. (1984). 'Using expert systems to manage change and complexity in manufacturing' In *Artificial Intelligence Applications for Business* (W. Reitman; Ed.). Norwood, NJ: Ablex, 149–158

Pople, H.E., Myers, J.D. and Miller, R.A. (1975). 'Dialog Internist: A model of diagnostic knowledge for internal medicine' In Proc. 4th IJCAI, Tblisi, 849–855

Shank, R.C. and Slade, S. (1984). 'Advisory systems' In *Artificial Intelligence Applications for Business* (W. Reitman; Ed.). Norwood, NJ: Ablex, 249–265

Shortliffe, E.H. (1976). *Computer-Based Medical Consultations: MYCIN*. New York: Elsevier

Smith, R.G. (1984). 'On the development of commercial expert systems' *AI Mag*. Fall, 1984

Smith, R.G. and Young, R.L. (1984). 'The design of the Dipmeter Advisor' In Proc. ACM Annual Conf., San Francisco, CA

Stefik, M. (1981a). 'Planning with constraints (MOLGEN: Part 1)', *Artif. Intell.*, **16**, 111–140

Stefik, M. (1981b). 'Planning and meta-planning (MOLGEN: Part 2)', *Artif. Intell.*, **16**, 141–170

Van Horne, J.C. (1983). *Financial Management and Policy*, 6th edn. Englewood Cliffs, NJ: Prentice-Hall

8

Knowledge-based Expert Systems in Auditing[†]

Jesse F. Dillard and Jane F. Mutchler

8.1 Introduction

Artificial intelligence (AI) is the area of computer science concerned with the design of systems that exhibit the characteristics associated with intelligent human behavior. Expert systems are a means of applying AI techniques within specific, complex domains such as auditing. The knowledge identification required to design an expert system, as well as the system, itself provides a means of identifying and explaining how human experts store, access, and process information. As far as applications are concerned, such a system can perform as an intermediary between human experts who provide the basis for its structure and knowledge, and users who use the system as a decision-making guide or task consultant.

Research related to expert auditing systems is applicable to two current areas in auditing. The first attempts to understand and explain auditor decision processes (see Libby (1981) for a review); the second attempts to automate auditing tasks, increase effectiveness and efficiency, and increase the consistency of decisions made by different auditors. The recent interest in statistical sampling is indicative of these efforts, and expert systems are a logical extension. Several of the biggest public accounting firms in the USA are moving toward the adoption of expert systems for auditing (Elliott, 1984).

Audit researchers are currently applying expert systems technology in several areas, including analytical review (Braun, 1983), auditor opinion formulation (Dillard *et al.*, 1983a), auditing by electronic data-processing (Hansen and Messier, 1982), and internal control (Dungan,

† We wish to acknowledge the contributions made to this research by Professors E.L. Hicks and K. Ramakrishna.

1983). This chapter examines research and development on expert systems in auditing. The example taken is the decision process used by an expert in formulating auditing opinions. Methodological issues are addressed, practical issues related to the complex domain of auditing are discussed, and theoretical aspects of expert system design are evaluated. Section 8.2 briefly describes expert systems that have been or are being developed for the auditing area, and Section 8.3 discusses the stages of their development. The methodology behind an expert system used to judge whether a firm is a going concern is described in Section 8.3, while Section 8.4 proposes evaluation criteria and discusses issues which should be considered when designing and constructing knowledge-based expert systems for auditing.

8.2 Expert systems in auditing

Hansen and Messier (1982) are developing an expert system to assist auditors using electronic data-processing in evaluating the reliability of advanced computer systems. They focus on software and the construction of a knowledge base. Advice Language (AL/X) (Duda et al., 1979) is being used to construct the system. The knowledge base contains 'if, then' rules provided by the expert, which are collected in an inference network and form the evidence–hypothesis relationships which represent the problem domain. The underlying model used in the AL/X inference engine is based on a subjective Bayesian updating model; that is, the expert provides both the rules and the likelihood ratios that indicate the strength of the rules. The weightings are established by having the auditing expert interactively respond to a series of questions intended to assist in arriving at well-founded conclusions about a particular problem. The knowledge base is a 'reconstructed' set of rules which experts perceive as plausible.

Braun (1983) is building an expert system which is to be a model of the decision processes used in analytical review procedures. He uses expert auditors and is attempting to emulate their decision processes in an expert system. The system, which is limited to the health care industry and specific audit areas, will contain weightings placed by auditors on various cues used in making the decision of interest. Braun's stated purpose is to determine the relative importance of the analytical review information compared with other evidence in reaching auditing decisions. He separates the rules (the knowledge base) from the system (the inference engine) that executed these rules, and recognizes that the major problem in constructing an expert system is the extraction of knowledge from experts. He proposes to use an analog learning system which identifies decision rules by exposing the expert to a series of examples identified from prior working papers and other historical evidence; the rules generated are then tested and revised. AL/X is used to build a decision model with logical Bayesian and context links.

AUDITOR is an expert system developed by Dungan (Dungan, 1983) which assists in assessing the adequacy of the allowance for bad debts. The system is based on AL/X and was refined through interactive sessions with expert auditors. The system's performance was tested using real and hypothetical cases.

All the systems described above follow the general methodology for expert system development in that the expert knowledge is gleaned from experts and is represented and encoded in a form that can be implemented on a computer. All are at rudimentary levels of development and use as the primary software AL/X, which is based on Bayesian inference rules. The inference engine and the knowledge base are constructed separately, and the main validation criterion is the predictive accuracy of the systems.

Expert audit systems should be based on a theoretical framework which has been verified by extensive investigation and hypothesis testing of expert auditors' decision-making behavior. It may be inappropriate to assume *a priori*, as has been the case, that decision processes in auditing are the same as in medical diagnosis or chemical analysis; this remains to be established.

8.3 Stages of system development

The development of expert systems can be viewed as a three-stage sequential process:

(1) task specification and system architecture,
(2) system testing and modification,
(3) system implementation and refinement.

The first stage yields a knowledge-based decision-support system and is carried out by identifying the task and human experts within the area, and representing the knowledge in such a way that it can be understood and encoded into a computer system. The decision hierarchy, decision points and linkages are identified. This results in a detailed description of the task and the requisite information processing for carrying out the task, and the resulting design provides a detailed description of the decision process. The types of database and prior information used and the sequence of use are identified, as are the analytic capabilities necessary to carry out the task and the point at which they are utilized, and the decisions that must be made in carrying out the task, their sequence, and their relationship to prior and/or future decisions. The system provides a means of testing the proposed structure in online interactive sessions with human experts. The intelligence in a first-stage system is the decision structure – its sequence, hierarchy, and component linkages – which provides the framework for building a sophisticated knowledge-based expert system.

The second stage modifies the structure constructed in the first phase by intensive testing with human experts and through the assessment of historical cases. In effect, the first-stage results (i.e., the prototype system) are viewed as a set of hypotheses to be empirically tested by multiple evaluation methods such as protocol analysis, formal decision theory, and sensitivity analysis, preferably carried out by a set of experts other than those who participated in the first stage. This process provides a detailed, systematic investigation of expert auditors' decision processes which results in more detailed and accurate models of expert behavior than are currently available from other sources.

As the structure is refined, it also can be made more 'intelligent' because the decision processes are better understood. The first-stage system confronts the user with the decisions that must be made, but requires the user to carry out the logical processes. The decisions are broken down into their lowest components so that the decision-maker is presented with the many intermediate decisions that will be combined by the system into the final decision required. This is intelligence only in the

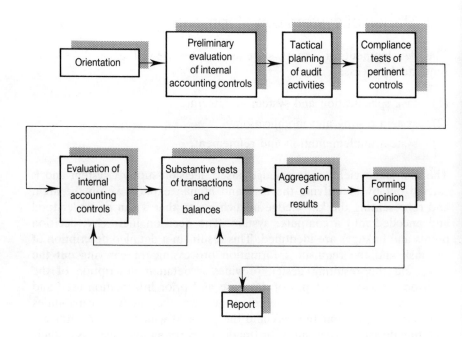

Figure 8.1   The auditor's opinion-forming process (Felix and Kinney, 1982).

sense that the intermediate decisions are aggregated, formatted, and presented to the decision-maker. In the second stage of development the intermediate decisions will begin to be 'compiled': not all the steps will have to be carried out by the user. The system will be able to infer the result. Hayes-Roth *et al.* (1983) found that this requires the implementation and encoding of decision heuristics as well as the availability of requisite databases, both of which are identified and/or validated during empirical hypotheses testing. (System interfaces with requisite databases and other decision-support facilities can present major difficulties in the construction of AI systems (Chandrasekaran *et al.* 1983a).)

The third stage in developing expert systems is to construct a system which contains extensive reasoning, learning, and language capabilities and which can be applied to more general and expanded decision-making tasks and situations. No AI system currently meets all these objectives in any one domain; the most sophisticated systems are currently in the area of medical diagnosis (see Hayes-Roth *et al.* (1983) for a review), but they fall short of meeting these requirements. It is, however, a goal which appears not too far beyond our grasp. The remainder of this chapter examines the design of an expert system through the first stage, using the going-concern decision as the auditing task of interest.

8.4 Expert system development for the going-concern decision

8.4.1 Problem selection

Given the current level of technological development, one of the most critical elements in the construction of a successful expert system is the selection of an appropriate decision task. The task should be fairly well definable and somewhat limited in scope; this will probably restrict it to a subtask or specialty task within the overall auditor's opinion-forming process.

Figure 8.1 shows the auditor's opinion-forming process (Felix and Kinney, 1982). Each stage can require many and varied judgment tasks, not to mention significant interactions between the cells. However, there is some sequencing of tasks. For example, compliance tests are undertaken before substantive tests, and the audit opinion is formed after the audit results are known. Thus, the opinion decision can be defined such that the auditing results are parameters whose values are known, reducing the magnitude of the decision task.

The different opinions the auditor can put forward are summarized in Table 8.1. In general, different sets of decision criteria are associated with each opinion category, so each can be viewed separately in terms of system design. That is, if it is assumed that the opinion decision can be

Table 8.1 Auditor opinion options.

	Not material	material	Very material
GAAP	Clean	Except for	Adverse
Unusual uncertainty	Clean	Subject to	Disclaimer
Scope	Clean	Except for	Disclaimer

viewed such that the results of the audit process are known parameters, a separate and distinct expert system can be constructed for each opinion category. Thus each could be the focus of an expert computer system. The focus in the rest of this chapter is on the 'unusual uncertainties' category in general, and specifically on the going-concern opinion.

Figure 8.2 shows that the issues related to uncertainty contingencies can be divided into two subcategories:

- those whose outcome, if not resolved in the entity's favor, would be material but not cataclysmic,
- those whose outcome, if not resolved in the entity's favor, would be cataclysmic; that is, would bring into question the entity's solvency.

The 'going-concern' opinion is a fairly well-defined task, so restricting the system to a manageable level of complexity. However, such a system could function as part of a more complete expert system for audit opinion-forming. An expert system addressing complex going-concern uncertainties can be adapted to deal with general opinion-forming.

Section 8.4.2 presents an example of an analysis of the task domain. By such an in-depth analysis the decision processes used in arriving at the going-concern opinion are identified in such a way that they can be encoded into an expert system.

8.4.2 Task domain

The subject of opinion decision is the general domain of interest. If uncertainty arises which can affect the financial statement results, the auditor decides whether a qualified opinion is needed. The circumstances giving rise to uncertainties can range from relatively simple litigation loss contingencies to relatively complex cases of entity failure.

As far as information processing is concerned, the major diagnostic task of the auditor is to construct a model for evaluation, given the

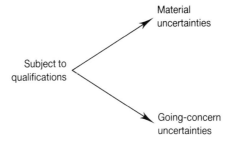

Figure 8.2 Uncertainty alternatives.

parameters of the entity being evaluated. Once reasonable standards are determined, an evaluation of the entity in relation to the standard is undertaken. Preliminary evaluations of auditors' behavior, together with experience in other complex domains and accounting problem-solving, suggest that the auditor's decision process appears to follow a hierarchical branching structure centered on a series of diagnostic questions. However, it does not appear that this structure is brought into play until there is reason to believe that an unqualified opinion is not appropriate. Support for this view is provided by the following statement, from Statement of Auditing Standards No. 34 (SAS 34) (AICPA, 1981):

> In an examination of financial statements in accordance with generally accepted auditing standards, the auditor does not search for evidential matter relating to the entity's continued existence because, in the absence of information to the contrary, an entity's continuation is usually assumed in financial accounting. Nevertheless, the auditor remains aware that auditing procedures applied primarily for other purposes may bring to his attention information contrary to that assumption. (Paragraph 3)

The results of some investigations (AICPA, 1981; Mutchler, 1984) suggest that, once there is reason to believe that the opinion may have to be qualified, the auditor assesses the following factors:

- management ability and plans,
- cash-flow potential,
- performance in relation to industry average,
- performance in relation to prior years,
- mitigating factors.

Specific diagnostic questions about these factors and the risk associated with the resulting opinion decision are addressed by the auditor and should be included in the hierarchical branching structure. Examples of questions the auditor might ask about the assessment of cash-flow potential and the risks associated with an incorrect assessment are:

- Has management prepared a cash-flow forecast?
- Is the cash-flow forecast reasonable and verifiable?
- Can bankers verify lines of credit?
- What is the degree of certainty associated with future sources of cash-flow?
- If I make an incorrect assessment, what is the expected value of the loss to the financial statement user, to the company, and/or to the auditing firm?

There are many specific risk assessment areas and related questions included in a hierarchical branching structure used by an auditor for the going-concern decision. For example, SAS 34 directly addresses auditors' decision-making in the presence of going-concern uncertainties. In doing so, it described 'contrary information' that may cast doubt on the ability of an entity to continue in existence, and points out 'mitigating factors' which may discount the significance of any problem. An analysis of each of these dimensions leads to auditing and risk assessments. Section 8.4.3 presents a detailed task analysis of the going-concern auditing decision as specified by SAS 34. Encoding the results of the task analysis yields a first-stage expert system. (This procedure will represent a complete first-stage system only if SAS 34 is a complete description of the decision process that coincides with experts' behavior. However, authoritative pronouncements provide an appropriate basis from which to begin developing the normative decision model.)

8.4.3 The normative decision model

The following analysis assumes that the auditor has cause to suspect that the going-concern opinion may have to be issued. The auditor begins by evaluating contrary information. The decision sequence is presented in Figure 8.3. First, the auditor determines whether the contrary information relates to solvency problems. SAS 34 identifies two classifications: negative trends and other indications. In evaluating negative trends the auditor determines whether there are recurring operating losses, working-capital deficiencies, negative cash-flows from operations, or adverse key financial ratios. Other indications of solvency problems are defaults on loans or similar agreements, arrearages in dividends, denial of usual trade credit from suppliers, noncompliance with statutory capital requirements, and the necessity of seeking new sources or methods of financing.

The auditor must also evaluate information that may raise questions about the continued existence of the entity in the future, indications that future solvency problems may arise. As shown in Figure 8.4, SAS 34

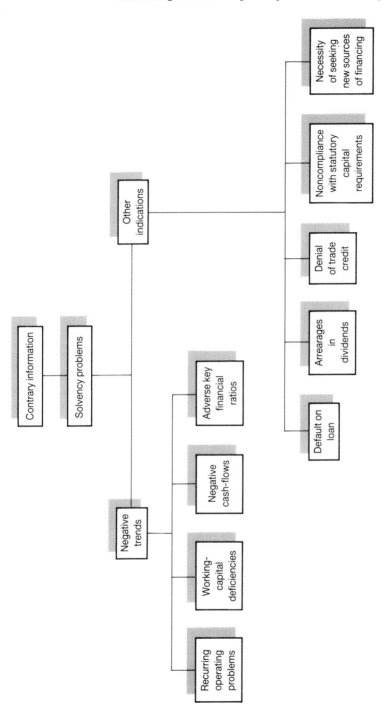

Figure 8.3 Evaluation of contrary information under SAS 34.

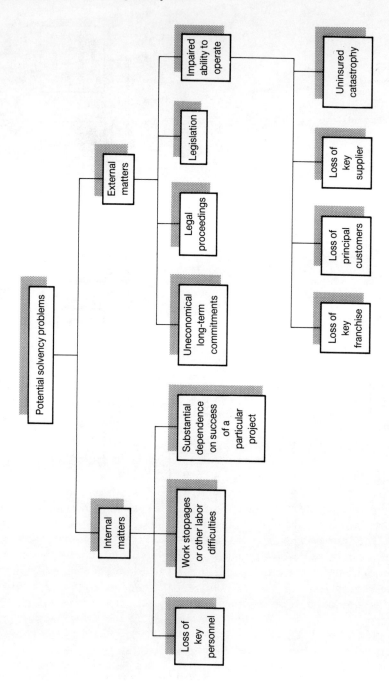

Figure 8.4   Evaluation of solvency problems under SAS 34.

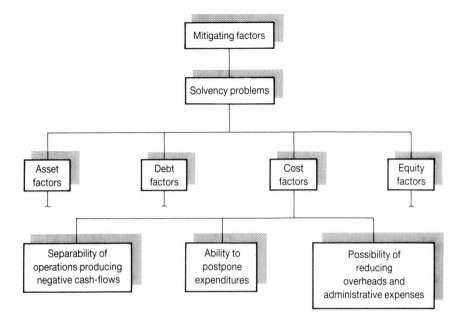

Figure 8.5 Evaluation of mitigating factors under SAS 34.

divides these into internal and external matters, giving specific circumstances to be considered under each.

The auditor is required to evaluate contrary information in the light of any mitigating factors which are present. As shown in Figure 8.5, SAS 34 classifies mitigating factors as relating to either solvency problems or to potential solvency problems.

Each cell in Figures 8.3 to 8.5 represents a decision, or set of decisions, that must be made by an auditor in making the going-concern decision according to whether certain circumstances apply or do not apply. The framework represents the first level of decision-making. The decisions can be represented by a series of 'yes/no/don't know' responses to queries about their existence or attributes that indicate their existence. At the second level of analysis, the potential impact of the identified factor is evaluated. For example, what is the moderating effect of mitigating factors on contrary information? Again the auditor is confronted with a decision or set of decisions that relates to the going-concern opinion, but in this case their relevance depends on the decisions made at the first level. For example, if there are no recurring operating losses, there is no reason to evaluate them in terms of mitigating factors.

For cases where contrary information and mitigating factors exist together, the decision process specified by SAS 34 is a rather complex one whereby each piece of contrary information is examined in the light

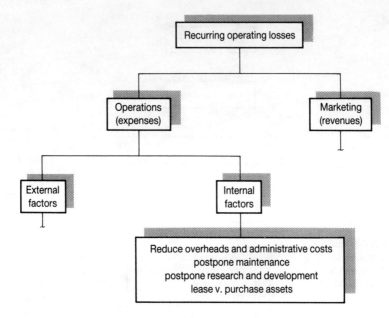

Figure 8.6   The SAS 34 decision process for recurring operating losses.

of the related mitigating factors to evaluate its impact on the financial position of the entity. This decision task is illustrated in Figure 8.6, using recurring operating losses and the related mitigating factors. The auditor must evaluate management's plans for remedying the problem. Possible plans include reducing overhead and administrative costs, postponing maintenance, postponing research and development costs, and leasing assets rather than purchasing them. The auditor must evaluate these plans to see whether they will achieve the desired outcome. This evaluation is in terms of the anticipated impact, the underlying assumptions, the auditor's knowledge of the business and management, and past performance as it relates to the issue under consideration. Each component is analyzed by the auditor, and the separate judgments are then combined to give an evaluation of management's plans for coping with recurring operating losses.

Contrary information can be indicative of underlying economic conditions. These conditions are evaluated in terms of

- rate of deterioration,
- temporality,
- amenability to internal corrective action,
- pervasiveness or segmentality.

If, having considered all relevant factors, the auditor still substantially doubts the entity's ability to continue in existence, the advice offered by SAS 34 can be followed:

> In such a case he should consider the recoverability and classification of recorded asset amounts and the amounts and classification of liabilities in light of that doubt. (Paragraph 11)

The auditor combines all prior judgments with the recoverability assessment in arriving at the final opinion decision.

The preceding discussion outlines the normative decision process described in SAS 34 for making going-concern auditing decisions. The decisions are identified and articulated in such a way as to be encoded into a first-stage expert system which thus enables this model to be tested against the auditor's actual decision processes.

8.4.4 Actual decision behavior

Prior research

Current research suggests that there are discrepancies between the normative decision procedures specified by SAS 34 and the actual decision processes used by auditors. Most of the auditors interviewed by Mutchler (1983) stated that since recoverability was not easy to measure, it was seldom a consideration in their opinion decision. Half the auditors interviewed believed that it was their duty to provide a signal to the user in the form of a qualified opinion when there were doubts about the continued existence of an entity, regardless of the recoverable status of the assets. One of the benefits of constructing a first-stage system is to gain a better understanding of the differences between what the auditor actually does and what the authoritative pronouncements state that the auditor should be doing.

Another issue requiring investigation is the basis upon which to evaluate the going-concern decision. SAS 34 gives the appropriate criteria as the recoverability and amount of assets, and the amounts and classification of liabilities. However, most of the research that has been conducted into the auditor's going-concern opinion has used entity failure as the appropriate criterion. Altman and McGough (1974) and Deakin (1977) compared the auditor's opinion decision with the predictions of a bankruptcy model. In both cases the bankruptcy model was a more accurate predictor of impending failure than was the going-concern opinion. Results obtained by Kida (1983) suggested that the auditor was clearly able to identify a firm having a going-concern problem. Whether or not a going-concern opinion would be issued to the firm was influenced by auditor cost variables such as the fear of possible legal suits by financial statement users, or of losing a client to another auditing firm. Auditor cost variables are not part of the normative (SAS 34) decision process.

The fact that the going-concern opinion decision may be made inconsistently by different auditing firms and/or auditors lends credence to the idea that this is complex domain in which an expert system could provide useful assistance. Furthermore, the construction of such a system would aid in understanding the reasons for inconsistencies and would be a step toward eliminating them.

Expert knowledge representation

The first step in system development is to represent expert behavior within the task environment of interest. Expert decision-makers are identified and their behavior represented in a meaningful way. The two most useful means of doing this are by in-depth interviews and verbal protocol analysis.

In-depth interviews are carried out first to gain insights into the auditor's thought processes. The interview structure is based on the task analysis. As more knowledge is gained, expert decision processes can be articulated more precisely, and more realistic cases can be constructed from the interview results and historical data such as working papers. Verbal protocols can be collected from experts as they make audit opinion decisions. Protocol analysis is explained by Newell and Simon (Newell and Simon, 1972), and its strengths and weaknesses are discussed by Ericsson and Simon (1980); it has been applied in accounting research (Bhaskar and Dillard, 1979; Dillard et al., 1982; Biggs and Mock, 1983; Hansen et al., 1981).

The cases used to collect protocols should be based on real data from firms that have received a going-concern qualification, and firms which appear to be having survival difficulties but which have not received a qualification, as well as firms with no problems. The protocols are collected by having the auditor think aloud during the analysis of a case, and these verbalizations are recorded, transcribed, and parsed. The analysis of these protocols provides the basis for representing and encoding expert behavior. This preliminary model of expert behavior is then compared with the procedures specified in the relevant auditing standards and commercial publications, and with the consultations with experts in the field, to gain insights into how the representation can be improved. The results of these comparisons provide the basis for designing the prototype first-stage system.

There is evidence that the going-concern opinion decision is a group decision (Mutchler, 1984). Once the verbal protocols are collected from individual auditors, they as a group can be asked to evaluate different cases. Such a procedure should provide interesting insights into individual compared with group decision-making processes. Whether the individual or group protocols can be used in the design of the system architecture depends on the actual decision-making procedures followed.

8.4.5 First-stage system

Research in areas related to accounting (Dillard *et al.*, 1983b; Ramakrishna *et al.*, 1983) suggests that the general architecture presented in Figure 8.7 is suitable. The task support system is a network of frames, each representing a decision–action state which is related to making the decision of interest. The guidance system is a network of frames which provide suggestions, rules, and methods for making the decisions required in the task support system; the guidance system would parallel the task support system. The task action system provides a package of support programs for data access, statistical analysis, and so on. The external interface system provides for the automatic production of requisite documentation, audit trails, and so on. The task support structure is the heart of the system. The structure is encoded in an information organization program that represents, organizes, and links the decision frames or episodes: that is, one frame represents each intermediate decision identified during the earlier phase of the study. This frame is linked to all other relevant frames as well as to the required databases and prior decision results. The resulting system provides a detailed description of the expert decision processes.

Software is currently available for constructing such knowledge organization systems. However, these systems provide only the structure, editing, and manipulation facilities. All the task-specific content knowledge must be constructed within the framework. A system within which an accounting-related decision task has been represented is ZOG developed by Robertson *et al.* (1977; 1979). The system has been applied in several different situations (Chandrasekaran *et al.*, 1983b; Fox and Paley, 1980; Mantei and McCracken, 1979; Ramakrishna, 1981). A prototype system for military procurement price analysis is currently being constructed using this system (Dillard *et al.*, 1983b; Ramakrishna *et al.*, 1983).

TASK SUPPORT SYSTEM

(a network of frames each
producing an information
structure)

GUIDANCE SYSTEM

(a network of frames of
suggestions, rules, methods and
further places to look;
highly structured)

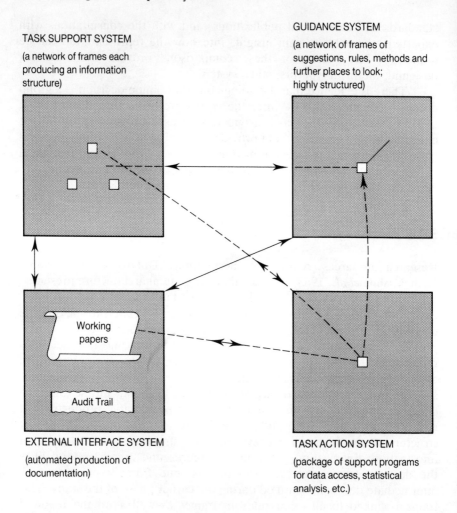

EXTERNAL INTERFACE SYSTEM

(automated production of
documentation)

TASK ACTION SYSTEM

(package of support programs
for data access, statistical
analysis, etc.)

Figure 8.7   Architecture of first-stage system.

8.5 Design criteria

Design criteria are needed for evaluating expert systems. The following
set of criteria, set forth by Bobrow (1975) in his discussion of
representation, are proposed:

- How do objects and relationships in the world correspond to the
  units and relations encoded in the expert system?
- In what ways do the operations in the system correspond to actions
  in the world?
- How can system knowledge be used in mapping the world state?

- How can information be added to the system without further external input?
- How are units linked to provide access to appropriate knowledge?
- How are two structures compared for equality and similarity?
- What knowledge does a system have to have about its own structure and operation?

(Several other sets of criteria have been proposed, by several authors; the reader is referred to Hayes-Roth *et al.* (1983).)

The first three criteria relate to how well the system corresponds to the 'real world,' while the others relate to the system's awareness of itself, and its ability to 'learn.' The first three require expertise in the domain of interest, and the related issues are legitimate auditing research issues; the others require AI expertise. The issues here represent fundamental AI issues that have yet to be resolved. This is not to suggest that auditing research should not address these issues, rather that fundamental theoretical development will also be required. The proposed criteria represent fundamental issues critical to expert systems research for scientific legitimacy as well as long-term real-world applications. It appears, however, that predictive accuracy is the criterion currently being used in auditing research. This leads to the question of what is the objective of the research: is it to explain human behavior or to predict an outcome or result of human behavior? And which of these is appropriate and under what circumstances? (See Waller and Jiambalvo (1984) for an interesting discussion of the related issues.)

From a short run application perspective, predictive accuracy is the appropriate criterion; prediction of bankruptcy is a good example of this, and linear models using a limited number of cues have been shown to be very good predictors of bankruptcy. Two observations can be made from the expert systems perspective. First, there is little about the behavior of the human expert that can be encoded into an expert system for carrying out the bankruptcy prediction task. Secondly, if the task can be carried out by an algorithm then there is no need to build an expert system to do it. In other words, predictive accuracy provides little in the way of guidance for designing expert systems. Prediction is a necessary but not sufficient condition for explaining expert behavior.

There is a need for more basic research into the behavior of expert decision-makers. The central determinant of effective use of knowledge is how it is organized, and issues of representation should come after the organizational structure of knowledge that is needed for problem-solving has been clarified. The methodology presented above provides a means for achieving this objective.

As more auditing expert systems are built, systems developers should become more mindful of system interfacing. The auditing task can be viewed as a series of intermediate decisions which are made by different people. These people could be viewed as specialists in their areas, and consulted in forming the audit opinion just as medical specialists are consulted during the diagnostic evaluation of a patient. Expert systems are being designed to carry out the tasks of these specialists. Thought needs to be given as to how these specialists should interact with one another and how they should interface with the 'opinion' expert.

8.6 Conclusion

The development of expert systems has been described, both in general and specifically as applied to opinion-forming in auditing. Two points need emphasis. The first is the importance of understanding the problem being investigated, and the second is the time required to construct expert systems (Hayes-Roth *et al.*, 1983) – much time is required to understand expert behavior. Three stages in system development have been identified. The result of the first stage is a knowledge-based system which represents a detailed outline of the expert behavior of interest, in this case the auditing opinion decision. The system provides a means of testing the proposed framework in online interactive sessions with human experts. The intelligence in this first-stage system is the decision structure, its sequence hierarchy and component linkages. These provide the basic components for building the more sophisticated knowledge-based expert systems of stages two and three. A methodology for developing an expert system for evaluating whether a firm is a going concern has been presented, along with evaluation criteria and issues which should be addressed when carrying out research on expert systems.

The primary objective of AI research in auditing is to describe expert human behavior by identifying heuristics and knowledge representation. These findings provide the basic foundation of any expert system in this area. One of the major benefits of research on expert systems is that it forces the researcher to examine important task domains in detail. This process not only contributes to the researcher's knowledge base, but can also lead to a self-examination by the auditing firm. This in turn can result in improved decision-making, fewer inconsistencies in the opinion decision between auditors, and ultimately in lower audit risk.

References

Altman, E.I. and McGough, T.P. (1974). 'Evaluation of a company as a going concern', *J. Accountancy*, (Dec.), 50–57
American Institute of CPAs (1981). 'The auditor's considerations when a question

arises about an entity's continued existence' SAS No. 34, AICPA, New York

Bhaskar, R. and Dillard, J.F. (1979). 'Human cognition in accounting: A preliminary analysis' In *Behavioral Experiments in Accounting II* (T.J. Burns; Ed.). Ohio State University

Biggs, S.F. and Mock, T.J. (1983). 'An investigation of auditor decision processes in the evaluation of internal control and audit scope decisions', *J. Accounting Res.*, (Spring), 234–255

Bobrow, D.G. (1975). 'Dimensions in representation' In *Representation and Understanding* (D.G. Bobrow and A. Collins; Eds). New York: Academic Press, 1–33

Braun, H.M. (1983). 'An application of expert systems to study the decision process used by analytical review information for audit decisions', Dissertation Proposal, University of Illinois

Chandrasekaran, B., Dillard, J.F. and Ramakrishna, K. (1983a). 'The design of an expert system for contract price analysis' Technical Reports I and II, Department of Computer and Information Science, Ohio State University

Chandrasekaran, B., Dillard, J.F. and Ramakrishna, K. (1983b). 'The design of an expert system for contract price analysis' Technical Report III, Department of Computer and Information Science, Ohio State University

Deakin, E.B. (1977). 'Business failures predictions: An empirical analysis' In *Financial Crisis: Institutions and Markets in a Fragile Environment* (E.I. Altman and A.W. Sametz; Eds). New York: John Wiley, 72–88

Dillard, J.F., Bhaskar, R. and Stephens, R.G. (1982). 'Using first-order cognitive analysis to understand problem solving behavior: An example from accounting', *Instruct. Sci.*, **11**, 71–92

Dillard, J.F., Mutchler, J.F. and Ramakrishna, K. (1983a). 'Knowledge based expert systems for audit opinion decisions' Report, Ohio State University

Dillard, J.F., Ramakrishna, K. and Chandrasekaran, B. (1983b). 'Expert systems for price analysis: A feasibility study' In Proc. Symp. on 'Federal aquisition research', Williamsburg, VA, US Air Force

Duda, R., Gashing, J. and Hart, P. (1979). 'Model design in the PROSPECTOR consultant system for mineral exploration' In *Expert Systems in the Micro-Electronic Age* (D. Michie; Ed.). Edinburgh: Edinburgh University Press, 153–167

Dungan, C.A. (1983). 'A model of an audit judgment in the form of an expert system', PhD Thesis, Department of Accountancy, University of Illinois

Elliott, R.K. (1984). 'Comment on "Auditing research in accounting doctorial programs" ' In *Doctorial Programs in Accounting* (T.J. Burns; Ed). Ohio State University, 228–236

Ericsson, K.A. and Simon, H.A. (1980). 'Verbal reports as data', *Psychol. Rev.*, 87, (3)

Felix, W.L. and Kinney, W.R. (1982). 'Research in the auditor's opinion formulation process: State of the art', *Accounting Rev.*, (Apr.), 245–271

Fox, M.S. and Palay, A.J. (1980). 'Machine-assisted browsing for the naive user' In *Public Access to Library Automation* (J.L. Divilbiss; Ed.). University of Illinois

Hansen, J.V. and Messier, W.F. (1982). 'Expert systems for decision support in EDP auditing', *Int. J. Computer Inf. Sci.*, 357–379

Hansen, J.V., Messier, W.F. and Biggs, S.F. (1981). 'Software development for implementation of artificial intelligence methods in EDP auditing' Research Proposal, University of Florida

Hayes-Roth, F., Waterman, D.A. and Lenat, D.B. (1983). 'An overview of expert systems' In *Building Expert Systems* (F. Hayes-Roth, D.A. Waterman and D.B. Lenat; Eds). Reading, MA: Addison-Wesley, 3–30

Kida, T. (1983). 'An investigation into auditors' continuity and related qualification judgments', *J. Accounting Res.*, (Autumn), 506–523

Libby, R. (1981). *Accounting and Human Information Processing*. Englewood Cliffs, NJ: Prentice-Hall

Mantei, M. and McCracken, D.L. (1979). 'Issue analysis with ZOG, a highly interactive man–machine interface' In Proc. 1st Int. Symp. on 'Policy analysis and information systems', Durham, NC, June 1979

Mutchler, J.F. (1983). 'A multivariate analysis of the auditor's going-concern opinion decision', PhD Thesis, University of Illinois

Mutchler, J.F. (1984). 'Auditors' perceptions of the going-concern opinion decision', *Auditing: J. Practice Theory*, (Spring), 17–30

Newell, A. and Simon, H.A. (1972). *Human Problem Solving*. Englewood Cliffs, NJ: Prentice-Hall

Ramakrishna, K. (1981). 'Schematization as an aid to organizing ZOG information nets', PhD Thesis, Computer Science Department, Carnegie–Mellon University

Ramakrishna, K., Dillard, J.F., Harrison, T.G. and Chandrasekaran, B. (1983). 'An intelligent manual for price analysis' In Proc. Symp. on 'Federal acquisition research', Williamsburg, VA, US Air Force

Robertson, G., Newell, A. and McCracken, D. (1979). 'The ZOG approach to man–machine communication' Technical Report, Computer Science Department, Carnegie–Mellon University

Robertson, G., Newell, A. and Ramakrishna, K. (1977). 'ZOG: A man–machine communication philosophy' Technical Report, Computer Science Department, Carnegie–Mellon University

Waller, W. and Jiambalvo (1984). 'The use of normative models in human information processing research in accounting', *J. Accounting Literature*, **3**, 201–226

9

EvEnt Assesses Risk Taking

Maia Rozenholc

9.1 Introduction

EvEnt is a business diagnosis expert system developed by EVALOG (France) for the analysis of small to medium-sized companies. One of its obvious applications is to evaluate their suitability to be granted loans. The system has been developed in cooperation with the Banque Hervet in Paris (in particular with their leading expert in credit evaluation), where it is used both to help in making credit decisions and for training non-expert loan officers.

This chapter describes EVALOG's experience in

- identifying the reasons why EvEnt's domain is a good application of expert systems technology,
- determining the choice of the tool used to develop EvEnt,
- structuring and building the knowledge base,
- validating the system.

9.2 Why EvEnt?

9.2.1 Domain justifications

Diagnosis/prescription applications

The domains of diagnosis/prescription and classification are the best known and best understood areas of expert systems application. The task of the knowledge engineer is to simulate an intelligent consultation between an expert and a user, which will help the user either to access knowledge or to deal with a new situation.

There is a whole range of diagnosis/prescription or classification problems. They range from the simplest kind of selection from a few options, like helping identify a plant disease, to more complex professional fields where the expertise is scarce or nonexistent, like predicting currency fluctuations. But whether simple or complex, the problem to be solved always involves finding out why a situation is the way it appears to be, or to what situation certain events will lead.

Business diagnosis

Determining the viability of a business comes down to evaluating its chances of performing well in the future. It appears that those who carry out this task assess past performance by carefully examining balance sheets from the last three years, and then extrapolate into the future, assuming a continuity that is rarely borne out by subsequent events.

Loan risk evaluation in banking

Lending and collecting money are the two main activities of all banks. Let us take the example of bank loans. When deciding whether or not to grant a loan to a client a bank not only has to consider its general risk policy, but also must estimate the customer's ability to repay the loan, capital and interest, in the specified time.

Unfortunately, most client companies' files are too often processed as paperwork and dealt with routinely. Lack of knowledge of a company's real weaknesses or strengths can lead to a wrong evaluation of its position and performance in its market. During a period of economic growth, and with little competition between credit establishments, the consequences of making mistakes are not extremely serious. At worst, such decisions stand a fifty–fifty chance of being correct. However, in today's less forgiving environment, it is extremely important to reduce judgmental errors as much as possible because bank margins have tightened, and banking – like any other profession – faces tough competition, and better relations with clients are necessary.

For a rigorous assessment of a company's capability to survive in a competitive market its balance sheets are not sufficient by themselves as a basis for an opinion. An expert does not rely on routine analysis of the books, but also takes into account

• quality of management,
• business activity: products and markets,
• earnings, financial structure, prospects of the company, and how it compares with the competition,
• production resources and facilities.

To collect reliable information about the client is very time consuming and costly. But then to synthesize correctly this data requires expert know-how. The interpretation that ensues from there, and allows the banker to substantiate his final decision, is the crucial stage of the loan-granting process.

In summary, the reasons that make EvEnt's domain interesting are that

- it is well known,
- almost all of the necessary data is obtainable,
- the assessment must be performed well,
- those dealing with this job on a day-to-day basis do not always possess the required expertise,
- the expertise not only exists, but is also verifiable by comparing the expert's predictions with subsequent events.

The existence and availability of experts in the domain brings us to consider the economic justification of building expert systems in this field.

9.2.2 Economic justification

Experts are too few in number and too expensive to employ for enough of them to be available in each bank. Large French banks, which have a specialized head-office loan department, each employ no more than two dozen business-analysis experts. These professionals each cost over $200 000 a year in direct and indirect salary, expenses, secretarial support, and so on. Each needs some two to three weeks to set down in writing one complete business evaluation. Since there are about 46 to 48 working weeks in the year, it follows that the expert will be able to diagnose about twenty companies per year. This puts the cost of each report at roughly $10 000, and, more important, it limits the number of cases that can be examined by even the largest banks to around 500 per bank per year.

Now, each branch of a bank may hold the accounts of thousands, perhaps tens of thousands, of independent, small to medium-sized companies, whose files should be reexamined every year. It follows that, because of the shortage of experts, this cannot be done properly. Because experts exist and the domain favors the technology, building an efficient and sound expert system would improve the situation. About 80 percent of an expert's knowledge can be embodied in a well-conceived expert system; the remaining 20 percent is concerned with difficult and atypical cases, for which the experts' intervention will always be required.

Let us suppose that the cost of developing a knowledge base containing the expertise of the best expert in the bank is about $200 000. Let us say that a branch has two members of staff dealing on a day-to-day basis with the loan applications. They are in the best position to collect from their clients the data needed for a full justification of any loan decision. Gathering these data can take two to three days. Therefore, they will be able to gather the required information for six clients a week, or roughly three hundred a year. Once the data have been collected, it takes some twenty minutes to load them into the system and for the system to reach a conclusion. If the system is run in only one branch the price of processing a file drops to less than $1000, and to much less if it is used in more branches.

If such a system can make it easier to reach a good decision 80 percent of the time without requiring the intervention of a human expert,

- the expert will then be able to concentrate on interesting, large, or complex cases,
- the more conventional cases will receive more professional attention,
- clerks will begin to adopt a more expert approach, since the expertise will be available to them,
- loan policy will be more consistent, as will the contents and structure of the applications.

There is, then, obvious economic justification for using an expert system to help bankers decide whether to grant a loan to a client. More cases will be properly handled, therefore decreasing the exposure of the bank, at almost no additional cost.

9.3 Choice of the tool

Once the domain of development of an expert system has been pinpointed, it must be decided what kind of tool to use to obtain the best possible formalization of the expert's knowledge. This decision is critical. One can either develop a specific tool, or choose one that is commercially available. The former option seems very attractive, as the tool may be modified and tailored to one's own requirements.

EVALOG's opinion is somewhat different. Software companies spend an enormous amount of effort, time, manpower, and money to develop high-performance tools. Therefore, unless building one's own inference engine leads to some dramatically different and important features, we do not think it good business policy to 'reinvent the wheel'! We do not believe today's knowledge representation mode to be ideal, but in its present state it can solve problems which classical programming techniques cannot.

We considered our needs and searched among existing tools for the one that suited us best. We wanted the tool to

- run on PCs because our clientele is (or will be) equipped with them,
- be easy to connect to existing databases,
- allow portability of the knowledge base to IBM mainframes,
- be user-friendly,
- handle incomplete or inaccurate data, as well as several files at the same time,
- use backward- and forward-chaining inference,
- provide for the use of substitution variables,
- be fast.

At the time we decided to proceed with the EvEnt project, the tool that seemed most appropriate was M1, the shell codeveloped by Teknowledge (Palo Alto, CA) and Framentec (Plessis Robinson, France). M1 was originally written in PROLOG, and has since been rewritten in C.

9.4 EvEnt's knowledge base

After we had circumscribed the domain of application of the expert system, and had decided on M1 for a programming tool, the next step was to define the general architecture of EvEnt's knowledge base, and then to build it.

9.4.1 Defining the general architecture of the knowledge base

Defining the general architecture of an expert system is certainly the most delicate and difficult stage of its development, one that is too often overlooked. To start writing rules without first carefully structuring the knowledge base will lead to the painful task of redesigning the whole system. The completeness and soundness of the knowledge base often depends on how the knowledge has been organized.

We believe that to be able to design a good system, it is necessary to understand fully all aspects of the problem to be solved and the way the system will be used. The general context in which the system will be used, who the users will be, what the idea behind using an expert system is, what the consequences will be on working habits, and so on are all points that should be considered. The whole problem has to be approached globally so that the knowledge base can be modified or augmented without the system having to be too complicated, which would create maintenance difficulties.

There appear to be no books on how to perform the task of the knowledge engineer. Interview techniques and/or psychological approaches are useful, but perhaps not quite enough. How to understand the expert's intellectual process, how his brain works, is taught nowhere – for it is not known. We believe that a general knowledge of the domain is important as it will compensate somewhat for this deficiency.

Very seldom will the expert describe explicitly all the commonsense aspects of his job and his working environment. If he is discussing these with someone who is familiar with the milieu, and with the vocabulary he uses, efficiency will be greatly increased.

To define EvEnt's architecture, and since our knowledge engineer is a banker herself, we took time to study what our chosen expert really did, and why he was recognized by his peers as being the leading expert in his bank. We accompanied him for a few days when he visited clients, and read quite a few reports he had written. It appeared that in his analysis of a business, he went systematically through five stages:

- management,
- business activity,
- earnings,
- financial structure,
- production resources and facilities.

We decided, after consulting our expert extensively, to make sure there were no other very important commonsense stages that he had skipped, that EvEnt should be organized in the same way as he organized his reports.

This organization around five headings seemed very convenient, especially since we planned to couple EvEnt to a classical financial analysis program. The system using the financial analysis results would then correctly interpret the financial ratios, and draw the right conclusions about the numbers.

9.4.2 Building the knowledge base around the five headings

Here we review the content of the knowledge base, with emphasis on the first two headings, for the sake of clarity.

Company and management

The first question EvEnt asks the user is the name of the company that is to be examined. The system then proceeds to collect all necessary information about the company: its legal structure, shareholders, strength and quality of bonds between shareholders and the company, and so on. If it has no access to the client's database, it sets about acquiring the necessary information. This is done in two ways:

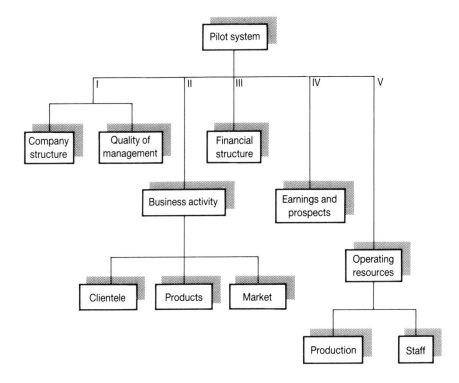

Figure 9.1   Structure of EvEnt's knowledge base.

- By a series of questions, asked by EvEnt, to which the user has to answer by choosing between options proposed by the system. The 'don't know' option, allowed by the inference engine, was forbidden by the expert who insisted on the importance of obtaining a definite answer to all questions.
- By deductions made by EvEnt from what it already knows.

If it does have access to the client's database, EvEnt can obtain any information contained in it. The system will ask about modifications since the last interaction, which may well have taken up to a year before. All relevant modifications will be taken into account by EvEnt. Simultaneously the database, and therefore the client's file, will be updated while running the consultation – this is of course true of any aspect of the company that is subject to change, of any stage of the consultation, and at any level of the process.

Quality of management is considered in EvEnt to be one of the most crucial aspects to look at when examining any company's past, present, and prospects. How many people are actually running the company? What are their ages and qualifications? Are they dynamic, how do they adapt to new and difficult situations? How homogeneous is the team, and is anyone outside the team regarded as indispensable? A company is shaped by its management, whose ability to run it efficiently and in its best interests must be given careful consideration.

The evaluation of the quality of management is mainly subjective. It can hardly be done without meeting those who run the business, and the idea one forms of them affects one's judgment of their ability to perform their job. This is one of the advantages of a system like EvEnt. If the user is the person who deals regularly with the clients, he will probably be in a better position than an expert – who might meet them only once or twice – to formulate a sound opinion. Furthermore, the way in which EvEnt asks questions, together with how it provides explanations that reveal the expert's reasoning behind those questions, can guide the user in how to assess the quality of management.

Business activity

The first thing EvEnt does – and, again, in case it is not connected to a client's database – is obviously to determine the domain of the company's activity. It may pursue several different activities, like for instance fabrication and distribution of products. Each activity should then be considered separately, so that its 'impact' on the company can be isolated. The system then proceeds, for each type of activity, to examine the quality of the clientele, the quality of the product(s), the market, and the sales organization and staff skills.

We consider as an example how the quality of the clientele for one type of product can be examined. The clientele's solvency is the first element the expert looks at. An otherwise successful business can be compromised if clients fail to settle accounts in a reasonable time. If the management is capable and the products are good, such a problem can be overcome by gradually shifting to a better clientele.

The diversification of the clientele is very important. If the company is independent (appart = independent) – which will already be known by the system from its assessment of management – and has only one client (number of clients), are both companies related to one another (link client)? Or, if it has a fair number of clients, what percentage of the turnover is attributable to the principal client (principal_client), and what percentage to 80 percent of the clientele (coverage)? Also of great interest is the average delay elapsed between invoicing and paying (delay_payment).

Some of the rules are as follows:

```
rule-220:   if solvability = no
            then index clientele = 0.

rule-221:   if number of clients = 1
            and (link client = no
```

                    or appart = independent)
              then index clientele = 0.

rule-222:   if number of clients = 1
            and link client = yes
            and delay_payment =< 60
            then index clientele = 100.

rule-223:   if number of clients = 1
            and link client = yes
            and delay_payment > 60
            then index clientele = 50.

rule-224:   if number of clients = N
            and N > 1
            and coverage = Y
            and Y >= 4
            and principal_client = X
            and X =< 50
            and delay_payment = D
            and D < 60
            and link client = yes
            then index clientele = 200.

rule-225:   if number of clients = N
            and N > 1
            and coverage = Y
            and Y >= 4
            and principal_client = X
            and X =< 50
            and delay_payment = D
            and D < 60
            and (link client = no
                    or appart = independent)
            then index clientele = 170.

rule-226:   if number of clients = N
            and N > 1
            and coverage = Y
            and Y >= 4
            and principal_client = X
            and X =< 50
            and delay_payment = D
            and D >= 60
            and link client = yes
            then index clientele = 150.

rule-227:   if number of clients = N
            and N > 1

and coverage = Y
and Y >= 4
and principal_client = X
and X =< 50
and delay_payment = D
and D >= 60
and (link client = no
        or appart = independent)
then index clientele = 120.

rule-228:   if number of clients = N
            and N > 1
            and coverage = Y
            and Y >= 4
            and principal_client = X
            and X > 50
            and delay_payment = D
            and D =< 60
            and link client = yes
            then index clientele = 100.

rule-229:   if number of clients = N
            and N > 1
            and coverage = Y
            and Y >= 4
            and principal_client = X
            and X > 50
            and delay_payment = D
            and D =< 60
            and (link client = no
                    or appart = independent)
            then index clientele = 50.

rule-230:   if number of clients = N
            and N > 1
            and coverage = Y
            and Y >= 4
            and principal_client = X
            and X > 50
            and delay_payment = D
            and D > 60
            and link client = yes
            then index clientele = 50.

rule-231:   if number of clients = N
            and N > 1
            and coverage = Y
            and Y < 4
            and principal_client = X

```
and X =< 30
and delay_payment = D
and D =< 60
and link client = yes
then index clientele = 150.
```

The rules are built here in such a way that the system only allows backward chaining. It needs to know what value to assign to index clientele, and so will therefore try to instantiate all the premises of the first rule concluding at index clientele, either by finding a previous instantiation in the 'cache,' or by asking the user to give one. The rule will succeed if and only if all premises are verified; if not, the next rule concluding at index clientele will be fired.

Financial structure and earnings

The financial structure is taken to consist of cash provided (used) by operations, cash provided by financing activities, cash used by financing activities, fixed assets, and liabilities. Earnings includes not only past operations – costs and expenses, revenue, and income – but also prospects like backlog and forecasts. Moreover, it reduces the figures to account for inflation, and compares the performance of the company with its competitors'.

Production resources and facilities

EvEnt seeks to determine whether the facilities are, among other things, adequately sited and in good condition, and whether improvements are needed or specific investments are planned. Are the facilities owned or rented, and under what terms? In examining production resources, the system deals with production equipment (factories, shops, and offices) and possible improvements or additional investments (compulsory or discretionary). EvEnt also takes into account the qualifications of the staff and whether it meets the company's needs, the working conditions and social atmosphere, and the quality of reporting.

The knowledge base consists of 450 rules and 5 meta-rules. It would have taken many more rules – probably over 1500 – had we used a knowledge engineering tool that did not admit variables in rules. For example:

```
rule-450:  if conclusion_management is M
           and conclusion_activity is A
           and conclusion_results is R
           and conclusion_financial_structure is F
           and conclusion_operating_resources is O
           then general_conclusion is G.
```

where each of the variables can take at least five different values. Rule-450 shows that each of the five headings gives rise to an intermediate conclusion. Following the expert's reasoning, the five intermediate conclusions are combined to give a final opinion on the strength of the company.

Six months were required to develop the knowledge base. We proceeded step by step, building one stage after another. In the first stage concepts were assessed on the basis of the expert's know-how and based upon a concrete example, a small pharmaceutical company. This allowed us to select the concepts to be formalized. Next, and with the expert's continuous involvement, we formalized these concepts and checked how the expert drew his conclusions from the values, given those concepts or parameters. At this point we began writing the rules modeling part of the expert's knowledge. This was difficult because we had to make sure that the inference process corresponded to the expert's way of reasoning.

Once the first intermediate conclusion corresponded to the expert's (as in his written report), we went on to the next heading. When we were finished we combined the five intermediate conclusions to come to the final conclusion.

Although skeptical at the beginning, our expert became more and more interested as our work progressed because, he said, he gained insight into his own reasoning process. What he regarded as 'flair' turned out to be heuristic rules derived from past experience and savoir faire. The rules of the domain he consciously used are mainly those he learned at school or from colleagues (the knowledge base contains both sets of rules).

9.5 Validating the knowledge base

We ran the system for more than 200 real cases, each time verifying that it came to the same conclusion as the expert. When it did not, we fine-tuned EvEnt so that it arrived at the correct appreciation of the file.

We then decided to cross-check the expert's decisions on files two to three years old, for which time had told whether the expert had been right or wrong. We concentrated on those cases where he had been proved wrong, and tried to establish, with him, why this was so. After reviewing a number of reports it became apparent that there was some consistency in the expert's misjudgments. We modified the knowledge base accordingly, incorporating a few additional rules the expert had consistently neglected, and reran those cases on the expert system.

When the system was able to reach a decision corresponding to what had actually happened with old cases, and to the expert's advice for current cases, the validation period was deemed to be over and the system ready for use.

9.6 Conclusion

In conclusion, we would like to emphasize that the successful development and application of an expert system in the management area requires

- the availability of the best expert in the domain, as recognized by his peers inside the establishment that will be using the system,
- the acceptance of the system by potential users,
- the very careful determination of the system's domain,
- the integration of the system into the general working environment organization.

In addition, it must lead to an improvement in the productivity and efficiency of intellectual tasks and, last but not least, it must yield an appreciable return on investment.

10

A Financial Management Assistant System

Véronique El Mernissi

10.1 Introduction

In this chapter we describe an expert system for financial management which allows small bank branches (with no expert financial consultant on their staff) to provide their clients with investment advice. The various stages in the construction of the system are described, beginning with the analysis of needs which permits us to choose an expert system generator. The generator itself is discussed, after which the characteristics of the model are examined. A short example of the syntax of the selected generator is given, together with a case study making use of this expertise. Lastly the transition from model to product is dealt with.

10.2 Analysis of needs

The first task is to set up two- to three-day meetings with the relevant experts to establish a precise definition of what their needs are. Since the system will be placed in branches, bank managers will want the system to operate on microcomputers, if possible IBM PCs or compatibles. This will be taken into account in the choice of generator. During the preliminary meetings, the various factors that will need to be taken into account are determined:

- the client's family, professional, and financial status,
- savings plans already held by the client,
- the client's objectives and plans,
- the bank's commercial policy.

Information on the client must be gathered and studied carefully before attempting any research into schemes and services that could be offered. This study should be supplemented by information contained in the bank's client database. The branch employee who uses the system will want to trigger simulations of the effects of seleted services and products for the benefit of the client. Both will need the system to be user-friendly.

Information handled by experts is usually one of three types:

- Boolean facts (e.g. 'the client is interested in financial markets' can be true or false),
- real fixed values (e.g. investment amount in $ = 10 000),
- symbolic facts (e.g. desired return = 'increase').

The use of variables is justified only for those simulations for which the client wishes to examine several scenarios. Some simulations already exist and are written in classical languages. Anyway, it is possible to get round the absence of variables by using external procedures.

The branch employee will also want to be able to answer the questions asked by a client interested in a bank savings scheme and who wants to know if it will be suitable for him. If it is not suitable the system may use information that is already available and propose another solution.

Starting with the requirements previously defined, we can choose the expert system generator. The requirements may be summarized as follows: the system must

- operate on IBM PCs and compatibles,
- be user-friendly,
- allow the use of external procedures (for the use of the bank database and simulation),
- accept both real and symbolic facts,
- use facts to reach a conclusion or verify a goal (to answer a client's question as to whether or not a product meets his needs),
- require no variables.

Our choice will therefore be a tool that

- has a 0+ degree inference engine (based on propositional logic),
- has interfaces designed so as to make the system user-friendly,
- grants requests for external procedures,
- allows forward and backward chaining (to allow the selection of products suitable for the client or to check whether a chosen product is suitable),
- has a specific built-in action which allows switching from forward to backward chaining if certain hypotheses prove correct.

We chose the Intelligence Service System, which meets all these requirements and is described below.

10.3 The Intelligence Service generator

Intelligence Service is an expert system generator which runs under MS-DOS on IBM PCs and compatibles with a minimum configuration of 512K and a hard disk drive. It is designed with an 0+ degree inference engine which also allows the use of counters (the modification of a fact value is allowed under certain conditions) and has at its disposal an assembly of expert and user interfaces which make the system user-friendly for those not used to operating computers. The experts use natural language for updating the rule base, and the user is guided in his research.

Intelligence Service provides two modes: the user mode and the expert mode. Thus it is available in two forms:

- the expert version is complete and allows the rule base to be modified, and the existing base to be consulted. Two modes are available, expert and consultant.
- the consultant version allows the bases to be used, but prohibits unauthorized users from modifying the base and restricts access to information considered confidential by the expert. The consultant mode is thus the only mode available.

The separation of the modes guarantees that the rule base cannot be modified or viewed by unauthorized persons.

10.3.1 Interfaces

The interfaces provide a multiwindow system with integrated menus. A special help system, displayed on-screen, is included with each window. Thus both experts and users will find the system user-friendly.

10.3.2 Rules and facts

The rules are in natural language and have the form if ‹condition› then ‹action›. Conditions are linked by the logical connectors AND and OR, and actions by the connector AND. They are identified by a header which allows them to be categorized.

The facts that make up these rules may be Boolean (true or false), real, or symbolic (belonging to a field). These facts may or may not be displayed, as the expert chooses.

Thus, in Backus–Naur form,

```
RULE:: =
‹heading› IF ‹condition›
      then ‹action›
‹CONDITION›:: =
(‹premise group 1›) or ... or‹premise group 1N›)
CONDITION
‹premise group 1› :: = ‹Premise 1› and ... and‹Premise 1N›
premise:: =‹symbolic fact› = "Symbol"
            3 ‹real fact› = value
            3 ‹Boolean fact›
            3 non ‹Boolean fact›
            3 ‹real fact› = known 3 unknown 3 undetermined
            3 ‹symbolic fact› = known 3 unknown 3 undetermined
‹ACTION›:: = ‹conclusion 1›
            and ... and ‹conclusion›

ACTION
conclusion:: = ‹symbolic fact› = "Symbol"
            3 ‹real fact› = value
            3 ‹Boolean fact›
            3 non ‹Boolean fact›
            3 ‹real fact› = ‹real operations›
            3 ‹built-in›
            3 ‹counters› = value
```

10.3.3 Built-ins

Built-ins allow specific actions to be taken which cannot be obtained by simple assignments, for example:

- proving goals,
- reinitializing the fact base,
- calling sub-expertise,
- calling external procedures.

The built-in 'goal proving' allows the inference engine to be switched to backward chaining during the execution of the action part of a rule. For example, suppose that a client would like to invest in a particular product, MidLongSavings. Before making the investment, we must make sure that the client has the right profile for MidLongSavings. This gives us the following rule:

MidLongSavings Profile   If the client wants SICAV MidLongSavings
                then   PROVE (the client has a MidLongSavings profile)

10.3.4 Calling in external procedures

Calls for external procedures are made on rule conclusions. For example, if one wishes to begin calculating the taxes paid by the client, then once the annual income is known we can write the following rule:

Taxation   If annual income = known
           and number of allotments = known
           then call "taxes" (‹annual income›,
           ‹number of shares›, ›taxes paid‹, ›tax bracket‹)

The information ‹facts› will be passed onto the 'tax' procedure by means of a text file, and the information ›facts‹ will be recovered in a text file by Intelligence Service. Information transfer is very rapid (about one-third of a second), and the procedures can be written in any programming language. It is thus possible to recover existing procedures used by experts at the calculation level, averaging modifications for data acquisition and recovery.

10.4 Model realization

10.4.1 Model goals

The model is not only a means of testing the feasibility of the system, but also a way of giving the experts confidence in artificial intelligence techniques and of validating the type of system one wishes to use. If a precise specification could not be drawn up by the experts this stage allows us to evaluate the following stage, and to define the windows to be used as well as the calls for procedures the experts wish to have.

It is often model evolution which allows experts to determine the characteristics, architecture, and completed specifications of a product. The model should contain a small but sufficiently representative sample of products for experts and users in order to validate system approach and utility. (In any case, it is no use including in the model a large number of products if some of them have similar characteristics.) Model realization may lead to questions about system choice in the function of the needs that will have appeared. The model also allows us to establish a more precise specifications sheet for product elaboration. It is only at this point that the duration required for product realization as well as external procedures can be specified. At model level we can rely on existing simulation software and on those where sources are available, or provide for the realization of a financial simulation.

10.4.2 The products considered in the model

For the model, the experts selected products from the real estate and financial markets that could satisfy short-, medium- and long-term objectives. These products may be differentiated in several ways:

- the market: real estate or financial,
- the proportion of shares or bonds they contain,
- the financial risk of the portfolio,
- the type of yield they provide (accumulation or income),
- the tax advantages linked to their specific nature (e.g., duration, geographical sector, type of yield),
- the geographical sector of the products making up the portfolio (e.g., France, overseas),
- the duration of capital immobilization,
- amount of subscription and shares.

We can thus classify the products in the following manner.

Short-term financial markets

SICAV ShortSavings: characterized by high risk over three or six months, or longer; made up of French bonds; they offer an accumulation-type yield.
SICAV MidLongSavings: characterized by high risk over 18 months to two years; made up of French stocks and bonds; they offer an accumulation-type yield.

Medium-term financial markets

SICAV MidLongSavings: characterized by average risk over the long term; made up of French stocks and bonds; they offer an accumulation-type yield.
SICAV Epargne Revenus: characterized by average risk; made up of French bonds; they offer an income-type yield.
SICAV LBI and CEA: characterized by high risk; mostly made up of French stocks; they offer a low-return accumulation-type yield. They provide a 25% tax allowance on the sums invested, up to a certain limit.

Fonds Communs de Placements (FCP): characterized by high risk; made up of foreign stocks and bonds; they offer an accumulation-type yield.

Long-term financial markets

SICAV MidLongSavings: characterized by average risk.
SICAV Epargne Revenus: characterized by low risk.
SICAV LBI and CEA: characterized by relatively high risk.

Long-term real estate markets

RealEstate real estate funds offer an average risk over the long term and are subject to real estate taxation. The investor needs to be in a position to retain his investment for a minimum of five years. Furthermore, capital gains made by investing in French real estate are tax-free up to a certain threshold, and the legal tender withdrawal allows the limitation of appreciation taxation to 25% (this should interest people who are already taxed over 25%). In contrast, income from such investments is taxed at the same rate as other income. This explains why in the following we will sometimes recommend capitalization products to people who are interested in income.

10.4.3 The rules of the model

The comments and explanations provided by experts at the initial meetings were formalized so as to represent both the linking of their different consulting phases and the rules they used.

   When the consultant version is used, certain information must first be taken into account to allow the consultation to begin. We start with a fact that we call the 'beginning of a session.' To begin the session we need information from the bank's client files on the family, tax, and matrimonial situation of the client. They are recovered by means of an external procedure (utilization of Call) in a temporary file, then the information obtained is added to the fact base (utilization of RedirectOn). Furthermore, the experts wish to have the exclusive right to modify share values and subscriptions for the different products, and to have an easy way of doing it. This is done by means of rules.

   We obtain the following initialization rules:

```
initInvestment IF begin the session
    THEN one share ShortSavings = 10000.00
        AND one share LBI_CEA = 500.00
        AND one share MidLongSavings = 1200.00
        AND one share Revenus = 6000.00
        AND one share FCP = 2500.00
```

```
initClientFile.1 IF begin the session
              AND name of the client file = KNOWN
         THEN Call "PRecov" ( ‹name of the client file› )
              AND file ready

initClientFile.2 IF begin the session
              AND file ready
         THEN RedirectedOn"DOSSIER.DAT"
```

After the initialization phase, the experts were interested firstly in the client's goals (tax objectives, interest for financial markets, the real estate market, sums invested over short, medium, and long term). This is expressed by the following rules:

```
tax.1 IF amount of taxes paid > 0.00
      OR
        tax bracket > 0.00
      THEN the client is taxed

tax.2 IF amount of taxes paid = 0.00
      OR
        tax bracket = 0.00
      THEN the client is not taxed

tax.3 IF the client has no portfolio
      AND the client is taxed
      THEN the client does not have all tax advantages

tax.4 IF the client is not taxed
      THEN the client has all tax advantages

obj.1 IF the client does not have all tax advantages
      THEN display tax advantages

obj.2 IF the client has all tax advantages = UNDETERMINED
      THEN display tax advantages

obj.4 IF tax advantages displayed
      AND the client does not have all these tax advantages
      THEN the client does not have all tax advantages

obj.5 IF tax advantages displayed
      AND the client does not have all tax advantages
      AND the client would like to benefit from tax advantages
      OR
        the client has all tax advantages
      THEN the tax advantages are known
```

obj.6 IF the tax advantages are known
    AND the client has a sufficient foundation = KNOWN
    AND the client has a comfortable foundation = KNOWN
    AND the client is interested in the real estate market = KNOWN
    AND the client is interested in financial markets = KNOWN
  THEN objectives checked

Investment Duration.1 IF amount remaining to be invested = 0.00
    AND amount of short-term investment = UNKNOWN
  THEN amount of short-term investment = 0.00

Investment Duration.2 IF amount remaining to be invested = 0.00
    AND amount of medium-term investment = UNKNOWN
  THEN amount of medium-term investment = 0.00

Investment Duration.3 IF amount remaining to be invested = 0.00
    AND amount of long-term investment = UNKNOWN
  THEN amount of long-term investment = 0.00

Investment Duration 4. IF amount remaining to be invested > 0.00
    AND amount of long-term investment = KNOWN
    AND amount of medium-term investment = KNOWN
    AND the client would like to make a long-term investment = KNOWN
    AND the client would like to make a medium-term investment = KNOWN
  THEN amount remaining to be invested = 0.00
    AND amount of short-term investment =
      ((amount remaining to be invested − amount of long-term investment)
      − amount of medium-term investment)

Investment Duration.5 IF amount remaining to be invested > 0.00
    AND the client would like to make a medium-term investment
    AND amount of medium-term investment = KNOWN
  THEN amount remaining to be invested = (amount remaining to be invested
    − amount of medium-term investment)

Investment Duration.6 IF amount remaining to be invested > 0.00
    AND the client would like to make a long-term investment
    AND amount of long-term investment = KNOWN
  THEN amount remaining to be invested = (amount remaining to be invested
    − amount of long-term investment)

Investment Duration.7 IF amount remaining to be invested > 0.00
    AND amount of short-term investment = KNOWN
    AND amount of medium-term investment = KNOWN
    AND the client would like to make a short-term investment = KNOWN
    AND the client would like to make a medium-term investment = KNOWN
  THEN amount remaining to be invested = 0.00
    AND amount of long-term investment = ((amount remaining to be invested

                    − amount of short-term investment) − amount of medium-term
                    investment)

Investment Duration.9 IF amount remaining to be invested = 0.00
           AND desired short-term characteristics checked
           AND desired long-term characteristics checked
           AND desired medium-term characteristics checked
        THEN investment breakdown taken into account

There are now different procedures, depending on whether the client desires consultation on a given product (he has heard about a product and wants to know if it will be suitable for him) or a more generalized consultation on the best possible investment. In the first procedure the system checks to see whether the product chosen by the client can satisfy his needs. If not, products that will satisfy his needs are proposed. In the second procedure the system determines all of the products that could be proposed to the client, and selects from them the most interesting. The following rules are used:

Profile.1 IF the client has a RealEstate profile = KNOWN
       AND the client has a medium-term FCP profile = KNOWN
       AND the client has a long-term FCP profile = KNOWN
       AND the client has a short-term MidLongSavings profile = KNOWN
       AND the client has a medium-term MidLongSavings profile = KNOWN
       AND the client has a long-term MidLongSavings profile = KNOWN
       AND the client has a ShortSavings profile = KNOWN
       AND the client has a medium-term Epargne Revenus profile = KNOWN
       AND the client has a long-term Epargne Revenus profile = KNOWN
       AND the client has a medium-term LBL_CEA profile = KNOWN
       AND the client has a long-term LBL_CEA profile = KNOWN
     THEN the client profile is determined

Profile.2 IF the client does not have a sufficient foundation
     THEN the client does not have an Epargne Revenus profile
       AND the client does not have FCP profile
       AND the client does not have a MidLongSavings profile
       AND the client does not have a ShortSavings profile

Profile.3 IF the client has RealEstate with us
       AND type of long-term yield<>"plus value"
       AND amount of long-term investment >= one share RealEstate
       AND the client will accept an average risk over long term
       AND the client is interested in the real estate market
       AND the client has a comfortable foundation
     THEN check RealEstate profile

Profile.4 IF the client has no RealEstate with us
       AND type of long-term yield<>"plus value"

AND amount of long-term investment >= RealEstate subscription
AND the client is interested in the real estate market
AND the client will accept an average risk over long term
AND the client has a comfortable foundation
THEN check RealEstate profile

Profile.5 IF the client has no RealEstate with us
AND amount of long-term investment < RealEstate subscription
OR
amount of long-term investment < one share RealEstate
OR
the client does not have a comfortable foundation
OR
the client will not accept an average risk over long term
OR
type of long-term yield = "plus value"
OR
the client is not interested in real estate market
THEN the client does not have a RealEstate profile

Profile.6 IF the client is not interested in financial markets
THEN the client does not have FCP profile
AND the client does not have a MidLongSavings profile
AND the client does not have a ShortSavings profile
AND the client does not have an LBL_CEA profile
AND the client does not have an Epargne Revenus profile

Profile.7 IF the client is interested in financial markets
AND the client has a sufficient foundation
THEN check MidLongSavings profile
AND check FCP profile
AND check Epargne Revenus profile

Profile.8 IF the client is interested in financial markets
AND the client would like to benefit from tax advantages
THEN check LBL_CEA profile

Profile ShortSavings.1 IF amount of short-term investment < one share
ShortSavings
OR
the duration of short-term investment · in months §< 3.00
OR
type of short term yield = "revenus"
AND age >= 45.00
OR
the client will not accept an average risk over short term
OR
the client will not accept a high risk over short term

AND the duration of short-term investment · in months §< 6.00
THEN the client does not have a ShortSavings profile

Profile ShortSavings.2 IF check ShortSavings profile
    AND type of short term yield <> "revenus"
    AND the client will accept an average risk over short term
    AND the duration of short-term investment · in months §>= 6.00
  OR
    check ShortSavings profile
    AND type of short term yield <> "revenus"
    AND the client will accept a high risk over short term
  THEN the client has a ShortSavings profile

Profile ShortSavings.3 IF check ShortSavings profile
    AND type of short term yield = "revenus"
    AND the client will accept a high risk over short term
    AND age < 45.00
  OR
    check ShortSavings profile
    AND type of short-term yield = "revenus"
    AND age < 45.00
    AND the client will accept an average risk over short term
    AND the duration of short-term investment · in months §>= 6.00
  THEN the client has a ShortSavings profile

Profile RealEstate.1 IF check RealEstate profile
    AND amount of long-term investment >= RealEstate subscription
  OR
    check RealEstate profile
    AND amount of long-term investment >= one share RealEstate
    AND the client has RealEstate with us
  THEN the client has a RealEstate profile

Profile RealEstate.2 IF check RealEstate profile
    AND amount of long-term investment < RealEstate subscription
    AND the client has no RealEstate with us
  OR
    check RealEstate profile
    AND amount of long-term investment < one share RealEstate
  THEN the client does not have a RealEstate profile

We have shown how each step of the consultation is carried out, but we have yet to show how the different steps are linked. The different research phases are triggered according to the order defined by the experts by means of the following rules:

phase.1 IF amount remaining to be invested = KNOWN
  THEN PROVE(objectives checked)

phase.2 IF objectives checked
    THEN PROVE(investment breakdown taken into account)

phase.3 IF investment breakdown taken into account
      AND establish client profile
    THEN PROVE(the client profile is determined)

Neither have we shown how the type of research was chosen; this is done using the following rules:

Type Research.1 IF the client is interested in a determined product
      AND the product which interests the client = KNOWN
    THEN do not establish client profile

Type Research.2 IF the client is not interested in a determined product
    THEN establish client profile

Type Research.3 IF the product which interests the client = "ShortSavings"
      AND investment breakdown taken into account
      AND do not establish client profile
    THEN PROVE(the client has a ShortSavings profile)

Type Research.4 IF the product which interests the client = "MidLongSavings"
      AND investment breakdown taken into account
      AND do not establish client profile
    THEN PROVE(the client has a MidLongSavings profile)

Type Research.5 IF the product which interests the client = "LBI"
      AND investment breakdown taken into account
      AND do not establish client profile
    OR
      the product which interests the client = "CEA"
      AND investment breakdown taken into account
      AND do not establish client profile
    THEN PROVE(the client has an LBI_CEA profile)

Note the frequent utilization of the word 'prove' (one speaks of a 'Built-in Prove'); this allows us to check whether a fact is true or false. Other rules allow us to obtain elementary information. They often use the data from the client's file, and essentially correspond to common sequences rules (e.g., if the client accepts an average risk, he will accept *a fortiori* a small risk, but not a high risk). These are rules which seem obvious, but an expert system cannot use them until they have been stated. To illustrate this, here is one of the rules:

foundation.1 IF the client has no SICAV
      AND amount of savings < 70000.00
    THEN the client does not have a comfortable foundation

foundation.2 IF the client has SICAV
    AND amount of savings >= 30000.00
  OR
    amount of savings >= 70000.00
  THEN the client has a comfortable foundation

foundation.3 IF the client has no portfolio
    AND amount remaining to be invested < 30000.00
  THEN the client does not have a sufficient foundation

Risk.1 IF the client profile is determined = UNKNOWN
    AND accepted risk over short term = "relatively high"
  THEN the client will accept a relatively high risk over the short term
    AND the client will not accept a high risk over the short term
    AND the client will accept a low risk over the short term
    AND the client will accept an average risk over the short term

10.5 From model to product

The model allows us to check the feasibility of an expert system for financial investments using the Intelligence Service software generator. It also allows us to compare an expert's reasoning before model realization (which may appear in the specification) with what was expressed during model realization. From this, the specification will be reviewed and the difference between the model and the product defined. The time necessary for product realization is then determined.

For a system of this type, the essential difference between the model and the product is in the number of financial products taken into account, with perhaps the addition of one or two others. The presentation of product rules is thus useless, since they are similar.

11

An Integrated Consulting System for Competitive Analysis and Planning Control[†]

Jaffer R. Syed and Edison Tse

11.1 Introduction

This chapter describes an integrated consulting system (ICS) for competitor analysis and strategy support to help business planners in industries characterized by a high degree of product differentiation and multiproduct production facilities. ICS is a computer-based business analysis tool developed by SRI International. Its primary aim is to analyze and predict competition in the industries by integrating the relevant business, marketing, technological, and cost factors.

The factor that distinguishes ICS from other methodologies is its ability to integrate detailed quantitative and qualitative knowledge of technology, producers' skill base, and the differentiated markets to arrive at results which closely reflect the 'real-world' behavior of the industry. By doing so, it overcomes the inherent weaknesses of highly mathematical models (removed from reality) at one extreme and of mostly qualitative institutional analyses (lacking in rigor) at the other. ICS can assess and incorporate the competitive reactions of all other producers to any change in the supply-and-demand patterns.

11.2 Background

A high degree of product differentiation and the use of flexible multiproduct production facilities have become the norm in many high-technology industries. This has greatly complicated the understanding of competition and the search for strategies. Companies are increasing their

[†] This chapter is published with special permission of Jean-Claude Rault, Chairman of the Annual International Conference on Expert Systems and their Applications, Avignon.

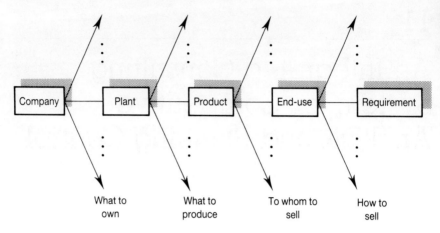

Figure 11.1   The decisions to be made by a firm in a competitive environment.

efforts to identify market segments and to match their products and services to the requirements of particular end-users. Efficient allocation of resources requires a company to have the production capacity, technology, and skills needed to produce the correct combination of products and services. This underscores the desirability of managing and processing information on technology, markets, and the nature of competition in these markets.

Planning is one of the most difficult and complex tasks facing management in today's high-technology industries. Problems requiring decisions by planners are depicted in Figure 11.1. Each box represents decision variables which span a set of possible options the firm needs to consider. The choices at each decision node are numerous, a useful decision support tool must reduce the number of options to a manageable size without discarding *a priori* any of the relevant options, and rank these options according to how well they meet the firm's goals. Typical decisions at each node include:

- *What to own.* These decisions relate to plant size, number of production lines, production technology, and location. For existing facilities a firm may need to decide on technology modification, capacity expansion, or plant shut-down.

- *What to produce.* For a given capacity and production technology a firm must match its product range with a desired combination of profits, market share, and related strategic goals.

- *To whom to sell.* Each product grade can be used for a number of end-uses which differ not only in their application characteristics but also in the characteristics of the consumers, such as size, institutional relationships, and level of sophistication. The firm needs to decide which consumer group it should target.

- *How to sell.* Each end-use has a set of demand requirements. Some end-uses are more sensitive to pricing than others. There are similar requirements for technical services, marketing, product quality, and product performance. The firm needs to select a combination of skills which will provide the market power to realize the desired sales.

These decisions must be made not in isolation, but within an integrated framework. In high-technology industries continual changes in the market environment are brought about by technology changes, product substitutions, and new uses. In this environment the assumptions which are made to simplify the planning process also change, and the essence of good planning is to recognize – and discard – those assumptions which no longer hold. Similarly, the discrimination which is necessary to make decisions in the face of an enormous amount of information becomes a handicap. In these situations a tool which uses all of the relevant knowledge in its rich detail, yet allows the planner to focus on the important pieces of information, can significantly improve the quality of decisions.

11.3 Approach

Optimization as behavioral rationality of economic agents plays a central role in conventional economic theorizing. In this theory, the firm is assumed to maximize its profits. In static models these profits are for the single period, and in multiperiod models the profits are treated as the expected value of the discounted profit stream for the planning horizon. The only decision variable the firms have is the level of production in each of the future periods. When we account for market imperfections such as friction in market adjustment processes, incomplete knowledge on the part of the decision-makers in the firms and the consumers, and a host of other institutional factors and product attributes which lead a consumer to view seemingly identical products differently, the optimizing behavior becomes quite untenable.

The institutional economists (Cyert and March, 1963; Kornai, 1971; Simon, 1976; 1978a,b) contend that firms use simple decision processes which focus on attaining some well-defined goals called aspiration levels. Depending on the outcome of a chosen decision, the firms adjust their aspiration levels upwards, engage in more complex decision processes, or adjust their aspirations levels downwards.

Thus, both individuals and organizations experience competition as a dynamic process, not a structural state. This process is punctuated by a series of events which are often caused by the competitors themselves in their efforts to improve their skill and competence or to gain an advantage over other competitors. Our model represents firms and consumers as purposeful objects exercising choice in their functional environment. The consumers are actually replaced by specifying a preference structure of their demand. The purposeful state of the firms is represented by three sets of variables:

- the aspiration levels,
- the means to achieve aspiration levels,
- strategies or actions to modify means and aspiration levels.

The purposeful object is represented as a process which exercises choice consistent with its purposeful state and its functional environment. It moves from one purposeful state to another in reaction to events occurring within or outside its functional environment. The functional environments are represented as data structures describing constraints as facts, rules, and procedures.

The purposeful state of the consumers is represented as a set of end-uses which are specified in terms of

- the requirements and their associated levels stated as qualitative values which the product must satisfy,
- the level of tolerance for each requirement stated as a qualitative value,
- the quantity demanded for the end-use.

The model simulates the decision processes of the firms and consumers, and the market adjustment processes. The decision processes of the consumers are subsumed in their preference structure.

One of the consequences of the bounded rationality of the firms is that their decision processes are sequential (Simon, 1978b). Another consequence is that the firms, faced with a problem, engage in progressively complex search processes for the solution. The structure of the model allows these processes to be simulated, and the user can interact with, control, or modify the simulation by specifying when these search processes are undertaken and what strategies a firm will choose.

11.4 Knowledge base of ICS

The global database is a company/technology/market database. It contains the available domain knowledge and a blackboard which is used to store intermediate knowledge generated by various procedural components of the system; it consists of six types of symbolic frame.

We have used ICS to model the polyolefins industry. Polyolefins are plastics derived from natural hydrocarbons. The competition in this industry arises primarily from product differentiation and other non-price factors. A typical polyolefins plant has the flexibility to produce several product grades by varying its operating conditions. Here we describe the frames suitable for process-related industries such as chemicals, paper, and steel.

11.4.1 Market frame

A market frame represents the information about various end-uses of the products of the industry. For each end-use a frame is specified as follows (the variables which are to be instantiated are enclosed in angle brackets):

```
market-frame(
    year(‹Year›),
    region(‹Region›),
    end-use(description (‹End-use-Description›),
    requirement(description (‹Requirement-Description›),
        value(‹Requirement-Value›),
        tolerance(‹Tolerance-for-Requirement›)),
    requirement (...
          .
          .
          .
    demand(total(‹Total-Demand›),
        product(description (‹Product-Description),
            demand(‹Product-Demand›)),
        product(...
          .
          .
          .
                )).
```

11.4.2 Market/technology frame

This frame represents the linkage between the products and the technology. A particular technology can be used to manufacture a number of product grades which can be sold in different markets. (Note that a market is defined by a product and a region.) Depending on the requirements of a particular market, more than one product grade can be sold in it. Similarly, but not very often, a particular technology may be able to produce a product grade which can be sold in more than one market; the firm will disguise the fact by packaging or other means. For each market a frame is specified as follows:

```
market/technology-frame(
    year(‹Year›),
    region(‹Region›),
    product(description (‹Product-Description›).
    technology(description (‹Technology-Description›),
        product-grade (description(‹Product-Grade-Description›),
            .
            .
            .
    technology (...
            .
            .
            .

                    )).
```

11.4.3 Technology frame

This frame contains the knowledge about technology in a generic sense –
information that relates to a typical implementation of the technology.
Information is specified for investment, plant operation, and recipes for
and characteristics of different product grades:

```
technology-frame(
    technology(description (‹Technology-Description›).
    basis(monetary-unit(‹Monetary-Unit›),
        capacity-unit(‹Production-Volume/Period›),
        year(‹Year›),
        location(‹Region›),
        nominal-capacity(total(‹Total-Capacity›),
            production-lines(‹Capacities-of-lines›)),
        product-grade(description (‹Base-Grade-Description›)),
        investment(total (‹Total-Investment›),
            exponent-up(‹Exponent-for-Larger-Plant›),
            exponent-down(‹Exponent-for-Smaller-Plant›)),
        labor (operators(‹No.-of-Operators›),
        maintenance-costs(‹Percent of Investment›))),
    product-grade(description (‹Product-Grade-Description›),
        characteristics(‹Attribute›, ‹Value›),
        characteristics(...
            .
            .
            .
        production-rate(‹Percent-of-Nominal-Capacity›),
        input(‹Input 1›, ‹Quantity›, ‹Units›),
```

```
input(...
        .
        .
        .
    )),
product-grade (...
    .
    .
    .
        )).
```

11.4.4 Technology/company frame

Generally, a firm will adapt a technology whether it owns it or licenses it. The most common differences resulting from the operation of the same technology by two firms are in the quality of the product and in some performance attributes. This is a result of differences in R&D expenditure or in the targeted consumer group within a market (one group may be more willing to pay for extra costs the company may incur in improving the quality of the product). The frame is specified as:

```
technology/company-frame(
    year(‹Year›),
    region(‹Region›),
    company(‹Company-Name›),
    technology(description (‹Technology-Description),
        product-grade(description(‹Product-Grade-Description›),
            characteristics(‹Attribute›, ‹Value›),
            cost-factor (‹Percent-Difference›),
            credit-factor (‹Percent-Difference›)),
        product-grade(...
            .
            .
            .
    technology(...
        .
        .
        .
            )).
```

The cost and credit factors are only for those special cases in which we do not disaggregate a market to account for a very small niche within a market for specialty products which a firm may serve.

11.4.5 Company frame

The company frame contains information about its plants:

```
company-frame(
    year(‹Year›),
    company(‹Company-Name),
    plant(location(‹City, State, Country›),
        technology(description (‹Technology-Description›),
        nominal-capacity(total(‹Total-Capacity›),
            lines(‹Line-Capacities›),
    plant(...
            .
            .
            .

                )).
```

We may have additional information about the company, such as joint ownership, upward or downward integration, or other institutional characteristics. If this information is relevant to the competitive process and we know the rules for processing it, we can also include it in this frame.

11.4.6 Company/market frame

This frame contains information about the company's capabilities which affect its sales of products in different markets. These capabilities are specified as company characteristics, such as marketing and service, which are needed to satisfy the demand requirements. The frame is specified as:

```
company/market-frame(
    year(‹Year›),
    region(‹Region›),
    company(‹Company-Name›),
    characteristic(description(‹Characteristic-Description›),
        product(description (‹Product-Description›),
            value(‹Characteristic-Value›)),
        product(...
            .
            .
            .

    characteristic(...
            .
            .
            .

                )).
```

11.5 Methodology

11.5.1 Architecture of the model

The computer implementation of the model uses a combination of logical reasoning procedures and analytical/algorithmic procedures, together with a global database which represents the knowledge about the domain as symbolically represented data structures. This model has been implemented on a Sun Microsystems workstation. The database and the logical reasoning procedures are implemented in QUINTUS PROLOG, a language suitable for processing logical formulae, and the analytical/ algorithm procedures are implemented in C language, a conventional programming language. The architecture of the system is shown in Figure 11.2.

The primary output of the system is the industry supply/demand matrix: a balance of demand in each market (identified by a product grade and region) with supply by each plant of each company. This matrix is the result of the competitive balance between the aspirations of each company in each market and its strengths in each market relative to its competitors in terms of ability to fulfill market (converter or end-use) requirements. Expert systems A and B are used to formalize the problem, which is solved for the supply/demand matrix; expert systems C and D are used to rationalize the solution and identify the strategies of the firms. We now discuss the methodology used in each of the components of the consulting system.

11.5.2 Market requirements and market power

Dimensions of demand

In order to understand the nature of competition and to formalize the concept of market power, we need to identify the dimensions of demand underlying the differentiation of products. Here we discuss their role in identifying markets and determining market power. We take the polypropylene industry as an example, although the underlying concepts are applicable to any industry with differentiated products. Polypropylene is a plastic resin which is processed to manufacture household items, appliances, and furniture, medical goods, packaging, fibers and films, and in transportation. These products are manufactured by different conversion processes, including injection molding, extrusion molding and blow molding.

There are seven basic production technologies, normally modified by the firms, which yield a number of product grades suitable for the above applications. The three basic product grades are homopolymers,

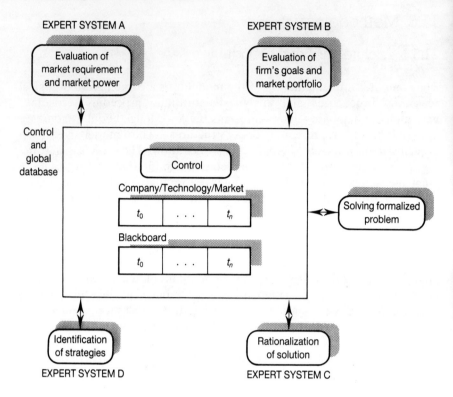

Figure 11.2　Architecture of the model.

copolymers, and block or impact copolymers. Requirements for the use of a particular product grade for a particular end-use can be classified along the following lines:

- *end-use requirements*: impact resistance, environmental stress-cracking resistance, tensile strength, clarity (for film in wrapping), color, melt index, stiffness;
- *conversion/processing requirements*: molecular weight, molecular weight distribution, melt index, draw-down, elongation, die swell;
- *converter*: level of sophistication, type, size.

This knowledge of the industry allows us to identify the dimensions of demand as well as the markets which differ along these dimensions:

- *pricing*: flexibility, quantity discount;
- *quality*: appearance, subjective factors;
- *performance*: objective and well-defined measurable criteria;
- *technical services*: R&D for conversion;

- *marketing*: delivery schedules, lot sizes, sales staff, sales offices;
- *institutional*: captive or contractual demand in addition to intangibles like 'buying from their own.'

Preference structure of consumers

Consumers' subjective assessments of a product are solicited from experts in the industry or are gathered through market research. The experts are asked, for each end-use, to rate the level of the requirement at which the average customer would find the product acceptable. The levels are defined on a qualitative scale of nine values: low, below-average-minus, below-average, below-average-plus, average, above-average-minus, above-average, above-average-plus, and high.

In addition to the requirement level the tolerance for the attribute level is also solicited. This is given as one of the four subjective levels: zero, low, medium, or high. This preference structure can be used to model the compensatory as well as the lexicographic nature of customers' preferences. Specifically, trade-off can be allowed between two requirements for which the preference levels are close, but not between requirements for which the corresponding difference in preferences is large.

For each end-use this knowledge is represented as the market frame. The market power of a firm depends on how well it meets the customers' preference for appropriate levels of attribute requirements, in comparison with its ability to produce goods with these attributes.

Capabilities of the firm

These requirements of demand depend not only on the characteristics of the product, but also on the characteristics of the consumers. The ability of a firm to distinguish these characteristics and gear its products and services to match them determines the market power of the firm. These abilities are derived from two sources: first, the firm's organizational structure, its production, marketing, service, and R&D facilities; and second, the firm's choices which define its aspiration levels and the implied efforts to achieve them. We believe that a firm's organizational structure and its allocation of resources and production across various markets are closely linked to its perception of its own market power compared with that of its competitors.

Market power of the firm

In order to determine the accessible market demand for a firm in the market, we represent the problem as a hierarchy, as shown in Figure 11.3. The top level represents the market power. The second level

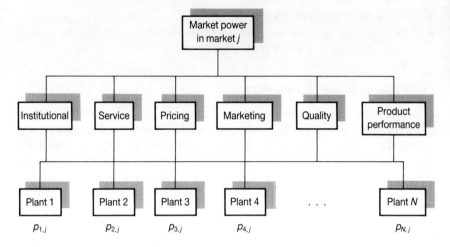

Figure 11.3 Hierarchical representation of the market power of the plants.

represents the requirements of demand which are important for the market power. (The relative importance of the requirements depends on the preferences of the customers for different end-uses, as well as the capabilities of the producers to satisfy these preferences.) The last level represents how each of the plant fares with respect to each of the requirements.

Evaluation of market power

The first step is to determine the weights for the requirements in the second level of the hierarchy. Next, for each requirement we determine the weights for plants denoting the capabilities of the plants or its owner. The overall weighting vector $(P_{1,j}, P_{2,j}, ..., P_{N,j})$ which represents the market power of the plants is then obtained by multiplying the matrix constructed from the weighting vectors of plants for each requirement by the weighting vector of the requirements. This is essentially a linear weighting scheme similar to the one used in the analytical hierarchy process (Saaty, 1980).

The weights for the requirements are determined by making pairwise comparisons of requirements with respect to the quantity of demand in the market which need to satisfy the requirements at a given level. For any two requirements i and j, these quantities represent, respectively, the quantities in which requirement i dominates j, requirement j dominates i, and requirements i and j are equally important. These quantities are then averaged to determine the weights for the requirements.

This averaging process also yields a requirement-sensitive demand

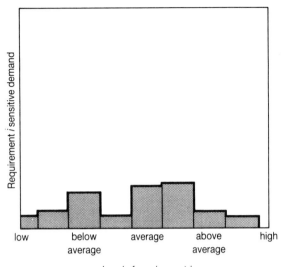

Figure 11.4   Requirement-related demand profile.

profile for each requirement (Figure 11.4); the profile is shown as cumulative quantities in Figure 11.5. It should be noted that the final quantity QR_i, the total market demand sensitive to the requirement i, is not mutually exclusive with similar quantities for other requirements. In fact, at each level the quantity of a demand should be interpreted as the quantity for which this requirement has, *to the consumers*, equal or greater importance than other requirements at the same level.

The fact that consumers have similar preferences for any two requirements (i.e., the requirement-sensitive demand for the two requirements is the same) does not mean that the requirements have the same influence on sales. For example, consider a segment of demand which needs requirements A and B both to be satisfied at the average level. At the supply side, requirement A is met by all of the competing firms at the average level, while requirement B is met at different levels, some below average and some above average. Clearly, the competing firms derive no selling advantage through requirement A of the segment of demand.

Thus market power is affected not only by the satisfaction of important requirements of the demand, but also by the level of differentiation in the potential supply of these requirements. To characterize the differentiation possibilities we use an index which reflects how the potential supply of a market requirement by the producers is measured on a qualitative scale from low to high. We call this measure the base differentiation index (Syed, 1987). A value of 0 indicates that the

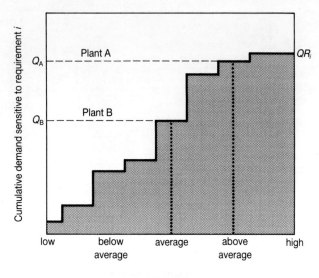

Figure 11.5   Comparison of plants for satisfaction of a market requirement.

supply from all producers is at the same qualitative level, while a value of 1 indicates that half the supply is at low level and half at the high level.

To reflect the overall importance of a requirement (from the demand as well as the supply side), we weight the total requirement-sensitive demands QR_i with the corresponding base differentiation indices. These weighted quantities are used to rank various requirements on the second level of the hierarchy shown in Figure 11.3.

In order to compare the relative weights of the plants, we use the information about the capabilities of each plant or its owner from the company/market and company/technology frames. This is shown in Figure 11.5 for two plants, A and B, which meet the requirement i at levels above average and average respectively. The quantities Q_A and Q_B represent the weights of the plants.

The market power represents a constraint on the sales which a plant can achieve in the market. As shown later these constraints manifest themselves in the sales aspirations of the producers and the resulting market processes which determine the actual sales.

11.5.3 Producer goals and sales aspirations

Aspiration levels are set by decision-makers in a firm according to the firm's own endowments and those of its competitors. The aspiration level is thus an element of the set of possible decision alternatives. The

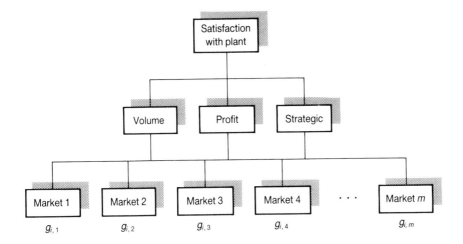

Figure 11.6   Hierarchical representation of aspiration levels for market portfolio.

determination by the decision-maker of the firm's aspiration levels is a process of learning about relevant environment and adjustment over time.

Aspiration levels for market porfolio of the firm

In order to formalize the problem of calculating the sales of various firms in the industry we need to specify the aspiration level for sales of each of the firms in each market. For this purpose we assume that a firm, given its capabilities derived from its organizational portfolio and its environment, will allocate its output among various markets so as to satisfy a set of goals. We call the allocation of the firm's output to various markets its market portfolio. The goals are profit, volume, and strategic. The profit goal is short-term or single period. The same is true for the volume goal, which essentially represents the desire to use all of the installed capacity. The last goal is strategic in the sense that the firm considers a market important from the point of view of long-term profits or survival. All of these goals depend on the firm's assessment of its market power, its installed capacity, and the demand in various markets.

For each item of plant, the desired production for various markets is determined by comparing the firm's goals with its production as a hierarchy, as shown in Figure 11.6. The first level represents the higher goal of the satisfaction with the plant, the second represents the goals which influence the higher goal, and the third represents the quantities (in terms of fractions of installed capacity) of production allocated to different markets.

Evaluation of aspiration levels

The firm's assessment of its market power, the market demand, its production costs, and its installed capacity define the constraints on its profit as well as its capacity utilization. We assume that, in order to allocate its output among various markets, the firm will use reasonable heuristics which are based in its perception of the range of industry profits and capacity utilization at the given moment. The heuristics are:

1. The satisfaction of volume goal of the firm by a market is high
    if
        the market size is large
    and/or
        the plant's capacity is small
    and/or
        the market power of the firm is high.
2. The satisfaction of profit goal of the firm by a market is high
    if
        the satisfaction of volume goal is high and its margin in the
        market is high.

The margins here are defined as the difference between the market price and the firm's delivered cost to the market. It remains to define what large and high mean.

Qualitative scales

We assume that firm's perceptions are shaped by the state of the industry. Thus the scales on which it evaluates its capacity utilization and profits depend on its competitors' capacity utilizations and profits. To construct the scale for capacity utilization we use the first heuristic and define a variable *capacity-util* as

$$capacity\text{-}util_{ij} = p_{ij}D_j \,/\, C_{ij}$$

where p_{ij} is the market power of plant i in market j, D_j is the demand in market j, and C_{ij} is the capacity of plant i when it produces the product for market j.

From the distribution of these mn variables we can define a range with intervals which correspond to qualitative variables between low and high. The approach we have taken is to use the standard deviation of the distribution and a scalar multiplier to define the range. This range is then divided into nine equal intervals which correspond to nine qualitative values: low, below-average-minus, below-average, below-average-plus, average, above-average-minus, above-average, above-average-plus, and high.

To construct the scale for profits, we define a variable *profit-util* as

$$profit\text{-}util_{ij} = margin_{ij} \times capacity\text{-}util_{ij}$$

where $margin_{ij}$ is a scaled measure of the difference between the market price in market j and the delivered cost of the product from plant i to market j. Note that the variation of production rate of a plant for different products influences the profits, and is taken into account by the variable *capacity-util*.

A firm's strategic goals are the same as its volume goal; i.e., it has decided to devote a certain capacity of the plant to be sold in a market for strategic reasons. Therefore, the qualitative scale for strategic goals is the same as the one for volume. But for strategic goals we use a scalar s_{ij} ($0 \leq s_{ij} \leq 1$) to determine the representative variable; s_{ij} represents the fraction of the demand in market j which is strategically important to plant i:

$$strategic\text{-}util_{ij} = s_{ij} \times capacity\text{-}util_{ij}$$

These scales and the market weights for a firm's plants are objective measures which depend on the state of the industry. These measures imply trade-offs which are derived from the market sizes, plant capacities, price-cost margins, and strategic markets of the industry. A firm may not choose to follow these trade-offs. For each of the three types of goal, the firm may choose to accept lower margins in a market or to increase the scalar s_{ij} to reflect higher desire for a market share. Whether a firm chooses to modify its preference or not, it has a basis on which to decide the direction to move and how to move.

The three non-commensurate goals can be compared by assuming that the intervals on qualitative scales for these goals represent the underlying trade-offs for the firm. To determine the market portfolio (i.e., the fraction of the capacity) of the plant, we normalize each of the vectors *capacity-util*, *profit-util*, and *strategic-util* for the plant. A lineaar weighted sum can be obtained by matrix multiplication.

11.5.4 Formalization of the problem

The problem is formalized as a set of constraints which represent the market power and sales aspirations of each producer's plants, the demand for products in each market and the capacity of each producer's plants. This capacity is related to the technology so as to take into account the instantaneous rate of production for different products. These constraints

	Market$_1$	Market$_2$	. . .	Market$_m$	Capacity
Plant$_1$	g_{11} x_{11} p_{11}	g_{12} x_{12} p_{12}	. . .	g_{1m} x_{1m} p_{1m}	C_1
Plant$_2$	g_{21} x_{21} p_{21}	g_{22} x_{22} p_{22}	. . .	g_{2m} x_{2m} p_{2m}	C_2
$\vdots$	$\vdots$	$\vdots$	$\ddots$	$\vdots$	$\vdots$
Plant$_n$	g_{n1} x_{n1} p_{n1}	g_{n2} x_{n2} p_{n2}	. . .	g_{nm} x_{nm} p_{nm}	C_n
Demand	D_1	D_2	. . .	D_m	

Figure 11.7 Formalized problem for supply/demand balance.

are shown in Figure 11.7. The columns represent the m markets for differentiated products, and the rows represent the n plants, one or more of which are owned by the same producer. The last column represents the capacity utilization of the production plants, and the last row the quantity demanded in each market. The entries in the table belong to three matrices which are defined as follows:

- p_{ij} The relative market power of the firms in different markets. In particular, p_{ij} is the relative power index of plant i in market j. These are normalized such that

$$\sum_i p_{ij} = 1$$

- g_{ij} The aspiration levels the producers have for their plants. In particular g_{ij} is the fraction of the capacity devoted to production for market j by plant i. These are normalized such that

$$\sum_j g_{ij} = 1$$

- x_{ij} The effective state which results from satisfying the aspiration levels g_{ij} of the producers with the relative market power given by p_{ij}. The x_{ij} give a solution which will most likely be different from the g_{ij}.

The market process will determine the realized sales of each plant in each market. The market processes are simulated by defining a function

$$f(g_{ij}, p_{ij}, x_{ij})$$

which represents a measure of the distance of the aspiration levels g_{ij} from the corresponding realized sales x_{ij}. These distances should be less if the corresponding p_{ij} is greater, and vice versa. The minimum value of this function will then provide an approximate measure of the disequilibrium in the industry. A simple form is to minimize the function

$$f = \sum_i \sum_j p_{ij} \left((g_{ij} - x_{ij}) / g_{ij} \right)^2, \quad g_{ij} \neq 0.0$$

over x_{ij}, subject to demand and capacity constraints.

Although we have specified the problem as an optimization problem, we are interested only in values of x_{ij} which give a value of $f(g_{ij}, p_{ij}, x_{ij})$ close enough to its minimum.

11.5.5 Rationalization of the solution

In this phase we test a set of hypotheses which have different levels of abstraction as well as different levels of confidence. The solution is tested for satisfaction of these hypotheses. The level of confidence can be used as the weight assigned to the hypothesis for assessing the general acceptance of the solution.

If the solution is unacceptable, the problem can be respecified by tracing the source of failure in the hypothesis to the purposeful state of the producers or markets and making the appropriate modification. The role of human interaction in this process is essential at this stage of development of knowledge-based systems. The rationalization process performs two tasks: first, it helps improve the solution by modifying the trade-offs for individual plants, and secondly, it sets up the information which will be used to identify the available strategies for each plant.

11.5.6 Identification of strategies

The knowledge developed in the rationalization phase can be used to reveal the underlying competitive processes, their intensities, and the reasons for them. This knowledge helps firms to identify strategies. The heuristic used for this purpose is as follows. Given the plants' market power p_{ik}, sales goals g_{ik}, and the realized sales x_{ik}, where i stands for the plants and k for the markets, it is reasoned that:

Table 11.1   Truth table for competitor analysis of a market.

Plant i has greater market power than plant j	Plant i is more 'satisfied' than plant j	Plant j is relatively more ambitious than plant i	Plant i is more 'satisfied' in other markets than plant j	Possible actions and comments
Plant i defends against plant j				
T	T	T	T	Best posture
T	T	T	F	Niche for plant *i*
T	T	F	T	Expect attack from *j*
T	T	F	F	Expect attack, *i* more vulnerable
Plant i attacks plant j				
T	F	T	T	Less incentive
T	F	T	F	Incentive to attack *j*
T	F	F	T	Least incentive to attack *j*
T	F	F	F	Strong incentive to attack *j*

For a given market *k*, and two plants *i* and *j*,
  if
        plant *i* has more market power than plant *j*
  then
        plant *i* is more 'satisfied,' in market *k*, than plant *j*
        unless
              plant *j* is more ambitious, in market *k*, than plant *i*
        or
              plant *i* is more 'satisfied,' in markets other than *k*, than plant *j*.

This is shown in Table 11.1 in the form of a truth table. We need to define the meanings of each of the above clauses precisely. For the *if* clause we simply compare p_{ik} and p_{jk}, which are proportional to the level of market demand for which plants *i* and *j* meet the requirements of customers. In a larger sense, a firm will be satisfied if its capabilities are such that its plants' sales in a market reflect them as much as possible. Otherwise, the firm is not taking advantage of its capabilities and the resource allocation is less than efficient. Thus, for the *then* clause we compare the realized sales x_{ik} and x_{jk} in terms of the fraction of the capacities of plants i and j.

To compare the relative ambitions of the two plants used in the *unless* clause, we proceed as follows. The given market power p_{ik} of plant i can be translated into a rough measure proportional to expected sales which are based only on the plant i and its owner's capabilities, given by $p_{ik}C_{ik}$. The desires of plant i are given by g_{ik}. Thus an unscaled measure of the ambition of plant i is given by $g_{ik}/p_{ik}C_{ik}$. A similar measure can be constructed for plant j, and since we are interested only in pairwise comparisons, the scale is unimportant. Finally, for the *or* clause, following the reasons for the *then* clause, we simply use the sums

$$\sum_{l \neq k} x_{il} \quad \text{and} \quad \sum_{l \neq k} x_{jl}$$

for plants i and j respectively.

To proceed with the competitor analysis of the market, it is not enough to know just the truth values of these clauses; we also need to determine the intensity of these values. These intensities can be evaluated through the use of the same variables which are used to determine the truth values. These measures are given as percentage differences calculated from the ratios of corresponding variables.

To evaluate the intensity of competition we use logical procedures which allow the user to home in on the causes, focusing in succession on:

- the producer,
- its plant in distress (given by a low capacity utilization),
- the markets in which the plant does not meet its sales aspirations,
- how it fares against its competitors in these markets, and
- why it fares badly against its competitors, i.e., what capabilities it lacks in comparison with them.

This analysis examines the actions or strategies the producer has the incentive to follow, and the expert can then assess whether the producer has the resources for these actions or strategies. This knowledge is used to specify the problem for the next time-period.

11.6 Example

We used ICS to determine the market share of various producers in the US polypropylene industry in 1983. This year was chosen because SRI International had estimates for market shares derived from market

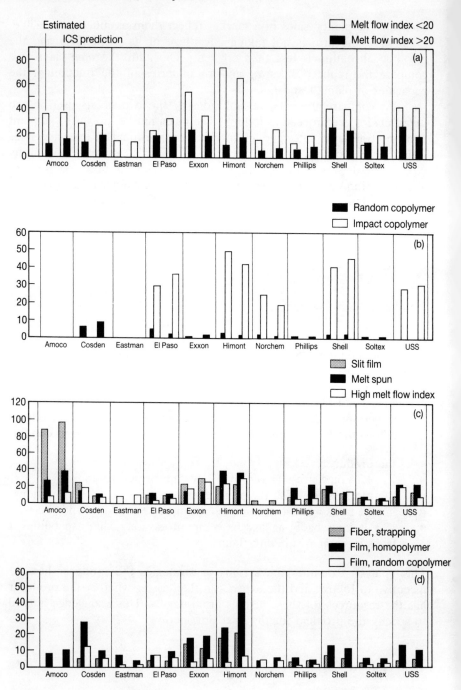

Figure 11.8 Market shares in the US polypropylene industry for 1983, as estimated by the industry and predicted by ICS: (a) injection molding of homopolymers, (b) injection molding of copolymers, (c) fiber, (d) fiber and film, (e) blow molding, (f) extrusion, and (g) exports (in thousand metric tons).

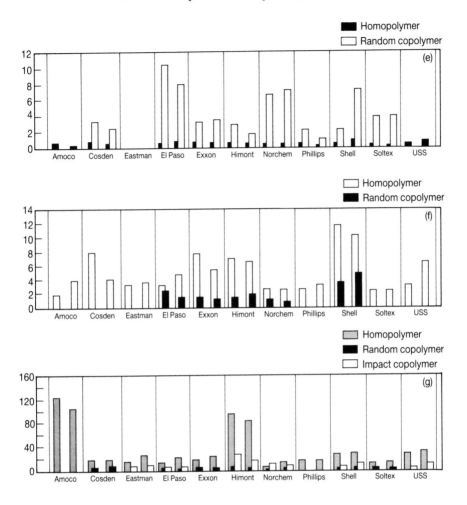

Figure 11.8   *(cont.)*

research and from responses from the producers in the industry. The knowledge base consisted of 11 companies, 19 plants, 17 markets, 41 end-uses and 7 production technologies with processes for over 100 product grades.

We have plotted the results in Figure 11.8 as bar charts for different groups of markets, with the estimated shares and those calculated by ICS shown side by side. Not only do the results agree very closely with the estimates, but the focusing procedures have revealed the competitive character of different markets and companies in a way which our domain experts have found reasonable.

The striking match of the market share estimates from ICS with those from an alternative source substantiates the conjecture proposed by the behavioral economists that, unless forced to follow more complex procedures, the firms use simple decision rules to set their sales goals for various markets and to determine trade-offs between profits, capacity utilization, and other strategic considerations. The polyolefins industry is a mature industry, and the simple decision rules used in ICS together with the detailed information about the industry were sufficient to produce credible results.

11.7 Status of ICS

ICS is currently being used to project how the industry supply structure might change in response to anticipated changes in demand patterns over the coming decade. It can be used in a similar manner to do 'what-if' analyses for possible new markets and new products. Another application might be the analysis of the industry's response to a new producer or to being restructured. Thus ICS has applications covering the complete range of planning functions, from investment and acquisition, through marketing and R&D, to production.

ICS is currently set up to analyze the US polyolefins industry, covering supply-and-demand matrices of all domestic producers, who serve a total of 97 markets. SRI International has evaluated 24 process configurations, representing all types of commercial polyolefins production processes, and has developed production processes for over 300 individual polyolefin grades.

Possibly the most useful feature of ICS is that it permits the user to analyze the result to find the key factors contributing to the competitive balance in each market. The interrogation procedures for the analysis can be used, for example, to compare the competitive position of one plant with that of other plants supplying a specific market, so as to find the relative strengths of producers and the degree to which each producer meets his aspirations. It will also indicate the character of each market, such as its sensitivity to product quality, pricing, and technical services. Thus, the interrogation system can be used to focus rapidly on the more important or sensitive aspects of each market or of each plant's product portfolio.

References

Cyert, R.M. and March, J.G. (1963). *A Behavioral Theory of the Firm*. Englewood Cliffs, NJ: Prentice-Hall

Kornai, J. (1971). *Anti-Equilibrium*. Amsterdam: North-Holland

Saaty, T.L. (1980). *The Analytic Hierarchy Process*. New York: McGraw-Hill

Simon, H.A. (1976). *Administrative Behavior*, 3rd edn. New York: The Free Press

Simon, H.A. (1978a). 'On how to decide what to do', *Bell J. Econ.*, **9**, 494–507

Simon, H.A. (1978b). 'Rationality as process and product of thought', *Am. Econ. Rev.*, **68**, 1–16

Syed, J.R. (1987). 'A hybrid approach to competitive analysis of an industry with application to polyolefins industry', PhD Dissertation, Department of Engineering–Economic Systems, Stanford University

Index

✓   **DATE DUE**   L.-Brault